AF255043

Cenerentola

John Campbell Rees

The TIMELESS Press

First published in the United Kingdom in 2019 by
The TIMELESS Press,
15, Stuart Street,
Treherbert,
Treorchy,
Rhondda Cynon Taff,
United Kingdom
CF42 5PR.

Also by John Campbell Rees
Winter Squad
Summertime Blue
Imogen's Quest

For My Family

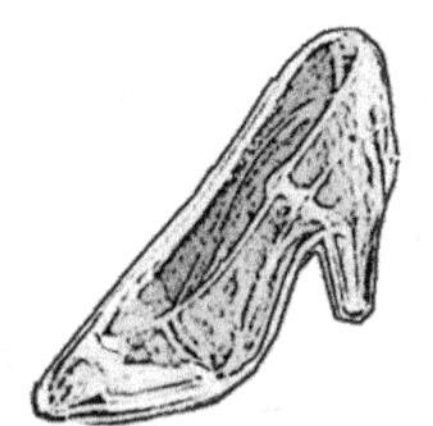 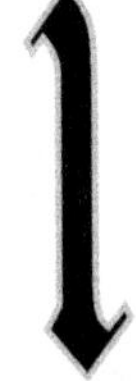 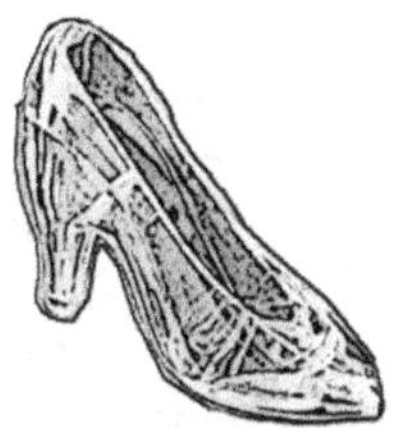

he room was as silent. As silent as the grave Gilbert du Fauché, Baron of Cenerentola had recently been deposited. The lawyer taking a sip of water was an infuriating break in the reading of the Baron's will. Thus far, there had been no mention by name of Chantelle,the late Baron's oldest daughter. There had only been a vague reference to his second wife and her daughters.

Chantelle's father had been a popular man with many friends who had come to pay their respects. All the gentry for miles around rubbed shoulders with fishermen and farmers. The cross section of Anserian society was completed by Countess Chrystine of Carlton representing the Queen, who was too advanced in her first pregnancy to travel.

'Finally, with no son, nor a nominated successor, the title Baron du Fauché of Cenerentola, passes to his wife.'

'Monsieur, are you sure about that?' asked Chantelle, who was twenty four years old, had been expecting to inherit the Baronial Chain. Her piercing grey eyes at the heart of her long face, were twice as sharp as usual, boring deeply into the lawyer. Her naturally pale skin had gone two shades paler.

'I am, Lady Chantelle. If Baron Gilbert du Fauché of Cenerentola had not wanted his wife to become Baroness, should have named someone else.'

'And that is the entire Will?'

'Why yes, Mademoiselle, that is everything in your late father's Last Will and Testament.' The lawyer closed the document and put it in his bag, denying Chantelle a chance to read it. 'I warned the Baron that he should have had such an important document written properly by an attorney. He insisted on doing it himself. Now I shall take it to Castello del Filippo to have the Archduke's Court grant probate.'

'Chantelle, my dear,' said the short, skeletally thin woman sitting next to the lawyer. This was Lady Livienne du Fauché, Chantelle's stepmother, 'you do not need to be mentioned in the Will. You are your Father's daughter. When I married your papa, you became my number one priority.'

'Thank you, Belle-mère,' Chantelle replied. Her step-mother had to say something, only Chantelle understood its true meaning.

Lady Livienne's priority, when she had arrived at Cenerentola House, eight years ago, had been to find a husband for Chantelle, as soon as she turned seventeen, whether she wanted one or not. That priority had been stopped dead in its tracks by the Baron. Chantelle no longer had her father to protect her from her step-mother's unwanted match-making. It must still be a priority for Lady Livienne, who would not be choosy about who that husband was.

Chantelle began to cry. How could her Father be dead. He had been healthy. Why did he fall so quickly to such a minor infection?

'As you can see, my step-daughter is distraught,' said Lady Livienne. 'I thank you for your attendance on this sad day. I ask you to withdraw, so the family can begin its week of isolated mourning.'

Chantelle stopped weeping, not because the grief was any less, but because she knew what was coming. The week of mourning would be horrible. The few remaining servants would work an hour each morning, to keep the place ticking over. Chantelle would be left with her step-mother and two ghastly step-sisters. Her dear young half-sister Madeleine had been unable to leave her school in Elizaburg, thousands of miles away. No need to guess who would be left doing most of the housework. The proprieties of mourning meant she could not leave the house. Then after the Mourning, with no inheritance, she would be unable to afford to move anywhere, unless it was part of an unwanted marriage.

Although everyone was wearing mediaeval French clothes, closer inspection would prove this was not mediaeval France. Too many trifocal spectacles, wrist watches and other anachronisms. This room was on Anseris, a world Humanity had arrived on, after a tortuous sixteen hundred year long journey, aboard the slower than light prison ship KHM#89. The crew members that arrived on Anseris were distant descendants of the original officers. Instead of a high technology prison colony, their ancestors planned, the crew created an agrarian world based on the European Middle Ages.

Captain Catherine Wellingford, the second commander of the KHM#89, was the author of the regressive settlement policy. She discovered an ethics free form of immortality. She expanded her life by jumping from one cloned body to the next. Even the League could not tolerate that level of infamy. Exiled on the juggernaut, at journey's end she had herself crowned Queen Kathyren of Anseris. Her immortality machine was the only advanced technology to survive the purge on arrival. Her reign became eternal.

There were twenty operational departments aboard KHM#89. As the journey progressed, their staff only married colleagues in their department. Jobs became family concerns and department heads became clan chiefs. When the ship arrived at Anseris, the land was divided into twenty Archduchies. Each department was given an archduchy to run as semi-indepedent fiefdoms. The department heads became the twenty Archdukes, and their clans became the aristocratic Great Houses.

The prison officers and convicts who travelled in suspended animation aboard the KHM#89 were brainwashed into accepting new roles. The prison officers became the Gentry and the prison stockades and the land around them became their estates. The convicts became the illiterate and superstitious peasants, who would do all the hard labour.

Fifteen hundred years after arriving on Anseris, the rule of Queen Kathyren, now called the Immortal Empress was ended. Earl Andrew Rushton-Browne, known as the Boatbuilder, discovered Queen Kathyren's secret and led the revolution that ended her reign of wickedness. The baby he rescued from the immortality system, grew up to become Queen Elizabeta, apparently free of the previous monarch's evil influence, and was declared the first Free Queen.

Queen Elizabeta's first child was a daughter, who unlike her siblings, looked exactly like her mother, and became Queen, beginning Female Primogeniture in the Monarchy. The primitive society that

Anseris became had no way of knowing the Free Queens had a third ovary designed to continue the parade of clones.

Change was glacially slow under the Free Queens, impeded by the aristocrats, who benefited most from the status quo.

T he first survey of the region that became Fiandre was done by space-probes before arrival. It assumed the large areas of flat land were close to sea-level with a temperate climate. It was designated as Flanders and the possible settlement sites were given Flemish names. Most of the land actually sat on a plateau, etched by deep valleys. Also, the climate was closer to that around the Black Sea, as was the flora and fauna. It was nothing like Flanders.

Jacob Griffin-Phillips, the first Archduke loved all things Italian renaming the areas Fiandre, the Italian for Flanders. Settlements now had Italian names, and the convicts settled there given Italian names. Sadly no-one in this part of the Archduchy could speak Italian It was as authentically Italian as pizza con prosciutto ed ananas.

A pedal taxi arrived as the rest of the guests in their horsedrawn carriages were leaving.

'Who the hell is this?' Lady Livienne was livid. 'Don't they know we are in mourning.'

Then a young woman wearing a brown and claret mourning dress emerged from the vehicle. Chantelle was overjoyed, it was her teenage half-sister Madeleine. They shared the same father, who had loved them, and was now dead. There were times when she felt more like a parent than a sibling, as Lady Livienne never displayed any love for her youngest child.

'Madeleine, is that you?' asked Lady Livienne. Every time her daughter, who had been sent to school in Elizaburg returned home she had changed a little. This time she had changed a lot. The girl was eight inches taller than when had last left for Elizaburg four months earlier. At twelve, Madeleine had been as chubby as the twins. Now she was tall and thin, half an inch shorter than Chantelle The most remarkable change was Madeleine's face, which appeared to have elongated and was now identical to Chantelle's. The Only difference was Madeleine had flame red hair while her sister's was ebony black.

'Oui maman, c'est moi Madeleine,' said the girl in Anserian French, the unofficial language of the Gentry.

'Je te l'ai dit, Madeleine,' Lady Livienne said curtly. 'Restez à Elizaburg jusqu'au la fin de l'année scolaire.'

'Stay in Elizaburg until the end of the school year, Belle-mère? How could she not be with her family at this time?' asked Chantelle, as she embraced her half-sister.

'But I told you to stay in the capital,' repeated Lady Livienne in Anserian English. 'Until the end of the school year. Are you incapable of understanding an instruction in any language? You missed the funeral anyway.'

'Oh no,' said the girl who was obviously distraught at the thought of missing her Father's funeral. I am sorry I am late Maman, the ferry was delayed by the storm swell at Zucca,'

'We must go indoors now, to begin our mourning,' said Chantelle, aware that people were watching them.

'Oh well, on the bright side, I suppose you being here saves me an extra few months of school fees,' said Lady Livienne, once the five women were safely indoors.

Chantelle watched as a look of horror crossed her sister's face. The girl obviously knew what was coming, but was afraid to ask.

'Months?' Chantelle asked her Step-Mother. 'She'll be going back in a fortnight.'

'Yes, Maman, I've only missed the last week before half term,' said Madeleine weakly. 'The rest of the term will be my Secondary Certificate examinations. A vital preparation for next year.'

'Next year?' asked Lady Livienne, who hated being interpreted.

'When I sit the Tertiary Certificate examinations to qualify for University,' said Madeleine. 'I know Papa arranged for Chantelle to become a mature student at Elizaburg University in September. I will join her as a student there in a years time.'

'The stuff of nonsense. You are both gentlewomen,' said Lady Livienne, who hated being contradicted more than being interupted.

'So?' asked Chantelle.

'As gentlewomen, it is your duty to make a good marriage. Then to run your homes and raise your children. You are both educated well enough for that. Over educated in fact. Those silly pieces of paper are the stuff of nonsense.'

'But I want a career in the Law, Maman, and Chantelle wishes to be a historian.'

Chantelle did not really know what she wanted to be. All she knew is her late Father had given her the opportunity to broaden her horizons. An opportunity her silly step-mother was determined to snatch away from her.

'The stuff of nonsense.' Lady Livienne was sitting in her late husband's favourite chair. 'You are home now. In two years you will be married to the man I choose. You are a pretty girl now, that should not be as big a problem as I am having finding suitors for Clementine and Citronella.'

These were Lady Livienne's twin daughters from her first, short lived marriage. Only a few inches taller than their mother, they were considerably bulkier, and with the penchant for orange and yellow dresses, they actually looked like the fruit they were named after.

'But that is so old-fashioned. The Queen says all women can follow their dreams of a career and fulfilment in her Kingdom.'

'And that is more stuff of nonsense. Women have but one career, to be wives and mothers. The Benedictian Kings understood that, during their century of strong male rule.' Lady Livienne preferred conservative King Benedict III. 'She is too flighty and radical. A mere slip of a girl.'

'But Belle-mère, you are thirty seven years old,' said Chantelle, 'just eleven years older than the Queen.'

𝕿 he Barony of Cenerentola in the South of the Archduchy of Fiandre is named after Cenerentola Island, a tiny speck of land, six miles wide from east to west and three miles from north to south.

The rocks Cenerentola Island is built on are porous, sucking up sea water from around the island. Bacteria living in the soil, that looks like cinders, or "cenere" in Italian, separated the salt from the water. They form large grey coated nuggets of salt. A stream of crystal pure water emerged from the highest point on the island, running eastwards to a small lake surrounding Cenerentola House, home of the Baron, then to a village, a mile downstream on the eastern tip of the Island.

Early in Anserian history, the island had been the temporary seat of the hereditary Archdukes of Fiandre. Controlling the source of the planet's best culinary salt generated wealth for House Griffin-Phillips. However they quickly moved the capital of the Archduchy to the strategically more important Ponte di Carla, at the narrowest point of the Great Rift Sea. Here the alien Aggelii's great stone bridge connected two continents. The island and the land around it passed to the Archduke's cousin, who became the first Baron Phillips-Forsythe of Cenerentola.

During the crazy years of the Emerald Bubble, when a vein of the green gemstones was discovered just outside Zucca, the Barons rebuilt the town called Castello del Filippo to be their capital, turning their back on the Island.

The bubble burst and the Barony was bankrupt. The Archduke of Fiandre stepped in, putting right the damage done by his cousins, who could spend money like water, simply could not get used to living on the salt income alone. The family was punished by being expelled from the Aristocratic Caste, where real power lay. They were allowed to keep the title of Baron but they became part of the Gentry, the minor landowning caste. The family was also forced to change its name, becoming du Fauché, the ancient French for hard-up, and a minor footnote in history.

'**M**aman is proving exactly what my friend Jadwiga says,' Madeleine said to Chantelle. 'Out in the country, the biggest brake on female emancipation is older women. They saw their dreams crushed, they're determined to crush the dreams of their daughters as revenge. Jadwiga says the cycle has to be broken.'

'I doubt Belle-mère would approve of her,' said Chantelle.

'Mama will hate her, despite her being a friend of the Queen.'

'Oh, that Jadwiga! How did you meet her?' Chantelle asked.

Everyone knew the Queen treated Jadwiga Smitz more like her sister than her friend.

'We attend the same school, she is a year above me. Or rather she was. Now she has her Tertiary Certificate and at university next year.'

'Oh, I see,' said Chantelle

'You'll meet her soon,' said Madeleine. 'She has a ten week internship with Monsieur Nouveauté's law firm. Her Majesty has rented one of the new houses in Zucca for her and her twin brother Janek. His bosses are sending him to the DuPré emerald mine. for a couple of months. Although he's joining the Navy as soon as he is eighteen. Despite what his parents say.'

'Look, Maddy dear,' said Chantelle, changing the subject, 'don't worry about what your mother says. We'll both be going to school next year. I'll get a decent lawyer to look at Papa's Will, to sort this mess out.'

'But I'll have to do my Secondary and Tertiary exams in the same year now. Both crazy and impossible.'

'Maddy darling, if anyone can do it, it's you.'

𝔄 century or so earlier, a religious cult, the Great Machine, based in the many belts of asteroids that orbited Fenzrii Beta, tried to invade the Anserian star system. The Fenzrians had not expected a long drawn out war. The Anserians saw an invasion from space by a technologically as a clear and present danger. They had been practising defending their home-world until their powerful alien friends arrived, for centuries. When the friends, the Aggelii eventually responded to a call for help, they acted as neutral galactic police. They saw the forbidden technology the Fenzrians were using, and the invader's fate was sealed. The Fenzrians were banished to an iron age existence on the other side of the galaxy. Fenzrii Beta was detonated to destroy the asteroids and any forbidden technology they contained.

The Aggelii then decided to quarantine Anseris, as they believed it was not yet ready for contact with the Galaxy.

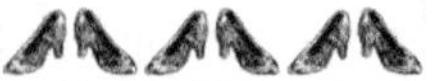

While waiting for the Aggelii, Queen Gertrude III of Anseris sent her daughter and niece on a diplomatic mission to neighbouring star systems. Princess Louise and Duchess Anita's ship became trapped in a hyperspace anomaly for one hundred years. When they returned the descendant of the conservative usurper Benedict I was on the throne. The Benedictians Kings tried to reverse many technological advances, turn their backs on the Anserolian System, and return Anseris to its previous pseudo-medieval existence. They failed, but set civilization back hundreds of years.

Following King Benedict IV death, three years earlier, his son Crown Prince David, stood down in favour of Princess Louise. Only a handful of men who worshipped the Immortal Empress opposed the new Queen, and they were defeated by their own stupidity.

The Queen's Suite in the Royal Apartment of Ellisford Castle had been completely refurbished by the new Queen. The heavy wood panelling and stiff mediaeval furniture she had grown up with, had been swept away. The suite now resembled a modern flat for the upwardly mobile in Elizaburg.

'Imogen, you should let our servants do that,' said the Queen's friend Jadwiga Smitz, 'we have enough of them.'

'Our servants, Jadzie dear?' asked an amused Queen.

'I know, I've be living like royalty, for too long,' the girl replied.

Jadwiga knew an encounter with alien technology had shown the Queen exactly what life was like for someone at the bottom of society, and given her a fiery determination to use her position to change things for the better. It had also changed the way the Queen spoke. The rounded royal vowels and aristocratic accent had been replaced with a rural accent. Here in the Queen's Suite she switched to a more relaxed plebeian vernacular.

'And miss this vital bonding session with my daughter, Jadzie dear,' said the Queen, as she dropped her child's dirty nappy into a lidded bucket, 'Tried actually a-washin' them monsters once did I. No wonder they used to say on ancient Earth "a woman's work ain't never done."'

'I suppose the Royal Nursery has her for long enough during the day,' said Jadwiga. It never ceased to amaze her how quickly her friend could switch between roles. At the door of her apartment, she stopped being Queen Johanna IV, the medieval monarch. Now minutes after arriving home in traditional clothes she was once more Imogen, in disheveled modern clothing, holding her freshly changed baby daughter who was curling her strawberry blonde hair, falling in a long ponytail.

The women moved to the living room. Jadwiga poured two cups of tea from a pot which accompanied the fresh sandwiches that had mysteriously appeared before they entered the room. Jadwiga used to try and catch the ghost-like servants, now she just took the luxury for granted. For several years the Castle had been her home. The girl had revolted against being taken out of school to become a domestic drudge. The Queen had taken pity on Jadwiga, arranging for her to continue in education and tried and failed to repair the breach in the family. Her mother had refused to take her home. The Queen had given her a room in the Queen's Suite in the Castle's Royal Apartment.

'Even with your servants, you looked absolutely exhausted.'

'That's because I be exhausted, Little Sister,' said Imogen, who had been an only child, so she called her three closest female friends, Duchess Anita, Countess Chrystine and Jadwiga Smitz, big, middle and little sister respectively. Only Duchess Anita came close to actually being the Queen's sister, because she was Imogen's cousin and they had been brought up together at Ellisford Castle.

'I've told you before, Your Majesty, if you want to be my big sister, you have to accept my Mother as well.'

'Then it's a good job it be only our private joke.' Imogen put her now sleeping baby daughter into her cot. 'You be a-headin off to Fiandre for a pre-college internship in Campo del Zucche next week. Then another shot at reconciliation in the last two weeks?'

'I have to try. She'll doom it to failure. She doesn't want me back. Thank the Angels it's only for the last two weeks of the forteen weeks I'm there.'

'Forteen weeks, the internship only be for ten?' asked the Queen

'Also, it's my friend Maddy's home town. She made it sound so beautiful, I decided to do my internship at a local law firm, sandwiched in my first holiday for four years.'

'That be Madeleine du Fauché?' Imogen asked. 'Such a shame I was prevented from a-gettin' to Baron Gilbert's funeral by the birth of madame over there. Lovely man, shame about his dreadful Wife.'

'Yes, that's right. Madeleine went home for her Father's funeral. I'm surprised she didn't come back to school last month?

'It probably be grief a-hittin' her harder than she imagined. Nothing to be a-worryin' about.'

'You're probably right.'

'Have you arranged for your bodyguard?' Imogen asked.

'What do I need a bodyguard for?' Jadwiga asked back. 'I won't be there alone. You know Janek's bosses are sending him to the office of the last emerald mine in the Barony for the Summer. Dad says it will be a good experience. Janek says he's just killing time before he can join the Navy, he's got no intention of staying in the Jewelry Trade.'

'Jadzie, like it or not, you's an important person now, and as almost my little sister, a link to me as well. So, Erik Franke is free, he'll jump at the chance of a paid holiday.'

'Uncle Erik is never free. His life is his duty to you and your Kingdom,' said Jadwiga. 'Did he ask you to have this conversation?

'No, his doctor and his boss have. They be worried about him. He needs a break, he won't take one. Even though everything he is a-workin' on can be put on hold.'

'OK, I'll try to make sure his working holiday is more holiday than work.'

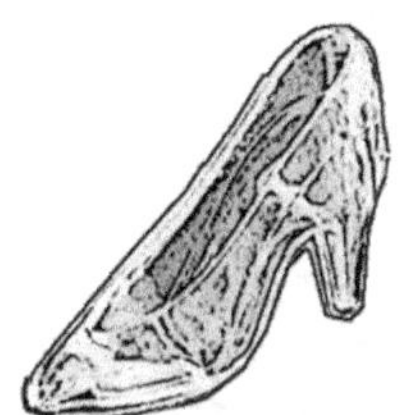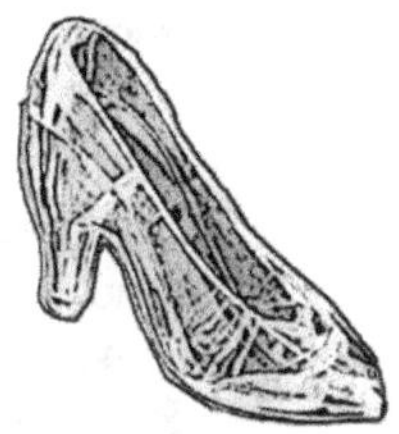

‘Did I hear you correctly. "You're not coming back." You are my servants?’ Lady Livienne asked the two women in the room. The house maid and scullery maid, who did the domestic work in the house, under the Cook's watchful eye.

‘As you know, Mistress, I was wed last week,’ said Carlota the former housemaid, who was taller than most women and towered over her former employer. Carlota knew this intimidated her old boss. As did speaking in a Deep-Country dialect.

‘I did not give you permission, as your employer you should have asked me first.’

‘Beggin’ your pardon, mistress, but your late husband, the Baron, gave his blessin’ last month.’

Lady Livienne vaguely remembered Gilbert saying something about it. She had been infuriated at the time, that he had not consulted with her. She would have to find a new housemaid. Also a new footman, as the stupid girl's new husband had inherited his Uncle's tavern in the village, and left the du Fauché's employ two weeks earlier. The tavern was not tied to the estate, so there was nothing Lady Livienne could do about it.

‘Shouldn't you be working your notice?’ asked Lady Livienne. Perhaps that would delay the search for replacement servants.

‘No, Ma'am, we did that before the late Baron passed away,’ Carlota replied.

‘Well, you can't go, not until I find someone to replace you.’

‘You can't a-stop to we,’ said Greta, the teenage former scullery maid, who normally did her best to be invisible to Lady Livienne.

‘Of course I can, I am your Seigneur.’

'Na, that were the Baron, who was a proper toff. But he stopped bein' our Seigneur when 'er Majesty started a-changin' all them Laws. A-bolishin' feudalism and the likes.' the girl said. She took a deep breath and continued, 'Tu es une femme donc c'est Seigneuresse. En tant que noblesse, vous devriez le savoir. C'est Français.'

'Get out! Never show your faces here again,' screamed Lady Livienne. Horrified that Greta had dared to speak to her in French, the third language of Anseris, used exclusively by the Gentry. What was worse, Greta had dared to correct her French in a perfect accent, much better than her own.

'If'n yous be a-payin' us our owed wages first,' said Magda, reverting back to rural Angerlish.

'What did you say?' Lady Livienne.

'Thirty Krona back pay for me an' forty-five for Carlotta.'

'Get out. I owe you nothing.'

'We'll see about that,' said Carlotta. 'Everybody in the village said we were off our heads a-workin' for yous. Well we weren't. We was a-workin' for the Baron and his daughters. Not for yous, you snotty cow, nor your inbred stupid twins, who are a waste of space.'

'*A*re you sure about this?' Lady Livienne asked Ray Payntor, one of her late Husband's oldest friends, who had been visiting Cenerentola when the Baron had died. Lady Livienne invited Payntor to dinner on this first night after the end of the official mourning. There was so much that her late Husband had refused to tell her about the time before she had met him. This man could fill in so many blank spaces. Naturally he accepted. Cenerentola House had the best cook in the Archduchy.

'Yes, milady, I took poor Angharad to hospital. The Angelbless was the nearest maternity hospital. If I had known what a disaster that place was, I would have taken her the extra few miles to the Royal. Then I had to go to work, I couldn't stay with her. I returned to the hospital at the end of the day, and the midwife on duty said both mother and child had died.'

'So who is Chantelle then?' she asked as she sipped her sherry.

'I don't know, milady.'

'Oh, come on Raymond, you've known me long enough to call me Livienne in private.'

'Thank you, Livienne.' The man relaxed into his chair and took his glass of brandy from the table.

'The thing is Gladys Simples was the only person who knew exactly who Chantelle is, and she has been dead for a dozen years.'

'What about Countess Jacqueline?'

'She was in labour at the same time as Angharad. No Livienne, I'm sure Gladys Simples knew that she would be set for life, if she could persuade poor Gilbert that some random female Fenzrian orphan was his daughter.

Ray could not believe that the stupid woman was swallowing his story hook, line and sinker.

'I have never seen Chantelle's birth certificate?' said Lady Livienne.

'If Gilbert didn't have a copy, I doubt one exists The Angelbless's administration was a joke. It burnt down shortly after Chantelle was born. Any records they might have had were lost.' He had burnt down the Angelbless Maternity Hospital, to hide the birth records of Chantelle. He had been waiting years, hoping to spring this trap on the filthy mongrel witch-child.

Ray Payntor knew the story he had just fed Lady Livienne was a load of old brozhnik. He knew the stuck-up old witch would germinate the seed of doubt he had planted. All to the detriment of the mongrel child of a man who was too stupid to realise he had been betrayed by his old friend Ray time and time again.

A nd where do you think you are going, Ella?' demanded Lady Livienne. She was standing at the top of the stairs, with her arms folded tightly over her chest. Chantelle recognised that look, her stepmother was about to do something horrible. It was best to just play along.

'I've just had my morning walk. I'm returning to my room, to change into different indoor shoes, belle-mére,' Chantelle replied, showing her stockinged feet. 'Then I was coming to see you.'

'First of all, you will never call me that again,' said Lady Livienne.

'But you are my step-mother, it is a common courtesy.'

'From now on you will address me as "Mistress", like all the other servants.'

'But I'm not a servant!' said Chantelle, who was shocked by this crazy outburst from her step-mother. Has the old cow flipped? Perhaps this was her way of grieving. This was how she expressed her shock at her husband's sudden death. Should she play along with this. No, her-step mother had to snap out of this now. Before she did something she would regret.

'No, Ella, you are.' Lady Livienne had walked down the stairs and was now one step above Chantelle.

'No! I'm not a servant, and my name isn't Ella, belle-mère.'

'You are. I learnt the truth about you last night.' The slap was sudden and painful. Lady Livienne had never physically chastised her, or her sisters before. 'I am your mistress, you will show me respect. Now curtsey, and say you are sorry.'

'I'm sorry, Ma'am,' said Chantelle now in a state of shock.

'As I was saying, first, you will never call me belle-mère ever again. From what Monsieur Payntor said, you are not actually my late husband's child. He says that poor Angharad's child died at birth. Madam Simples told Gilbert you were poor Angharad's daughter there is no evidence to support that.'

'That's ridiculous. Look at your daughter, Madeleine, we share the same Father. We're nearly identical.'

'I see no resemblance' said Lady Livienne in full flow. 'You are a stranger's child he spoilt and coddled. I promised my late husband that you would be looked after, but that was when I thought you were his child. I know now, you are nothing but a parasitic drain on this estate, you must now repay all the kindness he showed you. You will do that through hard work.' An evil glint appeared in Lady Livienne's eyes. 'I'll get Monsieur Nouveauté to draw up indenture papers. You must sign them or become a homeless pauper.'

'That is outrageous...' Chantelle did not get a chance to finish her complaint, as another slap stung her cheek.

'First, did I give you permission to speak, girl?'

'Second, Chantelle is far too grand for a mere housemaid. Now your name is Ella. You must accept that your old life is a cinder, Ella

'Third, you will move to the servant's quarters, and wear livery when you are on duty. You may have one afternoon a week off, plus any free time after church on Sunday morning and before you serve Sunday supper in the evening.

'Fourth, you will do whatever the Cook tells you to do, without question. Do you understand all of this, Ella.'

'Yes, Ma'am,' said Chantelle, still in shock.

'Now, go to your new room in the servants' quarters, change, then report to Cook. And this time, curtsey.'

Her ancestors had unquestionably obeyed orders for centuries. Something deep inside her clicked on.

'Yes, Ma'am.'

𝕴t was late, and Chantelle was feeling exhausted. She had been working non-stop all day, on the Cooks ever lengthening list of jobs. She certainly didn't feel like a gentlewoman at the moment. She currently didn't look like one either. Even though the sumptary laws had been revoked a year ago, ordinary people still mostly wore linen, and the burnt orange kirtle was pure linen.

A knock on the door. 'Can I come in?' asked Madeleine, whose hair hung long and loose like a titian curtain.

'Of course you can Maddie. You don't need to ask.'

'I do, the rules governing the servant's quarters demand it,' Madeleine said in a sheepish voice.

'Those rules also say you shouldn't be here,' said Chantelle.

'I'm so sorry about what Maman has done.'

'The Mistress, and by the same rules I must always call her that now, and call you Miss.'

Madeleine began to cry. 'Why did Papa have to die? It's so horrible without him.'

Poor Madeleine, thought Chantelle as she wrapped her arms around the sobbing girl. 'Ah! The rules be damned.'

'I thought you might want some of your things,' said Madeleine when she recovered some composure. She emptied the bag full of the twenty-first century level of technology that was the norm in rural areas of Anseris. 'She couldn't reset the laptop, but I'm afraid you will have to re-download all the books in the reader.'

'Your wearing my new blue outfit,' said Chantelle.

'You have to admit all my other traditional clothes are far too small, and I can't keep wearing the ready-to-wear mourning dress. Maman would have a fit if she saw me in any of the properly fitting city-style clothes I wear there.'

'Well, I was going to give you something to wear. I suppose the mistress has cancelled your trip to the seamstresses at Castello del Filippo?' asked Chantelle.

'Yes and no, Maman went through your room, as she moved me in, saying, "What does a housemaid need this sort of dress for? It's yours now,"' said Madeleine with a growing look of horror as she remembered the event. 'But the seamstresses of Castello will be busy for weeks, not making new clothes for me. Just altering your newer clothes to fit me. She says it will save money. Why is she penny-pinching? The estate is profitable and Father's stock portfolio is awesome. We are not as hard-up as our name implies.'

'A lifetime of genteel poverty has made her a miser and a terrible snob,' Chantelle said to her half-sister. 'After all, look at what she did to my hair.'

Like all women from the aristocracy and the gentry trimmed but never cut their hair. It had been long enough to sit on. It had been a sign of wealth and privilege. Just as she had been stripped of that privilege, she had been stripped of most of her hair, when Lady Livienne had cut it level with Chantelle's armpits.

'You'd be en vogue in Elizaburg,' said an envious Madeleine. 'Remember when I came home with the Queen's short hairstyle Everyone, including Papa, was annoyed. Despite my copying her Majesty's hairstyle. Madeleine's lovely red hair had grown to her waist.

'However, it gets worse,' Madeleine said, 'Mother declared that everything in the room was now my property. I said no, but she replied it had all been Papa's which he'd lent to you, as his work of charity. Now it was all mine, to dispose of as I saw fit.'

'Again, I refuse to be surprised.'

'Then she said, since Greta left, there is a vacancy for a scullery maid. I could always renounce my family and join you in the servant's quarters,' said Madeleine, with some iron returning to her voice. 'So that is what I am here to do. I suppose that will be my bed.'

So tempting, they had been a team sharing the housework during the mourning. Then Chantelle's moral compass sprung back to North.

'No, Maddy dear, don't do that,' said a horrified Chantelle. 'I appreciate the gesture, but I don't want you to suffer. Besides, I need an ally on the other side.'

'To spy on Mama and the twins? But why?'

'Maddy dearest, there was something very wrong about the way Papa died. Before she arrived, and introduced a strict separation between employers and employees, I could go anywhere in the house. As a servant, I can once again go anywhere without being noticed, freedom to investigate. However, a set of eyes with the family is always useful.' The two young women hugged.

'Oh, I wish our Aunt Bronwen was here. I know she would help,' said Chantelle.

'She's lived out in Pendragon for twenty years, so she would always be too far away to help,' said Madeleine. 'I've never met her.'

'Advice from a distance is better than no advice at all,' said Chantelle. 'Now, I have to be up at 5am in the morning. It's best if you go now.'

'OK, Chantelle.'

'You have to call me Ella.'

'But that is not your name?'

'I know, but it is what must be done.'

Chantelle knew she had to sleep, worry kept her awake. She had no way of knowing if her step-mother had poisoned Madeleine's mind. Was her half-sister had already betraying her.

She knew there was no love lost between Madeleine and her mother. Her Father told her Madeleine had been the surprise. Lady Livienne had been miserable during the entire unplanned pregnancy.

Open hostilities between mother and daughter broke out last year. Lady Livienne decided she did not want Madeleine to spend any more time in Elizaburg. The city was a hotbed of radical ideas. Instead of a proper education and career, Madeleine should attend her old finishing school in the old royal hunting lodge near Castle Stark. This would prepare her for la Saison du Débutante and marriage.

This had horrified Baron Gilbert, a firm believer in equality for women. He refused his wife's request as he agreed with the Queen, who called la Saison an unedifying cattle market which the Benedictian Kings had started. Naturally she would have no part in it, and canceled it.

Satisfied that her half-sister was firmly on her side, Chantelle turned over and dropped into a deep, all encompassing sleep.

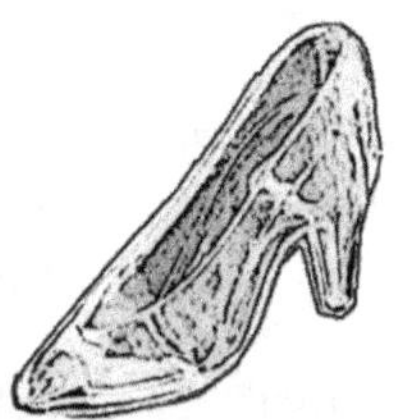 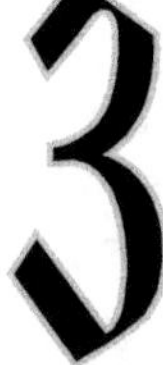 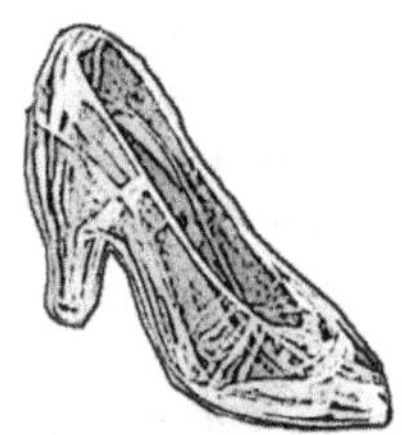

3

Lady Liùienne had forbidden television and radio from inside Cenerentola House. They were bad influences, full of progressive ideas and terrible modern music. She had no idea how Madeleine kept so up to date with events in Elizaburg. She had allowed the use of telephones. If she had known how powerful the Internet, that piggybacked the telephone line, was at spreading information, she would have banned that as well. Instead she tried ignoring the technology which was becoming more common.

The news online was full of the march that had taken place the previous day in Elizaburg, against the Fenzrian minority. Organised by a new political group called White Hand.

'There were nine hundred and forty six Fenzrian prisoners of war at the end of the conflict,' Madeleine said to her half-sister, 'including your Mother's ancestors.'

'Even today, the Fenzrians make up less than half a percent of the entire population of the Kingdom. Fenzrians are such a tiny minority which is still too many for the meat-heads and the bone idle,' said Chantelle.

'Who are feeling the pinch since the liberation of the Serfs,' Madeleine continued, 'If your Fenzrian relatives weren't here, the White Hand would be picking on the former serfs instead.'

Serfs, descendant of high security prisoners brought to Anseris aboard the prison ship KHM#89. The Serfs continued to be punished for their ancestor's crimes in life-long penal servitude. In the new liberal world of Queen Johanna IV, th injustice of Serfdom had been abolished.

'Oh, don't worry, Serfs won't escape the attention of the White Hand for long. The White Hand is powered by laziness and a sense of entitlement. Fenzrians are currently an easier target.'

'Ella, you're not paid to discuss politics, you're paid to work,' said Lady Livienne as she walked into the room.

'And talking of a sense of entitlement,' said Madeleine.

'I heard that young lady,' said her Mother. 'I didn't think I was entitled to an easy life, because I was dropped into a willing nest unlike some around here.'

'Whatever,' said Madeleine as she left the room. She would finish the conversation with her sister later.

The Fenzrian who became prisoners of war during the invasion would never have been allowed back into the cult, whoever won the war. The Cult of the Great Machine forbade unauthorized contact with outsiders. Prisoners were deprogrammed and started new lives in what were politely called re-education camps. The prisoners were rapidly becoming Anserian, so the Aggelii decided they were no longer a threat and it would be cruel to make them share the exile of the other Fenzians, and rip them away from their new homes.

The camps evolved first into the villages and then the towns. A high security prison was built between one of these new towns and the city of Randau. Many Fenzrians worked in the prison, so the town's name changed to Cacharau, the Welsh word for Prisons.

By the coronation of Queen Johanna IV, Cacharau had a population of over three thousand, almost all being pure Fenzrian. Cacharau was one of three prosperous communities on Gwener. The Fenzrians are hard working and efficient. They succeeded at whatever they turned their hand to. Fenzrians had moved to all parts of the Kingdom, some had married the locals, so thousands of people could now call themselves fully or partially Fenzrian.

The Fenzrians could still use the psychic interface technology common on the rest of the human inhabited worlds throughout the galaxy. After centuries of disuse, the local Anserians needed gene therapy to reactivate their psychic interfaces. The Benedictian kings tried to destroy this sort of technology. In backward looking rural areas using the psychic interface was classed as witchcraft. Calling Fenzrians witches and warlocks became a common insult.

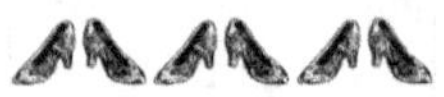

Twenty four years earlier, when Chantelle was born:

C enerentola might have been a rural backwater where people hated all newcomers on principle. Under Francois du Fauché and then his son Gilbert this was not the case. They welcomed their exotic new tennents. The small Fenzrian community was soon an integral part of Cenerentola village. When Baron Gilbert du Fauché married a Fenzrian woman, making her Baroness Angharad, there had been widespread celebration. They had also celebrated the news that the young Baroness was having her first child. The baby would be born in Elizaburg, the Kingdom's capital. Thousands of miles to the West, where the villagers thought the Baron had an important job in government.

The young Baroness went into labour three days after her husband had been sentenced to six months in prison for seditious libel. Her husband had put his name to a letter criticising the King's choice of location for a new airport outside the city of Tintagel.

'Why did they have to send him to prison, straight away?' asked Angharad, 'that's just cruel and unusual, even the King knows that.'

'It's not the King who is the problem here, it's the Chessmen,' said the Baron's friend Ray Payntor. He was referring to the Political Police, whose black and white chequerboard uniform earned them the nickname "The Chessmen". 'It's one chessman in particular. You know some of them hate your people.'

'A lot of people hate my people, Ray. Not just in the Political Police.'

'But one of the Chessmen must have persuaded that bastard of a judge not to delay incarceration, as is standard practice, given your condition. It's not as if Gilbert had been convicted of that serious an offence, or that he would do a runner anyway.'

What Baroness Angharad did not know was that Ray was the Chessman who had convinced the judge to impose such a cruel sentence. He knew she would never know that.

'I'm so glad that Gilbert has a friend like you,' said Angharad, just before she doubled up with another contraction.'

'Ray, this isn't the Royal. I'm booked in there to give birth.'

'You need help straight away. This old banger is not the a state of the arts ambulance you need. Once the staff of this place see your notes, they will transfer you to the Royal in a hospital on wheels.'

He knew that would definitely not happen. The Angelbless would hold on to Angharad, regardless of the amount of specialist treatment she required. Ray didn't expect Angharad to be seen by a midwife for hours. Before Angharad and Ray passed through the doors, a midwife met them, proving him wrong.

H er name tag read Gladys Simples. 'What's your name dear?'
'I am Baroness Angharad du Fauché,' she replied.

'Oh!' Everyone had heard of Baron Gilbert du Fauché and his wife. 'So this is your first child, dear?'

'Yes, my first.' Why did this woman ask such a stupid question. All she had to do was look at her data-pad. Sadly she was too distressed to notice the midwife didn't have a data-pad.

'Just like my daughter. Married a year ago and about to have my first grandchild,' the midwife said conversationally.'

Angharad was not interested in conversation. All she cared about was easing the pain. Gilbert, sometimes I hate you, she thought.

Why did you sign that letter, I told you not to. I knew the Chessmen would not like it. Then some protesters had vandalised the building site. Despite there being no evidence, Gilbert and his fellow signatories had been arrested for encouraging the protesters. One of the protesters said that Gilbert had told him to attack the site if the letter didn't work. Gilbert's barrister had tried to get that man's testimony thrown out, it had obviously been gained under torture, but the judge refused. Gilbert and his associates had been found guilty and sent to jail.

'Your admissions letter says you need quiet, because of your blood pressure,' said the midwife. 'Don't worry, I'll soon have you in a bed in a side room.'

A bed thought Angharad, somewhere to rest her feet, to lessen the upcoming ordeal. She let the midwife dress her in a surgical gown and help her on the bed.

'Where's Ray? Angharad asked, desperate for a friendly face.

'Who dear?' The midwife annoyingly answering one question with another.

'The gentleman who brought me in, replied Angharad.

'I'm not sure, dear. I have to fetch some paperwork. I'll check while I'm out.'

'You can't download my notes?'

'I'm afraid not. This place is out of the Loop. Never in it, in fact. The Royal will print your notes and send them over by courier.'

idwife Gladys Simples had every intention of returning to her patient until she saw her unmarried and heavily pregnant daughter, Jacqueline sitting in a wheelchair. Oh brozhnik! she thought, the child's coming early. Way too early.

Anserian society believed marriage before parenthood was the right way to do things. Becoming pregnant before marriage was tolerated if the parents married before the child was born. Having a child and remaining single was a source of shame for the pregnant woman while she was obviously pregnant. Once the child was born, the shame switched entirely to the good for nothing father who had abandoned his responsibilities. In a few hours Gladys could stop lying about Jackie's marital status.'

'Jackie, love. What ya doin' ere?' she asked, knowing the answer.

'Mum, its started,' said her daughter. 'My waters broke at the tramhalt as I was going to work.'

'Come with me, dear, I'll make sure everything goes smoothly.'

'I'm sorry mum. Getting myself knocked up by my ex-employer's son. Normally it would have been fine because he can't, you know, do it. The atmosphere that night was so different and he did it on the one night a month he shouldn't do it.' The young woman began crying. 'I thought Eddy really loved me.'

'There, there, Jackie. Life's just too short for recriminations, especially when you've a young one to look after,' Gladys said.

'He went off to be with his family and mourn for his brother, before I could tell him about the baby. He could never marry me. No matter how convincing I was, I'm still a pleb...' the woman's body was racked with another contraction, '...and he's a Ristoze. But that was months ago. I thought Eddy loved me enough to have set me and the baby up all comfy. I haven't heard from him at all.'

'We'll manage somehow dear. Now, how often are them contractions coming.'

'Every five minutes, I reckon. What with getting here on the sneltram, I haven't been checking'

'It's OK Jackie, your here now,' said her mother reassuringly. Inside Gladys was far from re-assured. The baby wasn't due for another month.

'It was fun though, Eddy passing me off as a Ristoze at all those parties and special events he took me too.'

'That's Ristoze for you,' Gladys said. 'Only pretending to be toffs when it suits them.'

'I miss him, mum. And I still love him.'

'Well 'e h-obviously didn't love you, otherwise 'e would 'ave replied to all them letters you sent 'im. Like I said, we'll manage.' Gladys was trying to keep calm, but her usual good grammar and diction had boiled away.

Gladys wheeled her daughter to the reception, and filled in the admittance forms for Jackie. Baroness du Fauché had a couple of hours to go before her baby popped out, Jackie was ready to pop right now. There was no way she was going to leave her daughter in the hands of her useless colleagues.

Ray Payntor left the hospital and disappeared for twenty-four years. He had gone to a seedy hotel that didn't ask any questions. It was not necessary in most places, but here he sterilised the bathroom as much as possible. Just to be safe. Then he carefully removed the titanium implants and watched in the mirror as his face sunk. He placed the bloodied metal in a container to sterilise it, and took a shiny clean piece of titanium from a box and slipped it into his mouth, then pulling his elastic skin into place, he had what he called his real face, the face of Stanley Silvermann.

Stanley had been born with the upper jaw and front of his face missing. He needed implants to keep his nasal passage open and to give him teeth to eat. For years he had been a deformed freak, making a living as an informer for the Political Police. One of the officers had seen possibilities in Stanley, and recruited him to his department. There several specialised implants were created for Stan, each one had several configurations, which gave him many different faces. A simple hair-dye and a change of accent gave Stan a bucketful of personalities he could adopt. The perfect spy, a man with literally a thousand faces.

Stanley was deeply conservative. He was loyal to the current royal family, who had saved Anseris from alien influences.

He desperately hated the Fenzrians. No matter how much they claimed they had assimilated, they would always be alien.

He had been sent to spy on the Baron du Fauché. When he discovered that the Baron, with whom he had feigned friendship, was married to a filthy Fenzrian he was disgusted. He made a promise that at the first opportunity, he would stitch up Baron Gilbert. He had made sure the Fenzrian bitch and the mongrel would not survive childbirth at the Angelbless the worse maternity hospital in Elizaburg.

We've had a phone call from Alfredsburg Prison,' said the ward Sister. 'One of their convicts has a wife in labour here. Anyone know anything?'

'Gladys admitted someone before her daughter came in,' said one of the midwives, 'I'll go and check on her after lunch.'

Except after lunch, everyone had forgotten the phone call and nobody checked on Angharad.

Why did nobody come? Where was Ray? Why had the judge been so cruel. These thoughts carouselled through Angharad's head. She did not know Payntor had sabotaged the bell to summon help. She pushed and pushed alone as her precious girl made her way from womb to world. Angharad fragile body was too weak for the process. There should have been a midwife, there should have been doctors. Her notes said she should have had a caesarean. That is why the child was being born here in Elizaburg, and not back home on Cenerentola Island. Instead of around the clock care, she was left alone, and her heart eventually gave out.

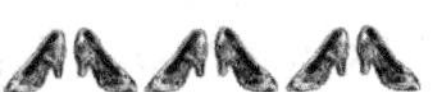

ladys should have been exuberant. A healthy grandson delivered to a healthy daughter. Except, she was full of doubt. Jacqueline's delivery had been far more complicated than she had expected so she had stayed longer than she had planned. Whatever had happened to that poor Fenzrian girl, whose husband had been so unjustly treated, she was well overdue now.

'Who delivered Angharad du Fauché?' she asked her colleagues.

'Who?' each one of them replied. They had recently come on duty and had not yet read the notes, that had arrived from the Royal Hospital's maternity unit, just before the previous shift ended.

'The noblewoman who came in this afternoon,' said Gladys 'Look her notes are here.'

'If she is a noblewoman, what's she doing here?' asked Sandra Millman, the ward secretary, who had no record of Angharad.

'I don't know. Her family must be all fur coats and no knickers, replied Gladys. 'I'll go and check.'

'For the Angel's sake Gladys, go home, I'll go and check,' said one of her colleagues.

Gladys and Sandra went anyway, knowing nobody would check Lady Angharad. The Angelbless was closing the day after she retired Maybe it was a good thing she thought.

She was horrified by what she found in the side ward. The poor girl was lying there dead, and her tiny daughter was delivered but in great distress. The old midwife rushed to the young child's aid. The pleasure from her own happy event was eclipsed by the feeling of betrayal she felt towards the poor woman dead on the bed. From that moment on, she decided she would do everything for the baby girl in her arms, including giving her a home while her Father was so cruelly incarcerated.

As she was cutting the umbilical chord, which still attached dead mother to living child, the door slammed open and another Fenzrian woman, in one of those new Guild Style outfits rushed into the room.

'Angharad, Angharad! Fy chwaer annwyl. Beth wedi'n wneud i ti?'* she said in Welsh. Gladys knew enough of the language to reply.

---

*'Angharad, Angharad! Ver kh-oo-ire annoil. Bairth wedee-n ooneyed ee tee?' She said in Welsh.

'Mae'n ddrwg 'da fi ei bod hi wedi marw. Mae'n ddrwg iawn gen i.'* she said then turning back to standard Angerlish, 'I was called away and she was forgotten by my useless colleagues. By the time I returned, it was too late for her, but the baby girl will be fine.'

Gladys saw the woman collapse to her knees and give out an almighty wail, tears pouring from her. The midwife continued with her work and eventually handed the child to its Aunt, who had calmed down, sitting next to her dead sister, sobbing intermittently.

'She is such a bonny little thing, My girls wre so sickly when they were born. Do you know what she is to be called , Miss?'

'I'm afraid not.'

'Not to worry. We'll call her Chantelle until we hear different. Do you have a key to her family home? I will take the babe there and look after her. Otherwise she will have to go into an orphanage until her father returns home. You will have to explain this to the staff at her home.'

'Thank you, Nurse Simples. I am due to return to Pendragon in a week, I can delay that for a while and help you.'

Gladys noted that being given something to do had galvanised the younger woman.

Please call me Gladys.

Six Months Later:

Baron Gilbert du Fauché had been released from prison that morning and been flown straight to Elizaburg. He was a broken man. He had received one letter from Ray Payntor, telling him his beloved wife was dead, as was the child she was carrying. All the life had drained out of him and he spent his time in prison as a dead man.

He had expected to find Maison du Fauché boarded up and empty. Instead he found it full of life. A matronly woman had answered the door. He had followed her to the drawing room where a young woman wearing City style clothes with a Pendragon hairstyle was sitting, reading a book. The matronly woman sat in the chair next to younger one, as if she belonged there, instead of withdrawing to the kitchen.

---

*'Mine throog dah vee ay bord he wedee maroo. Mine throog yee-own gen ee,' she said, then returning to standard Angerlish.

'Gilbert, we weren't expecting you until Wednesday,' said the younger woman, who had stood up and now hugged him. He now realised it was Angharad's sister. It, made sense, nothing else did.

He could hear at least two babies crying in the nursery on the third floor. The girl brought a tea tray from the Kitchen. A few minutes later she returned with a tray of sandwiches. The girl snagged a snack and sat on the settee with the other woman. A fourth woman started singing, on what sounded like the third floor, obviously in an attempt to quiet the children.

'This is Gladys Simples,' said Bronwen, 'that is her younger daughter Avril, and you can hear her elder daughter Jacqueline singing,' said Bronwen.

'Yes, but why are they living in my house, as if they belong here?' asked a very confused Gilbert du Fauché.

'I think, Gladys should explain things,' replied Bronwen.

'So my Lord, as you could not be contacted, I took control of the situation, and with Miss Bronwen's help, we brought young Chantelle home,' said Gladys, finishing the story.

'I thank you Mistress Simples, and of course you Bronwen,' said the Baron.

'I only supplied a front door key. The Simples have done all the rest. I knew you were due home this week, so I've taken some holiday time to help you adjust.'

'When I arrived back in Elizaburg, I was in a living nightmare, now I appear to be in a waking dream. You say young Myfanwy survived. May I see her?'

'Of course you can my Lord. You are her father, you have every right to see her.' Gladys took a tube from the wall and blew into it.

'Yes mum, what is it?' said a younger female voice.

'Jackie, his lordship has arrived a day early. Bring little Chantelle down with you, so he can meet his daughter.'

'We were going to call her Myfanwy, after her Grandmother,' said the Baron.

'It's not a problem. I didn't know what name you wanted. We call her Chantelle because the Gentry usually like French names.

Although, it's not as if she has got used to having a name, and she hasn't been registered yet, only you can do that.'

'No, I shall take her home to register her as Chantelle Angharad Cenerentola du Fauché. You would be surprised by how much babies understand...' Then he spotted the child, in the perfect white robe and lacy bonnet that had been bought for the child's naming day. 'Oh my darling girl. I might not show it, but I love you. You are also loved by these good women. You will never know your Mother's kiss, but I know you will always be happy.'

When Chantelle was four years old:

'Gladys, I think we may be turning a corner,' Baron Gilbert said to the woman sitting next to him in his study. 'The estate is about to break even, for the first time in centuries. If I sell the last packet of land in this city, it will be a certainty.'

He was talking about the land the house stood on. Property prices in Elizaburg's old town had sky-rocketed over the past eighteen months. The four city blocks around Maison du Fauché, which had been worth shillings were now worth hundreds of thousands of Krona.

'Yes dear, but do you still have to sell this old pile?'

'I'm sorry, Glad, you have called this house home for four years now and it's been my home in the city all my life, we have an emotional attachment,' said the Baron, 'but you know I have to sell the whole parcel of land, no exceptions, before the current property bubble in this city bursts. It is the only option. Profit from the sale will guarantee the estate remains profitable in the future.'

Months ago, Baron Gilbert had decided to relocate his family, as he now regarded the Simples as his family, back to his ancestral home. Back to Cenerentola House, in the Archduchy of Fiandre. Thousands of miles to the East.

Gladys had agreed with him that it would be far better for Chantelle and her grandson Len to grow up in the country. Away from the crime, grime and unpleasantness of the City.

Jackie Simples now a qualified Midwife and had a new job in in Fiandre. Avril Simples would make family history by studying Medicine at the University of Genova, also in Fiandre.

Chantelle and Len would be starting school, at the excellent new school Archduke Michael and the Sisters of the Merciful Charity of Angels to All Children had opened on the Island.

It was a shame that he would have to remain in his current job here in Elizaburg until his current contract ran out.

'Your heart belongs to the Island and its people, Gilbert' said Gladys. 'You wish you could be moving with us.'

'I do, but I can't. I have to stay here in Elizaburg. It breaks my heart I have to stay here, thousands of miles to the west, whilst my daughter grows up on the Island. I'll miss her terribly, and you. You've kept me on the straight and narrow.'

'Well, if you keep away from politics, there is no reason why you can't do that yourself,' Gladys said. 'It's more important that Chantelle has some continuity. If you can't be there, me, Jackie and Len will be continuity for her in her new home,' said Gladys.

'No continuity for you, moving so far east,' said Gilbert.

'Me and my Frank always planned on retiring to Tintagel,' she said. 'He passed away before we had chance. An island of the south coast of Fiandre is just as good.'

'It's going to need a lot of work done to renovate the place. Work that should have been done years ago,' said Baron Gilbert.

'Questionable plumbing?' asked Gladys.

'That could do with upgrading along with the electricity supply. Before you can move in the masonry and the roof need serious attention.'

'Nothing major then, Gilbert.'

There were those who said the Simples had taken advantage of Gilbert. Nothing was further from the truth. As a former political prisoners, he had a hard time finding well paying job. Income from the estate had to be ploughed into the estate. He had been as poor as the Simples, without their experience of being poor. He worked like a dog to turn things around. They had shared their meagre lot him. Now he wanted to share his wealth with his new family.

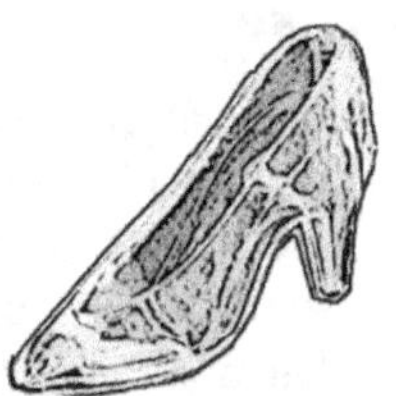 **4** 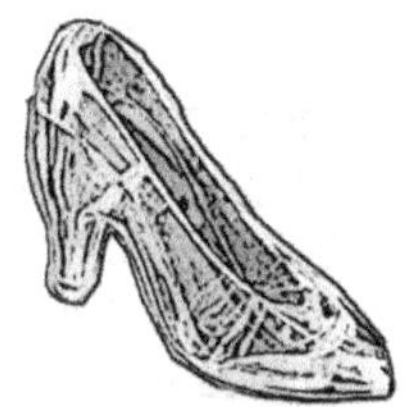

Lady Livienne du Carrefour had first married when she
was seventeen. Her husband's family sat at the head of Clan Carrefour, had never really approved of Jacques' socially inferior but politically important young cousin, who the astute match-makers had chosen to be his wife.

They did not approve of Jacques' chosen profession either. He was one of the last remaining Oath-sworn Knights who took part in Tourneys. On a planet so entrenched in its fake medievalism, Jousting had always been popular enough for a good living to be made. The sport was now dominated by plebeians and their sponsors, and was now seen as beneath the dignity of the noble classes. It was so much safer than it had been on mediaeval Earth, but Jacques still died accidentally at the first Tourney of 5868 CGE.

Her rich in-laws refused to support the widowed daughter-in-law who failed to produce a male heir. Lady Livienne's neighbour, Baron Gilbert du Fauché, was a middle aged widower, and rich enough to maintain her lifestyle. Every Baron needed a Baroness, so she persuaded herself that she loved him and his funny radical ideas, and set about persuading him that he loved her.

She had been married for five months, when to her horror she discovered she was pregnant again. Gilbert was ecstatic when he heard the news. Livienne pretended to be happy, but was miserable the whole time. The arrival of her third daughter did nothing to improve her increasingly sour world-view.

Madeleine passed from wet-nurse, to nursery maid, to nanny and finally to a governess. Lady Livienne insisted her daughters would not go to the plebeian school in Elizaburg that Gilbert had chosen.

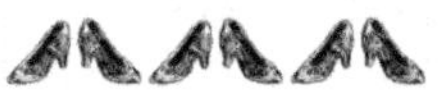

When Chantelle was Eight Years Old:

Chantelle was feeling lonely, so much had recently changed in her life. She had enjoyed the wedding. Aunty Jackie had looked beautiful all in white. The satin kirtle, the fancy lace surcotte and a bride's long pointed steeple henning were so pretty. Her aunt had gone to live in Castello del Filippo with her new husband Earl Edwin. Aunty Jackie

was now Countess Jacqueline. As threatened, Len, or Viscount Leonard, as she now had to call him had also gone to live in Castello del Filippo. Fortunately Granny Glad was still living at Cenerentola, but she was getting old and becoming more and more forgetful.

'Have you told Chantelle yet?' the Countess asked her mother.

'Told me what?' asked Chantelle as she walked into the kitchen.

'Haven't I told you about knocking doors, young lady,' said Granny Glad.

'Sorry, Granny,' said Chantelle, 'but told me what?'

'Your Papa has remarried. She is Lady Livienne du Carrefour. A widow with a pair of three year old daughters. Identical twins called Clementine and Citronella.' said the Countess.

'Orange and Lemon,' said Chantelle. Does that mean I will have a new mama and sisters coming to live here?'

'No dear, they will remain in Elizaburg. Your Papa is still an important man in the city, but will visit here regularly, try keeping him away.'

'Papa will still visit.'

Good, I didn't like Elizaburg, when I visited him.'

'Of course. Now, Leo is here, pour a glass of lemonade for him and one for yourself, and go out into the garden to play. There's a good girl,' said Aunty Jackie.

Auntie Jackie only said that when she wanted to say something private to Granny Glad. So Chantelle went outside and sat beneath the pantry window to eavesdrop

'What did Gilbert see in that terrible woman?' asked Granny Glad

'The same thing any healthy man sees in a woman,' said the Countess

'But she's such a small and bony creature, Jackie.'

'No accounting for taste, mum.' Aunty Jackie giggled. 'And she's trapped him the way only a healthy and fertile woman can.'

'Apparently not the case. They were wed for months before the happy news, or so Sarah-Anne Ellisford-Taylor told me.' There was a time when class conscious Gladys would never have casually dropped an aristocratic name into a conversation. There was a time when she would never have mixed with aristocrats, especially not distant cousins of the former Royal Family.

'Now that's intrest'n.', Mam,' Jackie said, dropping into the Elizaburg accent of her youth. 'Doz gentry and ristoze is a laughin' lot.'

'Inbred and stupid, the lot of them. Everything that is wrong with the Gentry can be found in Clan Carrefour.'

'You only say that because Livienne's father-in-law sacked me,' said her daughter, 'but he was clever enough to cut his dreadful daughter-in-law off.'

'Not really, it means that Gilbert is saddled with her now. And don't forget, getting sacked by old man Carrefour was your own fault. You were caught aping those who were your social betters.'

'If he hadn't, I would never have met Edwin, mum. And now I am stratospherically higher up the social scale than the Carrefours.'

'Which nearly went horribly wrong,' said the older woman. 'And when your Aunty Jackie tells you to go outside and play, she means it, Chantelle Angharad Cenerentola du Fauché! Not go outside and eavesdrop!'

The pantry window was shut and Chantelle could hear no more.

'**S**o you must be Chantelle Ingrid. Angels! You really are a witch child,' said the woman her Father had married. She was tiny, barely five foot tall. She could easily be mistaken for a child, if she had not been wearing a loose wimple and veil only respectably married women wear. Oh yes, she was also pregnant, but even her bump was tiny.

'Angharad,' Chantelle said, 'Chantelle Angharad Cenerentola du Fauché.' Then quickly adding 'Belle-mère.'

'Whatever,' said the tiny woman. 'I'll have to sack that nurse-maid and get her a proper governess.'

'Gladys Simples is not a nursemaid, dear,' said her Father. 'She saved Chantelle's life and tried to save her poor mother, my first wife. She earned more than my eternal gratitude. The Simples are almost family now.'

'Most of her family have moved to Castello del Filippo, now Aunty Jackie is the Countess, Papa,' said Chantelle.

'Oh, so that woman's daughter is the plebeian gold digger who got her claws into Earl Edwin,' said the tiny woman. 'Oh yes, she's persuaded him that her little bastard is his son.'

'What do you mean, Chantelle goes to the pleb village school. Gilbert, that has got to stop. I will definitely hire a governess. Much better than the Merciful Sisters and their associates in the village. Especially as the twins have one back in Elizaburg.'

'Until we come home to the Island. then the twins and our little one will go to the village school. You know I believe every parent, regardless of rank, should send their children to their local schools. Equality of education is the only way forward.

Chantelle really did not like her new Step-mother. Calling her a "Witch child" was a dreadful insult. Also why was she saying such horrible things about her almost family?

If she is now married to my Papa, and no longer a widow, why is she still wearing widow's green?

'What are you staring at girl?' the woman asked Chantelle.

'Widow's Green,' Chantelle replied without thinking.

'The stuff of nonsense girl. I wear green because I like green, no other reason.'

The day just got worse when she met twin squabbling toddlers Clementine and Citronella. Rude and bad tempered, just like their mother. Unlike their mother they were fat. In their orange and yellow outfits, they really did look like an orange and a lemon.

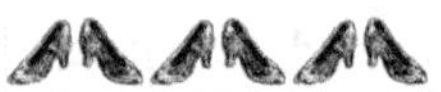

C hantelle was overjoyed to learn her Father was coming home. It helped reduce the grief after the death of Granny Glad. At eleven, her father had asked her if she wanted to go to secondary school in Elizaburg or Ponte di Carla. It had been so tempting, being with him, but that meant being with that woman and here awful daughters. There were now three of them, Madeleine had been born a year after her Papa had married that women. She had diplomatically told him she hated Elizaburg, and wanted to stay in Fiandre. It was the truth, but not the whole truth. That would hurt her Father's feelings.

Chantelle had spent the past year studying typing, and then how to use the new word-processor her father would be bringing with him. She had also learnt filing and basic book-keeping. Everything she needed to be her Father's secretary.

hat do you mean, you refused Lord Derek's proposal?' asked

W the angry Lady Livienne. 'His mother and I both agree you two are a perfect match.'

'I refused because Papa would never allow it. Also poor Derek only asked because his mama forced him to.'

'He's twenty one, high time he settled down.'

'He is settled down, with Brian, who is such a lovely fellow. Lord Derek's mother should accept her Son is homosexual.'

'Lord Derek is not a pervert.'

'Exactly, he's just gay. Some people are, live with it.' Chantelle laughed. 'Besides, he might be a lovely bloke, but he is also inbred and stupid, a bit like you.'

'You spend far too much time with Countess Jacqueline,' said Lady Livienne.

'I'm surprised a dreadful social climber like you would object to me mixing with an aristocrat.'

'Aristocrat my eye. That woman is a gold-digger, the ultimate social climber!'

'I was talking about Earl Edwin.'

'Livienne, Chantelle! Enough of this.' The door to Baron Gilbert's office slammed open. 'Livienne, stop trying to marry my daughter off, this isn't Gingerwall. And Chantelle, please be civil to your Belle-mère, for my sake, if nothing else.'

Chantelle followed her Father into the office and sat at her desk.

'Don't log-in just yet, I need to discuss the fishing rights with you,' said her Father.

'What about them, don't they belong to everyone?' she asked.

'Not any more. The King has changed everything.'

Fishing Rights were one of the few things on Anseris that were mutually owned. Everyone living in a coastal community, whether peasant, plebeian, gentry or aristocrat owned one share in their local fishing commune. This was about to change.

'He has ordered the demutualisation. People will have to buy fifty shares at first, which then can be traded on a stock market. Eventually all the shares will be tradeable.'

Sensing her Father was about to let off steam, she remained silent.

'It's fundamentally wrong. Privatizations and demutualisations are massive frauds by government against the people. By giving everyone the right to go and get free fresh protein from the seas, Archduke Andrew Rushton-Brown, the Boatbuilder, saved us all from the great famine at the end of Queen Kathyren's reign. Of course now, only the fishermen use that right, but it still belongs to everyone. So the fundamentally stupid will spend good money to buy something they already own, then sell it for a quick profit. They don't care it will deprive the fishermen of an independent income.'

'You've lost me,' said Chantelle. 'The fishermen will still fish the waters of the Mare di Napoli.'

'The people pushing the King for this change are the owners of big fishing conglomerates, like my old friend the Commander. They will buy the shares and prevent the independent boats from sailing in the waters they control. Everyone who wants to work on the sea will have to work for them.'

'And employees never get as good a deal as the self employed if it's not in the boss's interest to give them a good deal.'

'Exactly, Daughter of Mine. Which is why I have a plan,' the Baron said.

'You always do, Papa,' Chantelle replied.

'Fortunately, the Fundamentally Stupid are far more likely to sell their shares to a member of the Gentry like me than someone they regard as an upstart, in other words the Commander. When I have enough shares, I will de-list them. Establish a new fishing commune which protects the rights of the independents.'

'Can we afford to protect their livelihoods?' asked Chantelle, perfectly aware of the Estate's finances, how much it could spend and how much it earned. 'There are those who say we should only be interested in short term profit. We have the money to do it, but it won't make a profit fast enough. They would advise against it on a business level.'

'You are my Daughter, not my wife. You won't let short sighted business considerations stand in the way of doing the right thing, where everybody can eventually make long term profit.'

Madeleine du Fauché hated living in the country. She was a city girl born and bred. She had left all her friends in Elizaburg. All her favourite places were in Elizaburg. This dump had nothing. Maman had insisted she have a governess in Elizaburg, who taught her fun things like embroidery and music. Here she had to go to the local school, all they did was the boring stuff like Maths and Angerlish. Not forgetting that three of the school's six teachers were Merciful Sisters, the definition of dull. What was worse, the horrible school treated everyone equally. It was full of horrible plebs who poked fun at her. She could do all the boring stuff well enough, in this school they did more of it than Madeleine thought necessary.

'Of course the plebs need to do the boring stuff well,' her Mother said, 'they have to work for a living.'

'Yes Maman, thank you.' That sort of made sense to Madeleine.

'But that is no excuse for you. As a daughter of the Gentry you should always be better at your schoolwork than those children. Unless you are a disgrace to the Gentry.'

Madeleine watched as her Mother marched imperiously out of her room. What had she expected, her Mother was such a hard woman, especially to her youngest daughter. Madeleine could feel the hot tears running down her cheeks as she started to cry. She heard her sobs and hoped her Mother could not. Maman hated what she called extreme displays of emotions.

C hantelle heard the sound of a crying child. It was coming from young Madeleine's room. She didn't know what to make of the child. Much of the time she would be as nasty and spiteful as the twins, displaying the same smug superiority of her mother. Then, when she thought she was alone, Maddy changed completely.

'Beth sy'n bod, Cariad?' Chantelle asked.

'Pardon,' Madeleine said through the sobs.

'Que fait il, ma cheri?' Chantelle asked in French, the language the Gentry used to infuriate the aristocrats above and confuse the plebeians below.

'No, Angerlish, Maman says I must improve my Angerlish. But I can't because I'm so stupid,' Madeleine said before dissolving back into tears.'

'Who says you are stupid, ma chère?'

'Mostly it's Maman, she says I'm also a disgrace to the gentry.'

'Well, Maddy ma chère, you are neither stupid nor a disgrace to the gentry. You are du Fauché, who were once Aristocrats and could be again if the King decreed it. How dare she say those things. You are just badly educated, which is entirely her fault. However, we can do something about that.'

'But that would upset Maman, and she would hate me even more than she does now,' said Madeleine, who had stopped crying. 'I try so hard to be like her and my other sisters. I think, maybe then she will love me. It doesn't work.'

'Don't use her as a role model. Be yourself.' Chantelle could see the child was smiling. 'And I know someone who will help you catch up. By the start of the next school term in September you will be on the same level as your classmates.'

A s soon as the builders completed the new schoolhouse, the Sisters of the Order of the Merciful Charity of the Angels for all Children arrived to teach the local children. At the same time the first two local women were sent to Tintagel to train as teachers. The last remaining Merciful Sisters were due to hand the school over, now that four qualified local teachers could take over at the start of the academic year in September.

Madeleine recognised the head-mistress Mrs. Glanville, even though she had been absent for most of the term Madeleine had spent in the village school.

The Merciful Sisters lived in the priory in Zucca and were rarely seen on the Island during the long summer holiday. So the villagers politely ignored the woman staying with Juliet and Hazel Glanville in the cottage on the edge of the woods. The Glanville had trained as teachers in Tintagel. They said the woman, who had arrived at the end of the school year, was their friend Andrea, who they had met in college.

Their brother Thomas had been appointed school janitor and had recently moved into the cottage at the side of the school. No-one saw it strange that a single young man would return to his family home so often. He was obviously smitten with the guest.

The villagers had been slightly shocked at the start of term, on a wet September Monday, when the Headmistress had arrived at work wearing a blue dress and insisting everyone call her Miss Spenser. She had last been seen wearing a Merciful Sister's brown robes, answering to Sister Simone. She had been the Glanville's mystery guest. The school's governors immediately asked Miss Spenser to remain as Headmistress after the Merciful Sisters departed. They were delighted such an excellent teacher would be staying at their school.

The wedding at Jule had been harder to ignore. They had all been invited, few had attended. It turned out Miss Spenser was really Lady Andrea Spenser, one of the Gentry. Her marrying a plebeian like Tom Glanville caused a stir. He returned home and his sisters were now living in the janitor's cottage.

The Baby, was impossible to ignore. Everybody had assumed Andrea Glanville was too old to have children. Once again, she refused to give up her teaching post. The Merciful Sisters had agreed to send a temporary teacher to the school for six months, to cover the radical concept of Maternity Leave.

'Lady Chantelle, to what do I owe this honour?' Andrea Glanville asked, despite knowing the answer.

'I know you are tutoring young Clover in the summer holiday.'

'She's so lucky to be alive. Peritonitis can be deadly.'

Madeleine knew Clover was even more bullied by the children than she was. She liked Clover, who had the strangest sense of humour. That just made the bullying worse. "Look at those two thickies", the children would say, "laughing at thicky things that aren't funny."

'Yes. Mrs Glanville, I have to ask you a favour,' said Chantelle. 'This is my half-sister.'

'Madeleine, yes, if Junior hadn't intervened I would be teaching her next year. You want me to tutor this little one?'

'If you can, I don't want to over work you in your condition.'

'Don't worry, Lady Chantelle, I'm not due until October. I just got very big very quickly, and will stay that way until junior pops out. Don't forget, I'm tougher than old boots.'

Madeleine liked this woman, she didn't have the usual seen but not heard attitude of Sister Priscilla, her current teacher.

'Well, child, introduce yourself?'

'I am the Lady Madeleine Livienne Coeur-d'ange du Fauché, Ma'am,' she said, curtseying.

'Well, Madeleine du Fauché, there are no titles here, just like at school. I will be your teacher. Don't worry, your summer holiday won't all be sitting at a desk. There will be some formal classes, but much of the time you will be learning outside in the garden, doing things that don't seem like learning at all. Oh, and as this is my house you will call me Aunt Andrea.'

'Oh, that sounds fun, Aunt Andrea' the girl said.

'Now, go and play in the garden with Clover, it is lunchtime.'

'Thank you, Ma'am,' Madeleine could see Clover, who was beckoning her out. This was not going to be as bad after all.

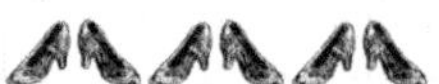

When Chantelle was Twenty

Since the summer at Aunt Andrea's cottage, Madeleine and Clover had become the star pupils at the village school. Their tutor's return to the school was delayed by another two more babies in the years after the birth of Frances.

At twelve years old Madeleine was offered the same choice as Chantelle. Either go to secondary school in Elizaburg or the new school in Castello del Fillipo. She had been so conflicted about leaving Fiandre now it was her home. She had become a country girl. Two things helped her decide. First, her friend Clover won a scholarship to the Princess Louise Academy, the prestigious boarding school outside Elizaburg, that Madeleine's father had chosen for his daughter. Second, when given the choice, Chantelle had decided to put half a world between herself and Lady Livienne du Fauché. Madeleine chose to do the same. Despite being her daughter, Madeleine was learning to hate her with every passing day.

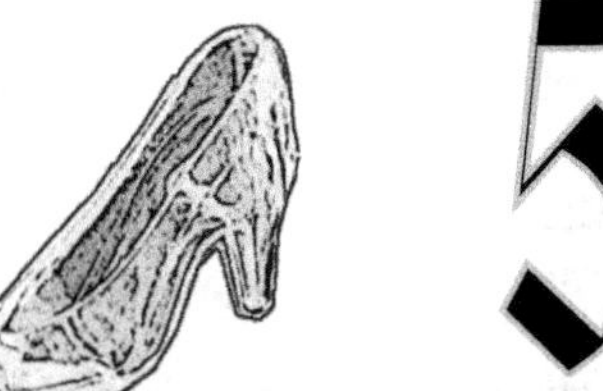

5

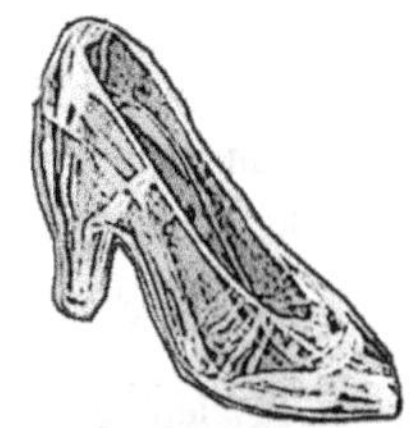

J **still can't believe nobody on the Home-world knows** I exist,' said the pale skinned young man standing with a trolley piled high with suitcases at the entrance to Tintagel Airport.

'Apart from you know who, there was no-one left to tell,' said his Mother. 'Your maternal grandparents died before you were born. As did your paternal grandparents. My sister Angharad, your aunt died a quarter of a century ago. Her husband Gilbert had started a new life for himself, so wouldn't have cared. Finally your Father was an only child, so you have no paternal aunts or uncles.'

'What about my cousins Chantelle and Madeleine?'

'What about them. As I have said before, Chantelle was eight at the time and Madeleine is a few months older than you.'

Bronwen Tudor regularly had this annoying argument with her son Aneurin. This was the third times in the past twenty four hours, it was getting old. However, could understand why his feelings were hurt, but why was he continually harping back to it. 'Look, you have to understand how frighteningly socially conservative Gwener is, which is why my grandparents moved to Cenerentola. If I had told any of my friends on Cenerentola Island, news would have filtered back to Gwener where most of our extended family still lives. What doesn't raise an eyebrow in Pendragon is the cause of a lifetime of shame, gossip and recriminations back there.'

'But we're going to live in a place called Campo di Zucche, known as Zucca, within the Archduchy of Fiandre.' said the boy, 'not on Gwener, which is in the Archduchy of Holywall.' I've no idea why the late King would chose to build the Institute in a place where they still insist everyone wears traditional clothing. So I have to get used to wearing short dresses with tights.'

'Damn it Nye, I wish my legs had been as good as yours, even in the knee length skirts older women wear in Pendragon. And they're called tunics and hose.'

'I suppose you have a point, Mam.'

'So. I'm off to get the hire car. Watch the luggage for me.'

'You my lad,' said Bronwen as climbed awkwardly into the rental car, have not got to get used to wearing veils in public again. Or wearing dresses with floor sweeping hems to trip over.'

Pendragon had never been tied to the silly pseudo-mediaeval clothing laws of the rest of the Kingdom, which were far too impractical for space habitats. It had its own style, a thousand years ahead of what she was currently wearing. Her black hair, usually cut into a very short station hairstyle would have been seriously at odds with this orange kirtle and cotehardie, or anything in her new wardrobe so en route to she had extensions added. Like all Fenzrians, her skin was almost white and contrasted with her ebony black hair. At five foot nine inches tall, Bronwen fell into the category of Fenzrian women who were tall and slender, but not skinny, with the perfectly proportioned figure that looked good in anything.

Right, let's see what POC they've tried to fob me off with because I'm wearing this get up. The headache wasn't helping, it had sprung from nowhere and would return to nowhere in an hour or so, like the others over in the past few days.

She was almost home, for the first time in seventeen years. So at a votive shrine in the concourse she lit a candle.

Seventeen Years Earlier:

She had studied Pathology and Criminology at Baaden Spitz University on the Northern Continent, but would have found it impossible to get a job on the Home-world back then. So she had moved out on the high frontier, on Pendragon Central Station.

Sometimes Bronwen found it hard to believe that the Archduchy of Pendragon was part of the same kingdom as the Archduchy of Holywall. Space exploration started two hundred years earlier, in the reign of Queen Johanna II. The moons orbiting the gas giant planet had also been terraformed by the Aggelii, but ignored by the original human settlers, who wanted nothing more to do with space travel. When the exploration bug once again bit on Anseris, these moons were quickly settled, becoming the Jovian Baronies. The asteroids and space habitats beyond the Baronies became part of the new twenty first Archduchy of Pendragon, ruled by House Thompson-Uther, the newest of the Anserian great houses. Despite its traditional form of government, it was the home of liberals and free thinkers. Anyone who did not fit in with the hidebound Home-world or unbridled capitalism of the Jovian Baronies.

Until Queen Johanna IV had arrived, Pendragon had been the most liberal place in the Kingdom, where all sorts of radical ideas rubbed shoulders with each other. All the social conventions that had been so important on the Home-world just didn't matter out there. You were more likely to see Archduchess Jane queuing at the tills in shops with the common people, than at a formal event.

Four years after moving to Pendragon, with its more liberal attitudes, she had met Aneurin's father. Edward Jenkins had been twenty three when he arrived to take a post graduate course in Dentistry at Pendragon University. A fellow Fenzrian, it had been lust at first sight. That the relationship had lasted three years was a miracle if you consider how far apart they were on social and political matters. Bronwen had embraced everything about life on a space habitat. Despite studying out there, Edwin hated Pendragon. Many of his attitudes were still back home on the island of Gwener. He wanted to go back to the Home-world as soon as he finished his course. Bronwen did not and was going to end the relationship.

She would never forget the day she had told Ned she was pregnant and the child would be a boy. This made things awkward. Unlike the Home-world contraception was legal, but frighteningly expensive. A termination, if contraception failed, was as illegal here as anywhere else in the Kingdom.

'You'll have to come back home with me to Gwener now,' Ned had said as soon as he heard the news.

'Or you could stay out here and take up the offer from Dave and Tony,' she had reply. 'You could be a partner in three years.'

'You know I always planned to go home one day, didn't you Bron?' he replied. Three weeks earlier he had announced he was putting that plan into action. Returning home Aberpumnant, his home town on Gwener. A town known as the most conservative places on Anseris, the polar opposite to Pendragon.

'Yes, but my career is on the up here, and so is yours. Why not stay here. Why move back to the Home-world?'

'But your career is changing now, and Gwener is the best place to bring up children.'

'Are you serious, Ned?' she asked. 'The infant mortality rate is shocking there.'

'Perfectly. Mam and Dad will help us set up our new home in Aberpumnant, I'll be earning enough to employ a couple of servants, so you won't have to do all the work. You'll have plenty of time to devote to good works.'

Bronwen was in a state of shock. Did he really think so little of her and her career?

'Of course, we'll have to get married now, and before junior becomes too obvious. It won't be the first time, and no doubt won't be the last.'

Obviously he did think nothing of her, or her career. 'No, I am not throwing away my education and training because you want to be the big man in a small household on Gwener.'

'But it's my son, I will decide what is best for him,' said Ned.

Everyone has a breaking point, and Bronwen had reached hers. This man was a problem, not a solution. If he wanted to go back to the Middle Ages on Gwener, he was more than welcome. She was having this baby and staying on Pendragon. She had no idea how much this snap decision would affect her life.

'Our relationship was already over, I was planning on telling you this at a better time. As you have said, we are not married, nor never shall be,' she said calmly but firmly. 'It is my child, I will look after him here on Pendragon.'

'On your own? You know what people will say?' Ned's voice was already high pitched, this bolt from the blue sent his voice up another two octaves.

'No, Ned. People, whoever the "People" might be, won't say anything. This is Pendragon. I'm earning more than you, as you said, enough to employ people to help me cope. More importantly I won't be on my own, I have a network of friends out here, who will be more than willing to help me, something I won't have on Gwener. I'll get six month's maternity leave. Then there is the free day-care, better health provisions, and of course the schools are so much better out here than Gwener.'

'I'll get a court order, take my son away from its unfit mother,' said Ned, who was becoming redder by the minute.

'No Ned, you won't, your not on Gwener, or anywhere else in Holywall now. This is Pendragon, you have no say over what happens to him, or me.'

'We shall see about that.' That was the last thing she heard him say, as he slammed the door behind him.

Eight months later. A week before Aneurin' birth:

Bronwen watched the changes in her body over the passing months, which until now had been scientific processes that happened to other women, and marvelled. A child was growing inside her. With its birth new life would be created. No wonder Angharad had been so happy during her pregnancy, despite the complications. What a shame it had all gone so horribly wrong.

'What are you thinking?' asked Eileen, her best friend, who would be with her during the birth.

The two women were admiring their handwork. They had been putting the finishing touches on decorating the nursery, which had once been the spare bedroom in Bronwen's apartment. Actually Eileen had done most of the decorating, Bronwen had sat in a very comfortable chair she would be using to feed Junior.

'About my sister,' replied Bronwen, 'everything was going so well, right up until the last minute. When that man took her to the wrong maternity hospital.'

'That was a totally avoidable tragedy, which would never have happened out here in Pendragon,' said Eileen. 'All of our hospitals are excellent.'

'It isn't going to bring her back. What if something happens to me? I would hate to see little Aneurin sent to Gwener and his crazy Father.'

'Don't even think that Bronwen,' said her friend. 'Aneurin, so that's what you are going to call the baby.'

'It was my Grandfather's name. I think Aneurin Tudor has a nice ring to it.'

'Was he a doctor?'

'No, he was a Cobbler, I'm the first person in my family to do anything in the medical field.'

Bronwen was an example of one variety of female Fenzrians, Eileen was the classic example of the other variety. A binary choice with nothing in between. Bronwen was usually tall and slender. Eileen was average height and curvaceous. She loved Pendragon and would never return to the Home-world. She assumed it was because like her ancestors, she had been born and brought up in the space habitats, and asteroids, just like Pendragon.

'Oh, I see,' said Eileen, as she leaned back and slid into her chair. 'He'd probably have something to say about the state of your shoes.'

'I don't doubt it. He made all my school shoes when I was a child and for Angharad. Of course she hated them, wanted something pretty, while Tad Cu made them practical and long lasting.'

'There you go, with your Welsh, out here the Fenzrian community sticks with Angerlish.'

'You wouldn't be able to read this then. A crazy letter send from somewhere in Gwener.'

'Actually sending a letter through the post, not faxing it,' said Eileen in disbelief, 'it must have cost whoever sent it a fortune.'

'Probably not Ned, He's not that blatant.'

The doorbell rang, its camera showed Eileen's husband was waiting by the front door.

'Come in Evan,' said Bronwen, 'I've unlocked the door for you.'

The two women transferred to the kitchen, where Evan had already put the kettle on. A small but comfortable room that was the heart of any space habitat home.

'What do you make of this then Evan,' said Bronwen, passing him the letter. Unlike his wife, he was a fluent Welsh speaker.

'Exactly what you would expect from some nutter in Gwener,' said Evan, 'I knew Ned was old fashioned, I never thought he was crazy as well.'

'You think it's from him? I assumed it was from one of his crazy friends.'

'Read it again, listen to the sound of the words, that is a man displaying his sense of entitlement for what he thinks is his.'

'Oh!' said Bronwen as the letterbox rattled.

It was another letter, this time in Angerlish and containing definite threats against Bronwen.

'Right, this makes it official,' said Evan, 'I'm reporting back to the station. I'm afraid you will have to come with me Bronwen, and you Eileen.'

It was over, and she now had her darling little boy sleeping in a crib at the bottom of her bed. Had it been worth all the discomfort.

Hell, yes. Would it be hard work? Again, hell yes. The real hard work was yet to come. For the next fifteen years she would have to guide this little boy on the pathway to manhood without any help from the Father, who had proved himself to be a complete madman. Whatever had she seen in him.

'So,' said Evan, 'I have arranged for a letter to be sent to Dr. Edward Jenkins, of Aberpumnant, on Gwener, in the Archduchy of Holywall, informing him that his son was born with a heart defect and died within an hour of birth. Included was a copy of the Death Certificate for the poor little mite we are claiming is his precious son.'

'Won't Edward check the facts?' asked Bronwen.

'From what my colleague down on Gwener said, he has become one of those crazy Space Deniers, like his parents. He claims he spent the past four years living and working in Elizaburg. If he has nothing to draw his attention to Pendragon, he won't look. He has told his crazy friends you are also in Elizaburg.'

'What about the crazy friends of his crazy friends? The ones who sent those other nasty letters to me?' asked Bronwen.

'They were arrested last night, Bron' said Eileen, 'Evan says they were planning something really stupid and now the Chessmen have got their hands on them. I doubt if they will be a problem again.'

'Do we know what sort of stupid Ned's friends of friends were arrested for?' asked Bronwen

'Who knows with the Chessmen,' said Evan, 'it's best not to be too inquisitive, unless you want the Chessmen being inquisitive about you.' On the whole the Crown Police, like Evan, hated and were as scared of the Political Police as everyone else within the Kingdom of Anseris. 'Just be glad those buffoons will never trouble you again.'

Ansersol, the star at the heart of the Anserian system, itself orbits Gansler Prime, a larger star four light years away. Every eight years, the Anserian system passes through the Transom Nebula, a cloud of dust and gas in interstellar space that also orbits Gansler Prime. For five days, on Anseris, there are pink and yellow skies at dawn and dusk, growing in length and intensity until on the sixth day the night is as bright as day. Humans called this event the Silent Night because the gas and dust vibrates at a frequency that overloads the auditory section of the brain, causing temporary deafness. This has no lasting effect on the human body. If it had done so, the Aggelii would have found another home for the passengers and crew of KHM#89.

The Silent Night interferes with all electrical device. At its peak there is no radio or television signal and the telephone network shuts down. In the years when only Anseris was a simple agrarian world this was no problem. Likewise on the terraformed moons of giant gas planets, the Jovian Baronies, on. For most of the space habitats in Pendragon, the effects could be catastrophic, with only the core of Pendragon Central being totally secure. Most inhabitants of Pendragon evacuated to the Home-world, where they would stay in a special resort on the Lonely Islands, isolated from Anserian society.

'I don't like this. I don't like it at all,' said Bronwen. This is your first evacuation. We all have to head down to the Home-world or a Jovian Barony for the Silent Night. Nobody likes it, but it is safer than staying out here when the system passes through the nebula,' said her friend Eileen.

The two women were in Eileen's office. She was a Registrar of Births, Deaths and Marriages. Every week Bronwen visited this office to supply causes of death for unexplained cadavers for their death certificates. It was how the two women, who were firm friends had first met.

'I'm more worried about Ned finding out about Aneurin.'

'Don't worry, yesterday the system generated an unnecessary NP4 Death Certificate. This error cannot be corrected for fifteen years, because those documents are issued under the King's Seal and untouchable. They make my records messy.'

'Why don't you do something about it then?'

'I would love too, but the Chessmen won't let me. They find these false documents, technically royal decrees, far to useful. Just for once, the mistake is going to be used by the good guys. You have the genuine documents. Aneurin's dad received a death certificate saying his son died at birth.'

'Fifteen years?' asked Bronwen. 'That's when Ned loses any legal claim on Nye.'

'Exactly dear,' said Eileen.

'Although we still have to go to the Lonely Islands for a week, the arse end of nowhere. What if Ned finds out about Nye during the journey.'

'We're going direct to an isolated and hermetically sealed holiday resort. have you seen the brochure? We pay for all this in our taxes,' said her friend. 'This was all explained when you first arrived, just after the last evacuation.'

'I wasn't really paying attention back then.'

'We chose to go there and quarantine ourselves.'

'Why bother?' asked Bronwen, as she picked up the brochure. 'There's no medical reason for a quarantine?'

'So no-one can get in and be offended by what we do, no-one can get out to cause offence back home. Which means Ned will never know you took little Nye to the Home-world.'

'I suppose so,' said Bronwen. So, the Lonely Islands. It will be fun, won't it?

'Sure,' said Eileen. 'It's going to be a blast.'

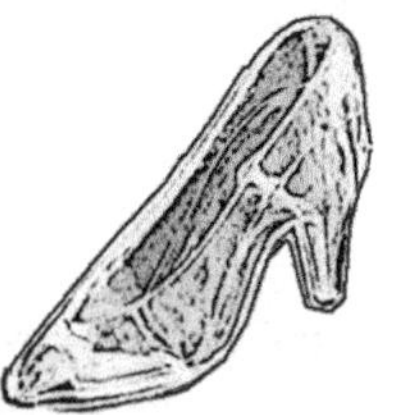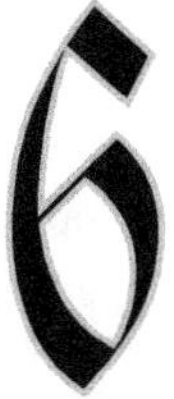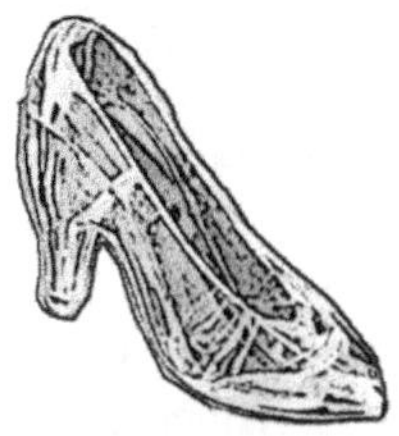

'And could you have found a bigger clunker if you tried?' Aneurin asked as his mother returned with the hire car. He wondered if the car had always been that shade of orangey brown, or if it had been resprayed that colour to camouflage all the rust.

'Nye, you know this heap is only temporary. Something to get us, and all the travel essentials to our new home. Everything else is being shipped, from Heavenward to Zucca,' His mother said as she climbed out of the large 4by4 vehicle. 'Just hopes we get there before it.'

'I suppose we will make a big entrance at our new home,' he said with a grin, 'after all, its all horse and carriages there.'

'Now don't be such a techno-snob, you know very well that motor vehicles are as common on the Home-world as any of the other advanced technological civilisations in the Galaxy. Even in places like Zucca.'

'You think, we only had interstellar contact for twenty years, before the War,' he said 'And then the Aggelii isolated us, for our own good.'

'The Aggelii only have our best interests at heart.'

'So they said, Mam, so they said. That was over a century ago.'

'We were too much at risk from the likes of the Fenzrians back then,' his Mother said, without a trace of irony.

'Look in that mirror, Mam, we are Fenzrians.'

'We are not that sort of Fenzrians, Nye. We're Anserfenzrians, our people have lived on Anseris for a century.'

'Mam, nobody uses that word any more, we're all integrated.'

'My point exactly, son,' said his Mother. 'Well, before we can think about travelling to the stars, we have to get to Campo di Zucche, aka

Zucca, which is in the next Archduchy. So we have at least four days of travelling ahead of us.

'So I had better start stowing the luggage?' said Aneurin.

'That's right, Son. Go to the top of the class.' Although her child prodigy son had always been at the top of the class. He completed the Primary Certificate, that fourteen year olds took to finish their basic education, when he was ten. If the Anserian universities had allowed students younger than fifteen, he would already be on his way to his Masters Degree.

Everywhere on the Anserian Southern Hemisphere is connected by the Angel's Highway network. Motorways and railways connecting all the continents and the Archduchies within them together. These indestructible super-highways had been built by the Aggelii when Anseris had been one of their colony worlds. Humans who inherited the planet still marveled at their construction. Now computersised cars sped down them at hundreds of miles per hour.

They heading for a place named Taunton by the end of their first day, Firenze for the second, Bardi for the third. Then two days on a considerably slower a human built motorway to the Mare di Napoli, Castello del Filippo and then finally to Zucca by the end of the fifth day.

Aneurin was sitting in the bar of the inn where they were spending their second night. The high speed five hour journey down the Angel Highway from the Guild City of Taunton in Carlton to the Fiandrian town of Firenze could easily have been a trip in a time machine. He had gone back five centuries to the early days of the Free Queens. Men in dresses, he would never get used to that. They are called tunics, he told himself. I will have to wear them once we get to our new home, or you won't fit in. He knew he would never get used to it, looking so stupid.

All the women wore dresses like his mother's. They all wore the traditional Anserian four strand braids. These were then pinned like a danish pastry around their ears, crossed over at the back of their heads. Just like the woman in Queen Kathyren favourite picture from old Earth. Anserians had forgotten the picture was a copy of the portrait of Cornelia Vetterlein a Victorian lady dressed in a vaguely Renaissance style dress and hairstyle.

When two youngsters in jeans, t-shirts and baggy tartan shirts walked into the bar, he was pleasantly surprised. He recognised them, they had been on the plane to Tintagel. Except they had been in First Class and vanished as soon as they arrived. Aneurin and his mother in Second had had to wait for their luggage at the airport.

'I don't care what your letter says, you can't come in her dressed like that,' said the Landlord, 'for a start this is the wrong Archduchy for all that tartan. Also I run a traditional tavern in a traditional town.'

'You know you can't do that,' said the girl, who looked a couple of years older than Aneurin. Her face was familiar, but he couldn't say why.

'Say who, your Father?' asked the Landlord.

'No, the Law,' she replied. 'Under section three, paragraph five point three of the Clothing Regulations Repeal Act, 5883, "No person nor organisation shall prevent a law abiding citizen from pursuing their lawful business due to the clothing preference for respectable garments by that citizen."' the girl took a breath, 'which is why my Mother can still wear all her trad clothes in Elizaburg, which is almost universally City Style now, and my brother Janek and I can wear what we are wearing in a place that is almost universally the traditional Country Style.'

'And what be you, a lawyer?' The Landlord was smirking, there were very few female lawyers on Anseris.

'Not yet, I start my Law Degree in October, so I will be.'

'And when you're properly qualified and all, then you can come in here a-quotin' the law at I. Might even be in a mood to be a-listenin'. You'd also know that law yous is a-quotin' doesn't come into effect in rural areas until 29th June, day after the Black Masquerade.'

The girl went bright red. She must have forgotten that the new clothing law was one which had a staggered implementation times, to stop them being to much of a shock to the Anserian Home-world's system. Aneurin had tried to delay the move until July.

'Don't come back, unless of course, you find somewhere to change into clothing that does not offend public decency.'

'Oh, for the Angel's sake, that is what we were going to do once we got to our rooms,' said the boy, finally chipping in.

'Well you should have thought about that before you arrived at my inn then, sunshine. So hop it!'

'Didn't I tell you, Jadzie, get Erik to check us in,' said the boy. The two youngsters left through the front door. Aneurin could not help but follow them.

to his sister, who was sitting on the front passenger seat of their car, busily plaiting her hair.

'Fat lot of good you were, Janek. And anyway, it was time for Erik's medication. I'm surprised he managed to drive us this far,' she giggled. 'No, I shouldn't laugh, but this place has pollen that makes normal pollen sneeze.'

'You know Jadzie, I honestly thought that for the first time ever you were going to say "do you know who I am?" to the Landlord.'

'Don't hold your breath. You'll never hear me say that.'

They had travelled in First Class, and now they had a driver. They could be Ristoze or Gentry, Aneurin thought. No, the boy had an urban plebeian accents. His sister, on the other hand had a well educated accent and could pass as a Ristoze. No, they were neither of the aristocratic nor yeoman castes. The Landlord would have clocked the gilded edges of a ristoze ID cards or silver edges of the gentry's straight away and would not have given them any of that grief. Only way to find out more is to talk to them.

'Hi, I'm Aneurin Tudor, but everyone calls me Nye,' he said to the boy, Janek, who was nearest. 'I saw you get off the plane back at Tintagel.'

'Oh, hello. I'm Janek, that's my twin sister Jadwiga,' said the boy, holding his arm out.

'Pleased to meet you,' said Aneurin, shaking the other boy's hand.

'You look Fenzrian, but you don't have a Gwenerian accent.'

'Born and brought up on Pendragon Central. My grand parents came from Gwener, but lived in a place called Cenerentola. My Mam moved to Pendragon as soon as she could. She still has the Gwenerian accent, we both siarad Cymraeg. You look and sound like Elizaburgers.'

'Our Mother would be horrified if she heard you say that,' said Janek, effortlessly switching languages to the Welsh of the Eastern Continent. 'Originally we're from a small village in the Penyresgryn Mountains, over the other side of Rift Sea from here. Jadwiga and I have lived in the Jeweller's Quarter, on the eastern side or the Elizaburg since we were nine,' He pointed to his sister, who still sat on the edge of the car's back seat, combing and plaiting her hair. 'She's got a ten weeks internship with a provincial lawyer in Campo di Zucche. I've got one with the last Emerald mine just outside town. You might have heard, she's going to be a lawyer. My parents think I'm going to be gemstone buyer.'

If not the children of the nobility, they were the children of a self-made man. Or they had the connections, an aristocratic patron, and were obviously going up in the World.

'Ah, here comes Erik. How did it go?'

'I found a local apothecary, she was marvellous. Knew all the local plants and recommended this nasal spray.'

The man was huge, a mountain of muscles starting to sag with age. He had "Copper" running through him like those sticks of rock with Tintagel down the middle. He was wearing a lose fitting knee length tunic and baggy trousers the Crown Police wore beneath their metalwork. No doubt he was trying to appear casual. Sadly, Erik's body language was far from casual. It was screaming out for a shiny breast-plate, helmet and a big sword to complete the uniform.

'And does it work?' Jadwiga asked, who was now had a Danish pastry behind her left ear, and was busily pinning one around her right.

'Brilliant, I can breath like the middle of Winter.' The man could see that Janek was sitting on a bench looking glum. He looked across to the doorway of the tavern and measured up the weaselly looking Landlord, who was standing in the doorway, making sure the young trouble makers didn't come back. Guessing what had happened in his absence, Erik walked towards the innkeeper, in that precise way policemen walk.

'Good afternoon, good Sir,' said Erik in that overly friendly tone of voice that was only heard in arguments. 'I understand you have a booking for myself and my employers.'

Aneurin didn't hear the rest of the conversation, as the two men had moved indoors and their voices were reduced to mumbles. However, within minutes the Landlord and Otto the barman were fawning over the two youngsters.

'Of course you have access to a bath, Councillor Smitz. My wife is lighting the boiler even as we speak.

'It's ex-councillor now. I resigned when the new Constitution passed, and didn't stand for election to the new Council.

'No, don't worry about your cases, Otto will carry them.'

So she was that Jadwiga Smitz, was she? The radical reformer. Everyone had heard of Jadwiga Anna Orlof Smitz, the friend of Queen Johanna, no less. Forget having an aristocratic patron, the girl and her brother had a royal patroness. Some even said the Queen calls this girl her little sister in private. Aneurin knew he had just benefited indirectly from that patronage. Earlier his Mother had been informed by the Landlady that the bathhouse was closed because it was a quiet night. There was no point, they had been told, in firing up the behemoth of a boiler for one tub full only.

'I can see by your smirk that you had been denied the use of the bathhouse,' said Jadwiga.

'That's right, Mistress Smitz.'

'Oh please, Nye, don't call me that. It makes me sound like one hundred and seventeen years old, not simple seventeen. Call me by my first name. Jadwiga.'

'OK, Jadwiga.'

'I do hate doing that. Pulling rank and getting services denied others,' Jadwiga said.

'You deserve some perks. Most girls your age go out and have some fun when school and chores are done. You went off to boring committee meetings, and spent all your free time with some of the dreariest people in the Kingdom.'

'Chores? Janek, Her Majesty let me live in the Royal Apartment in Ellisford Castle. No chores there. That's one hell of a perk.

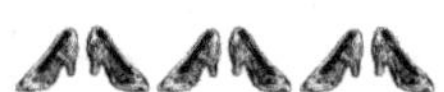

The Sea of Naples was once a deep crater created when Aggelii remelted the planet's molten core as part of the terraforming process. The arrival of liquid water and an oxygen/nitrogen atmosphere had flooded the crater and neighbouring rift valley. This put the Sea of Naples at the eastern end of what the later human settlers called the Southern Continent. Where the bay joined the Great Rift Sea was near the narrowest point between the Southern Continent and the imaginatively named Eastern Continent. This was called the Golfo di Gibilterra because of the mountain on either side resembled the Pillars of Hercules on Earth.

'Much changed?' asked Aneurin. They had driven on through the night to Castello del Filippo, where they had stopped for a break, to watch the Anersol rise over the sea.

'Nah, it's the same as I remember it. The new town is bit bigger, I suppose, but the Sea remains the same.' Her exhaustion was shining through. Unlike her son, Bronwen had not been able to get a few hours extra sleep en route. There was no auto-steer on human roads.

'So, first exit on the roundabout then eastwards to our new home.'

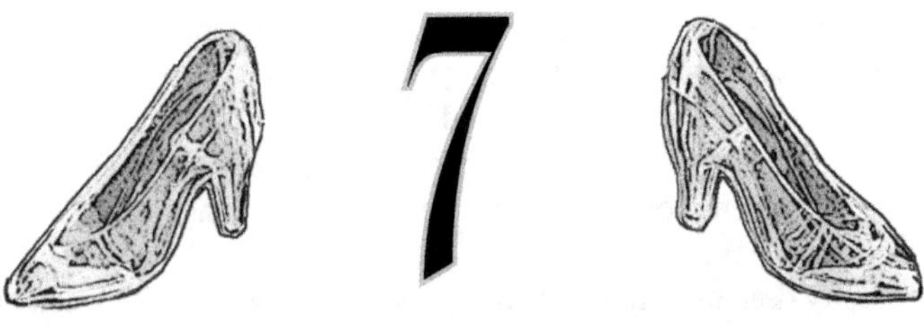

7

T**he sports-car easily climbed the hill and entered the** old town of Castello del Filippo. Up to the market square and then right, past the church and up to the Settler's castle that gave the town of Castello del Filippo its name. Like so many places on Anseris these days, the old town, on its easily defensible hill, looked down at the modern towns below that shared their name and worried about its future. Old Baron Claude Phillips-Forsythe, who had started the expansion of the town, had been a shrewd businessman, wisely investing the profits from the Emerald boom. If he had been in charge when that bubble burst, his family might still be part of the Aristocracy. It was just bad luck his grandson had all the sense of a Cald, the fish most prized by local fishermen. Recently, Gilbert du Fauché had rehabilitated his family's fortune, and Castello del Filippo was booming. Perhaps it was time to restore that family to the Aristocracy, let them be Phillips-Forsythe again.

The car was being driven by Viscount Leonard Edwin Griffin-Phillips, only son of Earl Edwin and Countess Jacqueline. Viscount Leo's grandfather was still teetering on, as he had been for the past seven years. Leo had only ever known him as a frail old man. He had met him for the first time as a teenager, at his grandmother's funeral. He had never known her and had never wanted to know her. What she had done had been unforgivable. He had only been there to make sure she was actually dead.

Leo climbed out of the car and handed the keys to a servant. His commission did not expire until midnight, so he was still wearing his naval officer's uniform. The blue gambeson, blue and white striped hose with blue codpiece and ankle boots with pointed toes, he looked completely anachronistic next to his sleek sports-car.

'Good afternoon Mama,' he said, with a courtly bow 'I trust you're well,' he said to the lady walking towards him.

'Another new car, Len?' asked his mother.

'Sweet, isn't she. And what do you mean, another new car, I have had my old one for two years. You'd swear I changed them every six months.'

'Sorry dear, my frugal upbringing showing through again. You know even after sixteen years, I still have moments when I can't believe all this is mine.' She kissed her son, who returned it, carefully avoiding the cloth of her wimple, then gave his mother a very plebeian hug. 'You had a much easier transition from plebeian to aristocrat.'

'Me, was I ever a plebeian?' he asked. 'I have lived in a mansion, a fortified manor house and then this castle.

'We still lived frugally in your first two homes,' said his Mother 'because neither of your first two homes belonged to us, they were Uncle Gilbert's. Angels give him rest.'

'I was sorry to miss Uncle Gilbert's funeral. How is Chantelle?' Leo asked.

'I haven't seen her since then,' said his Father. Last time I saw Gilbert, he said she was going off to university in Elizaburg. She's probably busy preparing for that.'

'OK, I suppose I did have a plebeian background. It came in handy when Grandfather had me packed of to naval academy at eleven. Most of the other fellows didn't know what hit them during the privation of first year.'

'Are you sorry to be giving up your naval career?' the Countess asked as they entered the castle's keep.

'I knew it was coming, I'll be twenty five in March, I have to start training for my proper job, sooner or later. Although long may Father becoming Archduke be delayed.'

'Even though our noble Queen has removed our political power completely?' asked Earl Edwin who was sitting in a comfortable chair in the central hall. 'Now Anseris is democracy.'

'Running an archduchy has always been juggling two jobs, being a CEO for a large corporation and being a large country's head of state,' said Leo. 'Neither of which gets the attention they deserved

You still have a powerful and important job, concentrating on that must be a good thing?'

'I could still stand for Governor of the Commmonwealth if I wanted to. But you're right, it's better to concentrate.'

Within the privacy of central hall, the two men hugged.

'As I know only too well. I have been doing the work of Earl and Archduke for years. Having you as my Prime Viscount will be a great help.'

'I heard you mention Chantelle du Fauché. You'll see her at the Black Masquerade,' said his father.

'Which will make that nightmare more bearable'

'Come now dear, I know it is fashionable to mock it,' said his mother, 'but I know you enjoy the Black Masquerade really.'

'I enjoy the ball, I don't enjoy the stupid make-up.'

'You would not be here today if it wasn't for that stupid make-up.'

'Strange. You always say it was a bucket of dirty water?'

When Leonard was 8 years old:

'You there, boy, who are you?' Earl Edwin asked the child sitting on a bench in the garden of Cenerentola House, reading a book.

'I'm Leonard Simples, my Lord,' the boy replied.

The Earl had heard that Baron Gilbert's tenants in Cenerentola house were called Simples and they came originally from Elizaburg. He had forced himself not to hope that she had been living in his family's Archduchy for the past four years. The housemaid who had made him laugh, made him think, and made him question all the notions of class and caste he had ever been taught. She had all the aristocratic grace of any fine and nobly born lady and in many cases three or four times the intelligence.

Ever since the sudden death of his older brother, and his elevation to the rank of Earl, his Mother had kept them apart. Mother had been horrified when she discovered his partner at all the best parties for the previous six months had been her junior housemaid. That he, Edwin Griffin-Phillips had been passing a plebeian girl off as one of the Aristocracy.

'Tell me, young Leonard Simples, what is your Mother's name?'

'Mum's full name is Jacqueline Gladys Angelsbless Simples. Everyone calls her Jackie.'

'And what is your Father's name?' the Earl could hardly contain his emotions.

'I have no father, my Lord. They call me Len the Bastard.'

'Take me to your Mother, young Leonard.' The Earl suddenly felt light headed. He climbed off his horse. The boy, her son, had to be his son also. He had already exchanged one set of sharp words with his Mother after he discovered all the letters she had hidden from him for the past eight years. The ones in which poor Jackie had pleaded for him to come to her, as she was in dire straits. There would be more sharp words when he returned home that night.

'Edwin Michael del Ponte Griffin-Phillips,' said Granny Glad, 'you've got a nerve coming here.'

'Technically, this is my grandfather, the Archduke's domain,' said the Earl, 'I have every right to come here.'

'Just because you can, don't mean you should,' Granny Glad replied.

'That should have been Earl Edwin, my Lord, how can I be of service.'

'I'll be of service with a heavy broom if you don't leave in five seconds.'

'Madam Simples, I can see why you would be angry with me, but your anger is misdirected.'

'So which of your noble parents are you going to blame for making you break my Jackie's heart nine years ago.'

'Neither made me do anything. I should have searched out the woman I loved then, and still do today. I didn't receive her letters. I believed her life would be easier for her if she forgot about me.'

'Brozhnik!' Granny Glad said.

Len could hardly believe his ears. Using the name of Evil Queen Kathyren's final defender was very naughty. He watched with a strange fascination. This was not how Granny Glad normally talked to a Ristoze. Especially not a Ristoze as powerful as the local Archduke's grandson. He was quite enjoying this novel situation.

'Angels you have been so stupid. So what changed your mind?' Granny Glad asked.

'When I discovered the letters my Mother had hidden from me. About the child, Jackie's son, our son.'

'Oh, how typically male and utterly aristocratic. I suppose you are going to cause my daughter more heartache by taking the boy away from her?'

'Mistress Simples, what sort of monster do you think I am?' the Earl asked. 'I fell in love with your daughter the first time we met. Now I want to marry her.'

Len realised that both adults were no longer talking to each other, but looking at him.

'Leonard, be a good boy and go back into the garden, there's a good boy,' said his grandmother.

This must be important. His Grandmother always called him a good boy and sent him into the garden when something important was being discussed.

'No, let him stay. Every child should know how their parents met and fell in love,' said his Mother, who had appeared like magic.

18 Months before Leonard was born:

You stupid son of Brozhnik,' Jackie Simples screamed at the young naval officer. 'I've just spent an hour polishing that floor, and you come through here with your stupid dirty feet and knock my bucket over. I'll have to start all over again. What sort of idiot are... Oh Angels, you're the Viscount. I'm going to be dismissed.'

Viscount Edwin looked at the woman and then at the floor, then the woman again. She wasn't crumpling, like lower class women usually did in this situation.

'However, as I'm going to be sacked, I have nothing to lose. So... You blithering idiot, do you have any idea how much work I have to do as well as redo this floor. No, you don't do you, because you're a Ristoze with no brain.'

'Guilty as charged. I am an aristocratic buffoon.' The Viscount picked up a mop and began cleaning. 'Don't worry, you won't be dismissed. I'd lose my rag if I had spent hours swabbing the deck, then someone thoughtlessly tipped dirty water over that deck.'

'Thank you,' she said, as she picked up another mop. Five minutes later, they were done.

'You're quite good at this, my Lord,' Jackie said.

'A year as a page aboard the Royal Yacht, then two years officer training at Tintagel aboard the training vessels based there. Given the circumstances, I'm Eddy, what's your name?'

'I'm Jacqueline Gladys Angelbless Simples, aka Jackie the third junior housemaid. I'm part of the skeleton crew.'

'A crew of how many?'

'Three on a Sunday in August, while the city swelters. Except as the lowest ranking servant, I am stuck here working while Hans and Sarah are nowhere to be seen.'

'Well, you could do with some help. What's next?' he asked her. 'I suppose you will be cleaning the fireplaces in the bedrooms next. Then polishing the brass around the grate.'

'No, you can't, you're a Ristoze,' said Jackie.

'Who has put you behind schedule?' asked the Viscount.

'You did, Eddy,' Jackie replied. So he continued helping Jackie until she was back on timetable.

Viscount Edwin had been surprised how much he had enjoyed what should have been a hot and boring afternoon, three days earlier. Jackie was unlike anyone he had ever met, so different from the vacuous aristocratic girls his Mother kept introducing him to. He wanted to see her again. This was the perfect opportunity.

'Can I help you, my Lord?' asked Jackie, 'although as this is my day off I shouldn't really bother.'

This was exactly the sort of reply that Viscount Edwin had expected from Jackie. The sun was shining and it lit her beautiful face. The blue outfit complimented her female contours perfectly.

'I'm heading off to Castle Rock, I heard you were also going there, so I thought I would give you a lift.'

'That is very kind of you, my Lord, but I couldn't possibly accept your offer, no matter how much I want to,' she replied politely.

'Oh, for the Angel's sake, why?'

'Because,' Jackie said, imitating the aristocratic accent, 'there should be no degree of familiarity between servants and employers or their family.' Then reverting back to her normal plebeian accent, but with the broad dialect she rarely used now. 'Them's de rules ay uv ter follow while I'm a servant. yer ma' would dismiss me on da spot.' She smiled beautifully, 'I'm not go'n ter be a servant forever, I'm go'n ter follow de family tradition an' become a midwife, I'm wait'n' ter take me entrance echzams so ay can start train'n' fairst as a nurse, dun a midwife. So ay can't afford a blot me copy book, like gett'n' dismissed without a reference.' Then under her breath, 'Again.'

'She doesn't employ you. That is the responsibility of the second viscount, in other words me. So hop in, I'm not going to sack you.'

'Ta, me Lord.'

'And remember, it's Eddy in here. Why did you learn how to do the aristocratic accent, you know you get fired if your caught.'

'Because all the nurses in the Royal are expected to talk posh on duty, regardless of their background.' She had switch back to ristoze. 'They all get elocution lessons. I thought I'd get one step ahead.'

'I'd say two steps,' said Eddy.

'Don't you think I could pass for a Ristoze. I'm lucky my skin is so pale and despite my job, I have perfect hands.'

'You're not dressed like a plebeian, the sumptuary laws still apply.'

'I have a licence to wear gentry and aristocrat level clothing. My Aunt is a dressmaker, I sometimes model her work. All my fancy clothes have tags with my licence number sewn into them.'

'I was wondering how you would get away with that outfit.'

'I'm modelling now.'

The Planet Anseris is larger than Earth, but takes the same amount of time to rotate around the star Ansersol. However, because of the shape of its orbit, the Summer and Winter Solstices fall on the twenty eighth day of June and December. Summer Solstice is celebrated with the Black Masquerade, the Winter Solstice has the Festival of White Jule.'

In the early Black Masquerades, the people would dance all night in black clothes, having the following day off. Now the rich had massive balls where the guests painted their faces, necks and shoulder thick white make-up and dyed their hair black. The poor in their best black clothes had a communal Solstice Supper and a sing-along.

Gladys Simples really did not need this madness from her daughter Jacqueline was going out on jollies with her boss on her days off.

She should have been at home studying for her exam. The man she so casually called Eddy was an aristocrat, the grandson of the sixth richest man in the kingdom. And here he was sitting at her kitchen table, talking nonsense about Jackie going to the Black Masquerade at Ellisford Castle with him.

Gladys, like her mother and grandmother had been midwives at the Angelbless Maternity Hospital. Prior to that her ancestress had been wise-women in the village of Angelbless, that had been absorbed by the ever growing city of Elizaburg. She had been a widow for six years and was finding it tough to make ends meet for herself and her two daughters. Even with the money that Jackie brought in from skivvying at the Griffin-Phillips Residence, things were hard.

'Mistress Simples, how nice it is to meet you,' the young man in a naval officer's uniform said to her.

'Pity the same can't be said for you, your Lordship.'

'Mum!' Jackie said, but it was obvious that her mother was ignoring her.

'I know your sort, having your fun with some silly little slip of a girl from the lower orders, then dumping them, with all the problems you cause, when you're bored.'

'I can assure you, Mistress Simples that my friendship with your daughter Jacqueline is purely platonic. She made it quite clear to me that she had no intention of being, as you said, some silly little slip of a girl from the lower orders. I value our friendship and would not want to spoil it.'

'It's true, Mum,' said Jackie.

'Oh, so you play for the home team. Well, you are a sailor,' said Gladys

'Actually I don't play for any team, Genophobia, I just can't bring myself to do it.' he said, with the emphasise on the word "it". 'I find the whole thing repulsive, gay or straight.'

'That's also true, Mum.'

'However, society expects me to to show the right preference. So, I require a young lady to take to the Black Masquerade. Just having her there means nobody, especially my Mother will care who she is. I'll bring Jacqueline straight back to her home immediately afterwards. Jacqueline has agreed to do this, I will provide everything she will need.'

The rich and powerful of each Archduchy made their way to the Archduke's palace for a ball hosted by the Earl and Countess of that Archduchy. The Archdukes attended a meeting of the Witan, the Kingdom's governing council at Ellisford Castle, on the morning before the ball. After toadying to the King and agreeing everything he wanted, The Archdukes would be joined by their wives and entourage for the King's Black Masquerade.

'Most of my friends and colleagues already think Jackie is high gentry or low aristocrat. She could easily pass muster at His Majesty's bash.'

'Your mother will be there. She will instantly recognise one of her housemaids.'

'Not in the Black,' said Jackie in an aristocratic accent. 'Not even you would recognise me.'

T hings had been going so well. She had been a great success at the Black Masquerade, so she had attended a number of other balls at the Castle and in Elizaburg. She started her nursing apprenticeship and he was promoted. They had stopped pretending they were not madly in love with each other. One night, when the Cosmos was supplying fireworks beyond human imagination, he had even overcome his phobia, and they went beyond kissing and caressing. However, it was the one night in the month that they should not have gone beyond kissing and caressing.

Then, everything had changed. Edwin received a new posting, commanding a small fishery protection vessel in the deep, icy cold waters of the Arctic Ocean. They should have had three weeks together, but his older brother died. Edwin, who became an Earl, went to his family for the official mourning, and never returned. When he was not on duty, he spent his life in Ponte di Carla in Fiandre. It was during this time Jackie discovered she was pregnant. She could not get in contact with Edwin. To make matters worse, when her condition became obvious, her apprenticeship was terminated. Her Mother had been right, she had been a silly little slip of a girl from the lower orders, used and then dumped.

Nine years later:

'I thought he had dumped me,' said his Mother, 'until today.'

'You see, young Leonard,' said the man claiming to be his long dead Father, 'my Mother, your Grandmother, had opened the first letter your Mother sent me, and stopped me receiving any further letters from her.'

'I hate her, she made my Mum so sad,' said the boy.

'But your Mother and I are to be married in the chapel of Castle at Ponte di Carla. Then your mother will be the Countess Jacqueline and you will be Viscount Leonard. We will be together as a family at Castello del Filippo.'

'Can Chantelle and Granny Glad come with us?' Len asked.

'I'm afraid that they will have to stay here, in Lady Chantelle's family home,' said Jackie.

'But don't worry,' said his Father, 'Castello del Filippo and Cenerentola are less than an hour's journey time apart. You will be able to visit each other regularly.'

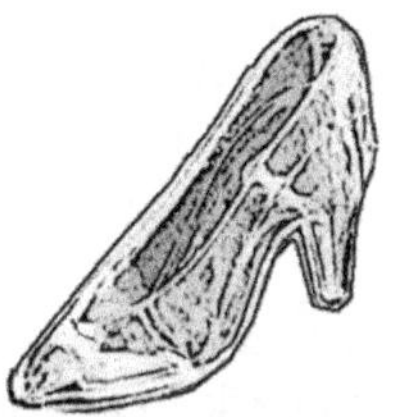 **8** 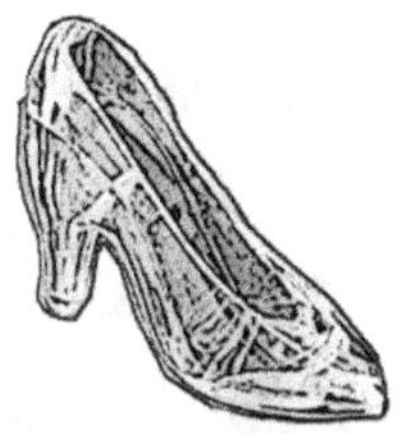

'That village is just an extension of Zucca on the other side of the channel,' said Aneurin.

'For the love of the Angels, don't say that in the Village,' Bronwen said to her Son.

'But it is, the village is on the easternmost tip of the Island, almost opposite the westernmost tip of Zucca.'

'The channel makes the difference,' Bronwen said, 'you have to make an effort to get to Cenerentola Village.'

'All this effort. The ferry is incredibly cool, but why didn't they just build a bridge?' asked Aneurin. 'The channel is only a couple of furlongs wide.'

Bronwen knew he would be fascinated by the ferry and the mechanism that powered it. Aneurin loved quality engineering and precision mechanics. The ferry ran for sixteen hours a day, keeping village and town connected.

'The channel is incredibly deep, and with the poor quality of the ground on the continental side, it was too complicated for mediaeval bridge building techniques,' his Mother replied.

'Any sensible colonists would have built a suspension bridge,' he said, 'but that was too modern for the whack-job who built Anseris.'

'Not all the blame can be laid at Queen Kathyren's feet, the Aristocracy's ancestors were just as enthusiastic about establishing an anachronistic world. So originally, this ferry was powered by donkeys on treadmills. With a real carrot on a stick?'

'The steam engine is better, but it's not very Mediaeval though, is it,' her son replied, pointing out the gleaming brass components. 'The current set up was what, on Earth, would be described as Victorian.'

'This set-up dates back to the reign of Queen Helena V, over two hundred years ago. When everything was steam driven.'

'It can't be the original engine. Can it?'

'Well, no,' Bronwen laughed, 'the actual equipment is updated and replaced every so often.'

'There is talk of replacing the steam engine with a new solar powered electrical one,' said the man standing to Aneurin's right. 'You on holidays here, Son?'

'No, I'm going to study at the Institute, Sir,' Aneurin replied politely.

'So I've come home,' Bronwen said. 'Mervyn Jones, how are you?'

'Do I know you, Madam?' asked Mr. Jones.

'Bronwen Tudor. Baroness Angharad's sister, Blod and Gwynfor Tudor's daughter.'

The man had gone bright red. Oh well, thought Bronwen, not everyone will remember me.

'Anyway, lad, a strong loop of metal rope just bellow the water runs to and from the island. A lever on the bow of the boat operates arms at either end of the vessel. If the lever was pushed to the starboard, the lower part of the loop was grabbed and the boat was pulled towards the island. If pushed to the port, the upper rope would be grabbed, pulling the boat back to the mainland.'

'Thank you, Mr. Jones.'

'Don't mention it. I'm the ferry's engineer, it's my job to keep the old tub running.'

Bronwen stood at the rail on the port side of the ferry looking out towards the rapidly approaching island, where she had been born forty one years earlier. Her self imposed exile was now over, and she was immersed in memories.

Damn it, she thought as a wave of nausea spread over her, this is a three minute trip, not long enough for me to get sea-sickness. Perhaps it was guilt over staying away for so long. Fenzrians gossiped and news of Aneurin would have quickly arrived at the main Fenzrian community on Gwener. Despite fake documents created to persuade Aneurin's crazy Father the boy had died at birth, she had been sure that Ned would see through the lie if he ever saw Aneurin, so she had avoided returning to the Home-world whenever possible.

'You look deep in thought,' Aneurin said. He had been talking to Mr. Jones and Chief Franchini, the ferryman, and was deeply impressed by the ingenuity of this vessel.

'Sorry love, I didn't notice you there,' she replied.

'You've been standing here for at least a minute, looking like death. I thought I had better wake you up, we're about to dock,' then with less sympathy he said, 'you still haven't seen a doctor about those headaches, have you?'

'They're nothing.'

'No Mam, at least one headache a day, everyday, is not nothing.'

'Double negatives, son,' she replied, correcting his grammar.

'Exactly, double negatives make a positive. You're feeling odd, aren't you? You should see a doctor.'

As he spoke the ferry gently hit the wall of the jetty. It produced an almost musical note.

'That's something I have never forgotten,' she said.

'How long has it been?' her son asked.

'Far too long,' a woman who had just boarded the ferry said in Gwenerian Welsh. She looked about sixty, but you never could tell with Fenzrians.

'Eighteen years. Is that you, Annie Roberts?'

'It's Annie Bowen now, and has been for a decade. Like I said, you've been away for far too long. There was a time you called me Aunty Annie.' The older woman had been Bronwen's next door neighbour when she had been a child. As a child, all Bronwen's parents' friends had been given the honorary rank of aunt or uncle.

'Well, I'm back now. My son Aneurin will be studying at the new Oceanographic Institute in Zucca. So I've bought a house there.'

'Dear Angels, this is your boy?' Annie asked, already knowing the answer. 'He's the spitting image of your Dad, Angels give him rest.'

'I think so too,' said Bronwen, swelling with maternal pride.

'Why did you keep him secret? Afraid of what people would say? I didn't think you were that daft. How many other secrets have you been keeping then?'

'More or less,' replied Bronwen, 'and only the one'.

'This isn't Gwener you know. Still water under the bridge now.'

'Excuse me, madam, but if you don't want to go straight back to Zucca, I...' Chief Franchini stopped and took another look at Bronwen '...Angels, is that really you Bronwen Tudor?' Merv said something about a crazy woman claiming to be back from the dead.'

'It is, Guerrino. You can tell that dozy so and so I'm very much alive, thank you. How are you?'

'I'm fine, but I have a timetable,' the man replied.

'Sorry,' Bronwen said as she scrambled off the boat.

W as it his imagination, or did everyone know his Mother in this tiny village. What should have been a five minute walk from dock to the outskirts of the village took two hours. They had been invited into three Fenzrian and two Anserian households on route, or six welsh-cakes and four digestive biscuits, with endless cups of tea.

'Angels, I've missed this place. Everyone's so friendly,' she said as they approached Cenerentola House.

'And I've kept you from them, gee thanks,' said Aneurin sulkily. 'That makes me feel so good.'

His mother turned and hugged him. 'There could have been half a dozen other reasons why it took me so long to come home,' she said reassuringly.

'I suppose so,' he said, hoping no one could see him. He was after all, still a teenager, and found expansive outbursts of emotion embarrassing and being hugged mortifying.

'And, it's a nice place to visit, but I don't think I could ever live here again. Too small and self-contained for me now. Zucca on the other hand is growing, Your Oceanographic Institute, also Elizaburg University is opening a field study centre and research labs in the field next door. The town is attracting more educational organisations I wouldn't be surprised if it doesn't have its own university by the end of the century.'

'Although it will probably be called Università di Castello de Filippo. Who wants to say they studied in a pumpkin field.'

'If you put it like that, "Pumpkin Field University" sounds wrong. Maybe it will be Università di Cenerentola.'

'"The University of Small Cinders" doesn't sound much better,' said Aneurin.

'The island is called that because that is what its unique soil looks like,' replied his Mother. 'Don't you think you're being a tiny bit too literal in your translations. Nobody actually speaks Italian here any more.'

'I suppose so, Mam,' he said. 'Anyway, we're here.'

They passed over a bridge then an expance of gravel to get to the front door of Cenerentola House. Even before they could ring the doorbell, the massive wooden door swung open. The Butler looked shocked for about two seconds before the mask of calm bored civility returned.

'Mistress Tudor, what a pleasant surprise,' he said.

'Thank you, Mister Bottles,' said Bronwen.

Aneurin couldn't help himself, he was smirking wildly.

'The young gentleman is not the first person to find amusement in my name and choice of profession. I do myself.' The man was trying hard to hide his smile and be the perfect professional butler.

'Thank you, Mr. Bottles. I've come to visit my Nieces and Lady Livienne, to pay my respects. Baron Gilbert was a good man.'

'I'm afraid that is not possible,' said the Butler.

'They are all here?' asked his Mother. He could tell she was worrying that they had gone to Zucca while she had been making all those house calls.

'Yes Mistress Tudor, but they are all indisposed.'

'Mister Bottles, who is it?' Asked a cute girl in a pretty blue outfit, her red hair in the Danish pastry style, but with her head uncovered. The cliché about eastern inbreeding sprung to mind. Don't let her be my cousin. Who else could she be?

'I 'm Bronwen Tudor. If you are Madeleine du Fauché, I am your Aunt.'

'Aunt Bronwen, do come in. I'm Madeleine. Ignore what Mr. Bottles said, he has to do what the Bitch told him to do.'

'M'Lady, there is a chance she might hear you,' said Mr. Bottles.

'Don't worry Mr. B. she already knows I call her that.'

'Yes Milady. Your Mother, the Baroness told me not to admit this lady.'

'And I'm telling you to admit her, and the cute boy she has in tow. Like I told you, her use of that title is under dispute and you should not address her with it.'

'Yes Milady,' said the Butler, who diplomatically retreated.

'It is nice to finally meet you Madeleine. You were a baby when I last saw you.'

'So I was told, by my Father.'

'This is your cousin Aneurin, I believe you are the same age.'

The girl had flushed bright red, but was now back to her normal pink and her smile gave her dimples.

'Pleased to meet you, Cousin Madeleine,' said Aneurin.

'And you, Cousin Aneurin.'

'You youngsters are being frightfully formal,' said Bronwen.

That's because she's thinking about banjo twanging easterners as well, thought Aneurin. Brozhnik to that. I think I'm in love.

'I'm sorry, yes,' replied Madeleine as she lead them into the drawing room. 'Please call me Maddy,' then giggled. She was staring at him, with a "you can call me anything you like," stare.

They were about to sit down when Aneurin saw a maid run into the room, wrap her arms around his mother and started crying. He was fairly certain that this was not how servants and their employer's guests usually interacted. Then he took a good look at the maid's face, she was so similar to Madeleine. Could this be Chantelle? This situation was bizarre.

'Oh, Aunt Bronwen,' said the weeping girl, 'I'm so glad to see you.'

'Chantelle, cariad. Beth sy'n bod?' asked his Mother in Welsh.

'Dw i'n drist iawn,' replied Chantelle, 'ar ôl i nhad farw.'[*]

'Er, what?' asked Madeleine, who had never learnt the other official language of the Eastern Continent, even though there was a large community of Welsh speakers living on her family estate.

---

[*] *'Chantelle carry-ad. Beth seen bawd?' asked his Mother in Welsh.*
'Do-ween drist yee-ow-en,' replied Chantele, 'are ole ee nhard varooo.'

'Mam asked Chantelle what was the matter and she replied she had been very sad since her father died,' said Aneurin translating from Welsh to Angerlish.

'Sorry, Maddie, I forgot,' said Chantelle, who then started telling her story.

Another woman burst through the door as Chantelle finished. She was small and wearing a hideous green outfit that made her look like a hyperactive frog. 'Madeleine, who are these people. Ella what are you doing. Pull yourself together, haven't you got work to do?'

'How dare you. How very dare you. You monster. How could you treat my poor dead sister's daughter so badly?'

'I'm Baroness du Fauché, I can treat the staff on my estate exactly how I like. Especially one of my indentured servants,' retorted Lady Livienne. 'I have it on good authority that the child you are referring to died at birth. That fraud was foisted on my family by the Simples. She has nothing to do with either me or you.'

'Yes Livienne, I know who you are and what a stupid woman you are. I saw Angharad lying lifeless in the Hospital minutes after Gladys Simples discovered her. She was busy saving my niece's life. I can assure you Chantelle is my niece, and your dead husband's child

'Oh really, and can you prove that?'

'Do I need to?'

'Yes, you do.' said Lady Livienne. 'I am not going to let that parasitic fraud steal any of my children's inheritance.'

'One man has told you that, and you choose to believe him over everybody else,' said Madeleine.

'Then why didn't my late husband never mentioned her in his Will, that is proof enough.'

'The lawyer couldn't read Latin well enough,' said Madeleine. 'Then he had the Will sent to Castello del Filippo before anyone could check it.'

'Shut up girl. Monsieur Nouveauté is an excellent lawyer,' Lady Livienne snapped at her daughter.

'Papa always said what a fool and a crook André Nouveauté is, not half the man his father Jean-Claude was,' said Madeleine.

'Since the ban was lifted, genetic testing is now common,' said

Bronwen, 'I will prove Chantelle is who she says she is. And if what Maddy says about the Will is true, then I will have even more proof.'

'How will you get a blood sample from my indentured servant.'

'Why does she keep saying that?' Aneurin asked.

'Because Mama forced Chantelle to sign Indenture Papers,' said Madeleine.

'Is that true, Chantelle?' Bronwen asked. 'In the Angel's name why?'

'It is, she refused to feed me until I signed,' said Chantelle.

'Oh, cariad. Don't worry, that's another injustice I will overturn.'

'How, will you overturn it? Leave this house and never return,' said Lady Livienne. 'Mr. Bottles, escort these people out. And you young lady, can go to your room,' she told Madeleine.

'I'm leaving. But don't think this is the end of the matter.'

'**A**unt Bronwen, I'm so sorry things turned out like that,' Madeleine said as soon as she saw her Aunt and Cousin.

'I thought you had been sent to your room?' Aneurin asked.

'That is no problem. I've always been able to come and go with nobody noticing,' she said. 'But I can't stay for long.'

'Here, my address in Zucca. You're always welcome,' said her Aunt.

'Thanks. I'm always in Zucca, There's more to do there.' She had tried to be brave and strong, but the emotions got to her. 'If Mama has her way, Zucca is as far as I am ever likely to travel.'

'My dear, what's the matter?' asked her Aunt.

'I came home for my Father's funereal, expecting to go back for the rest of term.' Madeleine sniffed. 'Mama told me was not returning. That I should spend my time preparing for marriage at seventeen.'

'You like school?' Aneurin asked. Was there anything not to like about his cousin.

'Oh yes, I want to be a lawyer. Chantelle was going to go to University in September. None of that is going to happen now. I hate my Mother. Why didn't she die instead of Father?'

'I'll find a way to spring both of you from the clutches of that dreadful woman,' said her Aunt. 'Go back to the House before you're missed. Next time you come to Zucca, phone me in advanced. We can start making plans.'

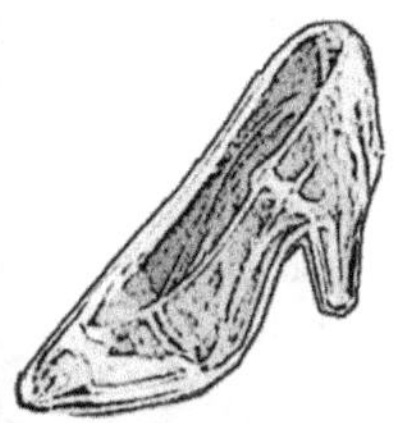 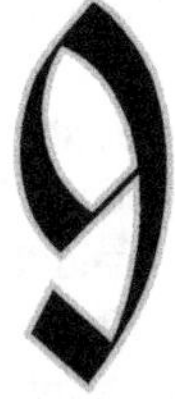 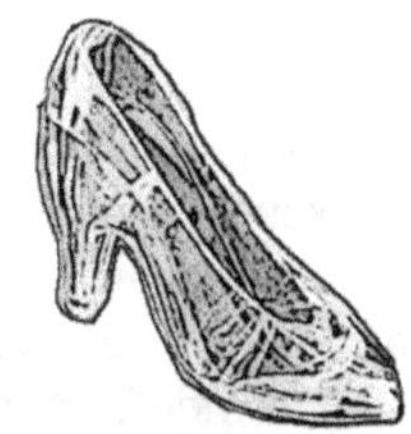

‘ƒfternoon, milady,’ the old woman said to Chantelle.
Everyone on the Island suspected her stepmother was treating her badly, and doing a good job at hiding it. Now they knew it was true. Her Aunt Bronwen had told them. The hot-heads wanted to do something about it. Calmer voices prevailed. It became another reason, if one were needed to hate Lady Livienne. Nobody on the Island had ever liked Baron Gilbert's second wife, and refused to call her Baroness. That would always be the title of the Baron's long dead first wife.

‘Afternoon Janice. How are you?’ Chantelle asked the women waiting at the jetty.

‘I'm fine, milady. My Henry's chest is playing him up again, but apart from that, it's all good. You off into town?’

‘Yes, I'm of to see my Aunty Bron.’

‘Saw your sister Lady Madeleine a-catchin' the ferry I missed, she was with them stupid twin sisters of hers.’

‘Yes, my ugly sisters are off to the Ugly Sister's orphanage, they regularly volunteer there. They want to join the Order.’

‘Really, milady. That's nice of them. I'd never have guessed. Not by the way they normally act.’

‘Every cloud has a silver lining,’ said Chantelle. ‘You now know my Step-Mother would not be happy if she heard you calling me milady.’

‘Oh hell to her. You are my Seigneuresse regardless of what she or the crooked lawyer says.’

The ferry arrived at the jetty, sitting on two of the seats were Madeleine and Aneurin.

Unlike her mother and sisters, Madeleine was loved on the Island. Only a handful of villagers remembered she was as rude as her mother and sisters when she first arrived. They now said it was water under the bridge.

'Thank you,' Chantelle said as she climbed aboard.

'Your welcome, milady,' said the boatman.

'Mam sent us to fetch you,' said the boy in his strong Pendragon accent, which echoed the New Zealand accent of ancient Earth.

'That's kind, but I do know my way around Zucca,' said Chantelle.

'But he doesn't, do you Nye?' her sister asked with a silly grin on her face.

'No, Maddy is giving me a guided tour. Mam is off to Castello For a job interview.'

'Good for her,' said Chantelle. Maddy and Nye were just staring at each other.

'So, the Queen wants everyone to learn how to use the Psychic Interface, if they can,' said Aneurin, spotting a copy of the Daily Truth lying unattended on one of the ferry's benches. 'So of course that rag is against it.'

"Witchcraft Legalised. The Queen is Under an Evil Influence." was the headline of the newspaper, In the past three years the Daily Truth had found its niche with the deeply conservative in society who believed the Queen was destroying every tradition of the Kingdom.

'The evil influence will be anyone Fenzrian in general and the Duchess in particular. You and Aunty Bronwen have a working psychic interface naturally,' said Madeleine.

'Of course, I'm pure Fenzrian, it's part of our genetic make-up Until recently we weren't allowed to use it,' Aneurin said. 'Chantelle has a working psychic interface, she inherited it from her Mother We've been spreading it through the Anserian genome for generations

'It's not an exclusively Fenzrian thing,' said Madeleine. 'It was permanently added to the human body by genetic manipulation, but has to be switched on by some sort of gene therapy. Most people could use it, but they are afraid of that gene therapy.'

'That's all very well, but what exactly is this Psychic Interface I'm supposed to have?' asked Chantelle.

The ferry had reached Zucca, and the three young people got off the boat. Once they had all regained their balance, Aneurin continued

'The nervous system is an electrochemical system which gives of a tiny amount of radio interference. The Psychic Interface magnifies and modulates this interference, turning it into a signal to control electrical devices.'

'So that explains the funny shiver I get when I am close to old alien technology,' said Chantelle.

'Sure. Mam will be able to teach you how to use the Interface, when we get to the house.'

'It's easy,' said Madeleine, 'I had the gene therapy with my friend about eight months ago, while it was still an illegal and a rebellious thing to do. I couldn't use it because I'd never been shown how. Aunty Bron has taught me how to knock lights on and off, just by looking at them. Believe it or not, all the lights in Cenerentola House work this way, the manual switches were added later. They are all linked to the control unit that looks like a glass crystal star in the Hallway.'

'There are a lot of pre-war devices that people now think are pretty antiques. They come from a planet called the Lambour, who could do all the simple things, but preferred it if you paid to make it pretty as well,' said Aneurin.

'So, Nye, how are you finding life on the Home-world?' Chantelle asked her cousin.

'It's fine. Everything is so much more relaxed here. I'm quite enjoying the reduction in pace.' He laughed. 'I'm even getting used to the dresses I have to wear.'

'Their called tunics, Nye,' said Madeleine. 'It's only until the Summer Solstice, then you will be able to go back to your old space clothes when the law changes.'

'To stick out like a sore thumb. The people here won't change their wardrobes overnight.'

'You don't want to be a trend-setter then?' asked Chantelle.

'No, thank you, I just want to fit in.'

Like a good little Fenzrian, thought Chantelle. The Curse of the Great Machine, as some people called it. The result of hundreds of years brainwashing by that crazy religious cult where uniformity and fitting in with the Cult's dictates were all that mattered.

'What about the difference in technology down here?' asked Chantelle.

'All my kit works fine, now that they have fibre broadband around here. Who knows, they might have Quantum broadband in a few centuries.' Aneurin started grinning, 'Did you see that ship with the full set of mast turbines yesterday? She was awesome.'

'The FQMV Estella Bianca del Propizio, the flagship of their fleet.' said Madeleine, 'built for their new concept of cruise holidays. Zucca won't forget her in a hurry.'

'Yes, in the eighteen months since she came into service, she has come into the Mare di Napoli twice, and until yesterday only called at Genova,' said Chantelle. 'Papa and belle-mére went on three day mini cruise last year. Father was in negotiation with the del Propizio Line, it was supposed to be a business trip.'

'He loved it. Maman was scandalised by what the women were wearing. Papa would have booked a full two week cruise this year,' her face dropped, 'Things was normal with him around. Angels, I miss him.'

Bronwen remembered being asked by her Grandmother why she wanted to cut up dead people. Her Granny had not been pleased to be told that the dead would not complain that there was no anaesthetic. So she quickly told her Grandmother that giving the grieving the comfort of knowing the truth about how their loved one died was very satisfying. Her Grandmother still thought it was a bit gruesome, but could see Bronwen's logic.

Studying Pathology had taken her to another continent. Practising Pathology had taken her off the planet for twenty years. She had been a lecturer at Pendragon University for ten years.

Since her return to the Home-world, Bronwen was surprised how much things had changed, and not just under Queen Johanna's rule. So many things had started moving forward during the reign of the conservative King Benedict III, the arrival of the new Queen had accelerated change. She was about to start her new job at the mortuary at Castello del Filippo's new General Hospital. She was only a part-time lab technician, there had been no vacancies for pathologists. She suspected she had been the only applicant.

'Professor Tudor, is that you?' asked the young man in scrubs and a white lab coat, when he finally realised who she was. 'I've only ever seen you in scrubs.'

'Yes, it's me, Dr. Sanders.' She remembered him as one of her first students at Pendragon University, several years ago. Bronwen was wearing the traditional orange outfit she had worn on arrival at Zucca, no wonder it took so long for him to recognise her.

'What are you doing here?'

'I'm your new mortuary technician, Dr. Sanders,' said Bronwen, who watched the look of surprise become one of sheer amazement.

'You are so magnificently over-qualified for that job. Why on Anseris did you apply for it? Although I'm glad you did, the post has been empty for too long.'

That was it, suspicions confirmed.

'Well, I have to do something,' Bronwen said to her new boss. 'Yes I have more than enough from my savings to retire into the Life of Reilly, but that's so boring. I need to be doing something constructive with my time.'

'OK, the locker room is through there. I wasn't expecting our management to employ a woman for a job like that. The building might be new, but the attitudes are still old. Have we even got female scrubs?'

'Not to worry, I've brought some with me. And ones which are suitable for Fiandre.' That meant long skirts for the women. She supposed she was lucky, she would be working somewhere that the hospital administrators classed as an Operating Theatre, exempt from the Clothing Regulations. The nurses and doctors working on the wards upstairs filled with state or the art equipment still wore mediaeval clothing.

Bronwen did feel guilty. Boredom was only part of the reason for getting this job. Chantelle believed someone had killed her father, and that it had been hushed up. Bronwen agreed with her niece, there was something strange about the death of Gilbert du Fauché. He had reportedly been at the peak of fitness immediately before his death. None of the doctors in a thirty mile radius had reported treating a normal throat infection, so where had he caught what turned out to be a fatal illness? Nobody else in the Archduchy had died from such an infection that spread throughout the body, ripping the immune system to shreds. Why had nobody noticed this? There had to be foul play involved in the Baron's death. To prove it, Bronwen needed access to the sort of equipment that could only be found in this mortuary's lab to answer those questions.

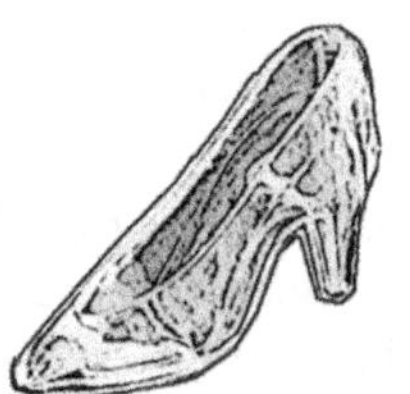 **10** 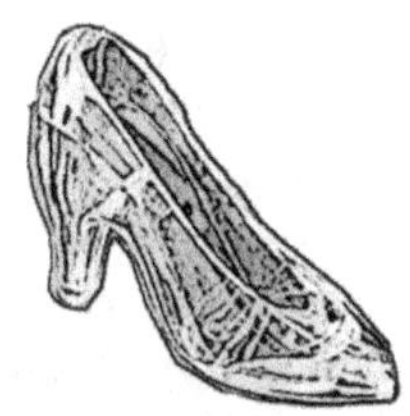

Amongst all the wicked things she did during her long reign, Queen Kathyren would occasionally do something good. Such as when she decreed the five Archduchies on the Eastern Continent would use Welsh as their official language. It had been her family's first language, this saved it from the mass extinction of other Earth languages. Now more people used Welsh as their first language than had ever done on Earth. The Eastern Continent adopted the National Anthem of Wales, which proudly proclaimed "Yr hen iath barhau" or "the old language survives" as its own.

The easternmost Archduchies, Gingerwall and Holywall, with no mineral resources, look East onto the wide Southern Ocean are rural and conservative. The mineral rich Nofogrod, Cymbriau and Dolffi look West across the narrow Rift Sea to the Southern Continent, are industrial and rebellious.

For centuries, Jadwiga's family had been peasants in Nofogrod, her male ancestors worked in the jewel mines, while her female ones kept home. The family had begun its rise upwards when Jadwiga's paternal great grandfather became an apprentices with a jeweler in Orlof. He then joined the Jeweller's Guild of Elizaburg, even though he and his wife never left Orlof. They officially became Middle Class, when her Father moved the family to Elizaburg after two years of compulsory military service.

Jadwiga had inherited her paternal grandmother's radicalism. She knew the old lady had despaired at her son's conservitive wife. The dislike and distrust was mutual, her mother hated Jadwiga having and contact with Nana Eirwen. Jadwiga sneeked weekly visits.

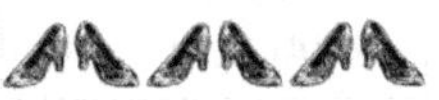

'So, you're originally from Orlof. I used to go hiking in the Penyresgryn Mountains' said Monsieur Nouveauté, 'I know that village well.'

Jadwiga knew the type, condescending idiots who were roundly hated by the locals. It was her first day at work and she was having an introductory chat with the head of the firm. His office was horribly decorated with dark wood panels and no windows. Even on a Summer day like today, it had lights blazing.

'My maternal grandmother was from even further East, from Holywall,' said Jadwiga. 'One of the groups of peasants brought to Orlov to dilute its radicalism.'

'Which had worked a treat,' said Andre Nouveauté, 'Orlov is now the most conservative place in that Archduchy.'

Don't I just know it, thought Jadwiga. 'My Father, Axlbrandt Smitz decided to resettle his family in Elizaburg. He had been stationed there during his Military Service.'

'Ah, that explains your curious lack of accent,' said her Boss in an annoyingly patronising tone. 'So how did you meet Her Majesty?'

'It was before she revealed herself. She told me she a nurse at Ellisford Castle and advised me to seek help from the Caretakers. I don't think she was expecting me to run away from home. I always wanted to be a Lawyer and live a completely fifty ninth century life. My Mother could only see marriage and motherhood as a career for her daughter.'

'Is that how you ended up at the Basilica in Elizaburg on the night King Benedict III died?'

'Yes sir. The nurse turned out to be Princess Imogen who was being crowned Queen Johanna IV at a meeting of the leaders of all the groups opposed to the old regime. I helped her change into her ceremonial robes, then guide her train. She remembered me from months earlier, and decided that she was now in a position of power and could help me fulfil my dream.'

'And your place in government? You are such a fascinating person to talk to, Jadwiga.'

'The Queen, appointed everyone present Royal Councillors, charged with creating a new constitution and modern laws and democratic government for the Kingdom of Anseris. I was chosen to represent the views of all the young people in the Kingdom. Although I didn't do much, just a grand title. I get credited for things that I had very little to do with. Now I want to do things normal girls my age do.'

'Well, I hope you enjoy your time with us, Jadwiga,' he said, 'Miss Wilson will show you around the building.'

Doing an internship in the time between completing school and starting university was not neccessary for students who wanted to be lawyers, but it certainly helped. Unlike the other girls her age, Jadwiga had no trouble when she was applying for internships. Her name alone made so many sexist old men, who would never have considered a female intern, forget their bigotry to gain the cudos of employing the Queen's young friend.

At this early stage in her career, Jadwiga thought her time as a Royal Councillor was a problem. An intern should not know more about the practical aspects of the laws of Anseris than her employer. So she lied about her practical knowledge. The glaring holes in her theoretical knowledge helped with the pretence. She was looking forward to filling those holes in university.

'This is a three storey building,' said Miss Wilson, the senior legal secretary. 'The main entrance, office and reception are here on the first floor of the building. It can be confusing because the main entrance opens out onto the main street of Zucca.'

The office she was working in was exactly as Jadwiga imagined it would be, old fashioned. Miss Wilson sat at one desk, facing towards the left hand wall of the building. Mr. Spain, the Articled Clerk sat at a desk facing Miss Wilson. Jadwiga would be sitting at the reception desk, facing the front door. Each desk had a computer, but there were folders, files and ledgers everywhere. Most of the business was still done on paper.

'If you follow me, we shall go up to the library and archive,' said Miss Wilson. In here is where we keep a copy of the Laws of Anseris, plus a record of case law and precedences. Next door is Room #1 where the Wills of all our living customers are filed.

When a customer dies and the Will receives probate, it is sent to the Will Archive in Castello del Filippo.'

'Do we not keep a reserve copy?' asked Jadwiga.

'No, we do not have the room, I'm afraid,' said Miss Wilson. 'If we need a will from there, we send a request and a copy is sent to us. Once Monsieur Nouveauté has signed and date stamped the request. The invoice for the document arrives a month later.'

'What's in Room #2?' Jadwiga asked.

'Conveyancing, contracts and licencing applications. Our bread and butter work. Then Room #3, is government stuff and special projects. It's not used very much.'

The two women walked back down two flights of stairs to the ground floor.

'As you know, that is Monsieur Nouveauté's office. Along the corridor is a meetings room and a small kitchen where we make tea and coffee and have our lunches' said Miss Wilson, 'How are your tea-making skills, you'll be spending a lot of time down here.' information for the next planning meeting.

'The biggest flaw in my plan was, how can I steal the Will from the Palace? Where would I hide it, in a pocketless ball gown?' asked Chantelle. 'I'd only have a tiny purse for my dance card.'

'Now you don't steal it. We will get the Archive to send a copy here,' said Jadwiga.

'And bill Nouveauté for the privilege,' said Bronwen.

'So how do I do that?'

'By putting a request in the diary of the Archivist at the Palace,' said Jadwiga, taking a slip of paper from a pocket in her surcotte's voluminous sleeves. Getting the boss's signature was so easy.'

'If it was so easy, why not just send it from the office?' asked Aunty Bronwen.

'He double checks the requests before they are sent to Castello del Filippo,' Jadzia replied. 'He would hit the roof if he found out I was helping you. He's in Lady Livienne's pocket.'

'Thanks for this, Jadwiga, but we wouldn't want you to lose your job over this.'

'There's not a worry of that. The Archivist won't know the request did not come from the firm, so won't ask why "Awful André", as he is known by all the legal profession in the Archduchy, wants a Will sent to you. Also Monsieur Nouveauté won't check up on why he has been billed for a will until I am long gone.'

'Again, pockets?'

'Sow a small one in your chemise, a few inches from the floor, so it's easy to access,' said Jadwiga, lifting her dress to demonstrate.

'That will make my life so much easier, not just at the Masquerade, but at work as well,' said Chantelle.

'You mean none of the Simples told you about that?' asked Jadwiga.

'No, they were bringing me up to be a gentlewoman who didn't need to carry anything, and gentrifying themselves in the process.' Chantelle went bright red. 'That makes me sound so upper-class and useless.'

'Don't let it stress you,' said Aunty Bronwen, 'I should have known that, with my middle class background. Years living on Pendragon kept that little trick away from me.'

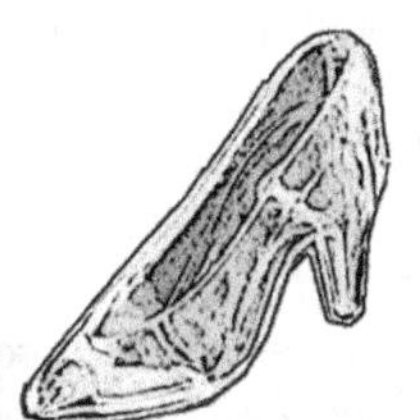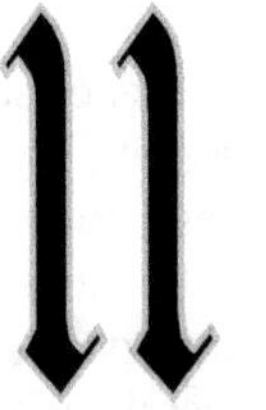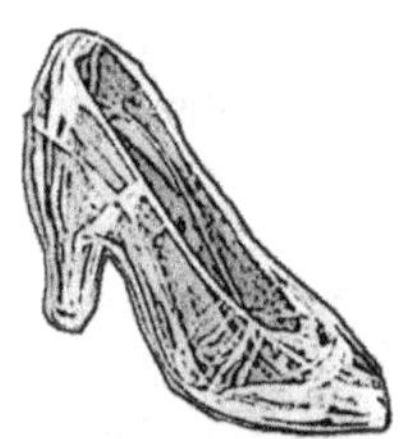

11

I t's 2pm in the afternoon of Tuesday, 9th June, 5885.
I should be in an Economics examination now, Madeleine
thought as she looked at her watch. Proper Economics, not
the Home variety. She was sitting on a chair in the garden,
supposedly practising her rusty embroidery. One of the many
"Wifely Skills" her mother wanted her to master. Chantelle
was pegging clothes on a line. Not many stitches were being made
and the line filled slowly. They were enjoying the conversation.

'It's a pond with pretensions,' said Madeleine to her sister. They
were discussing the small body of water surrounding the tiny spot
of land Cenerentola House was built on.

'As I said, it depends on your sense of perspective, I like to think
of it as a small lake,' said Chantelle. 'Either way, it meant that the
original builders didn't have to dig a moat.'

'No, they just built circular curtain walls around the shoreline,
making it nice and regular,' said Dave Bottles. Madeleine could see
he had slipped out of the house for a quiet cigarette, leaving the
Butler persona indoors.

'In the sixteen centuries of human history on Anseris, there have
been seven buildings on the spot, five houses, a boathouse and the
kennels for the guard dogs that patrolled the original prison stockade
that became Cenerentola Villager. The first Cenerentola House was a
square tower within the walls. This was purely defensive and had no
domestic frills. 'The second house was a round tower which had
a great hall at its base, and rooms for the family above, and was
surrounded by outbuildings. The third house had a doughnut shaped
building surrounding a central tower, which burnt down when it
was three hundred years old,' he dragged on the cigarette, and blew

out the smoke, to emphasise his point. 'The fourth house retained the doughnut structure, but it enclosed three square towers at its heart. Each house became less and less castle-like, and a large manor house replaced half the doughnut when the current Cenerentola House was constructed two hundred years ago.

'Each time a new house was constructed, the rubble from the older house was spread evenly over the islet, raising the level higher and higher above the water 'When the current house was built, soil was brought over to level the garden around the house with the top of parapets and turrets of the curtain wall.'

'I never knew that, Mr. B,' said Madeleine. 'Does that mean that the underground boathouse was once an actual boathouse?'

'Yes milady. There was always a defended door with a jetty with a roof within the curtain walls. Now it's completely buried several feet below the garden, with a passage connecting it to main house The outer entrance to the boathouse on the lake is now a cavernous doorless arch on the southern side of the wall.

'Granny Glad brought her brother-in-law, Uncle Ron out of retirement in Tintagel, he renovated this place. It was when I first arrived here,' said Chantelle to her sister. 'Of course, I don't remember what it was like back then. Although I've seen the photographs, so its probably best that I don't.'

'They removed the dilapidated drawbridge and portcullis and built a solid stone bridge from the house to the road on the other side of the moat.'

'Which has a water main and sewer connecting the house to the Island's water supply network,' said Chantelle. 'Uncle Ron was in many ways a genius.'

'It was always artistically maintained to be rustically charming said Madeleine. 'Now it all looks so down at heel.'

'Well, it could do with a coat of whitewash on the stonework, and the guttering needs cleaning.' Chantelle was emptying the content of her vacuum cleaner into one of the bins.

'Pappa always used to say it was on the to-do list. Just there were more important things to-do.' Madeleine had followed her sister was wrinkling her nose.

'I'm sure that plastic film recycling bin shouldn't smell like that?'

The content of normal bins smell badly, it's in their nature. The content of this bin naturally smelled sweetly. All the plastic items that clogged up the ecosystem on Ancient Earth had been made from mineral oil and were almost indestructible. Similar plastics on Anseris were made from a vegetable oil and broken down easily by a species of worms bred for the purpose, which lived in specially designed bins. Every week, a bottle of oil was removed from the bin and sold back to the plastics companies, who used it to make recycled plastic film, packaging and carrier bags. The bin was supposed to smell like almonds, it currently smelled like rotten fish. It was also supposed to be full of fluid; it was a dry as a bone.

'Something has killed 'em worms. That bin needs to be cleaned, and the dead worms burned,' said the Cook a few minutes later, after she had examined the bin with the help of two long sticks.

'OK, so where do I begin?' asked Chantelle.

'No, Ella. This needs to be done by professionals, with special suits,' said Dave Bottles.

'Oh nonsense Mr. Bottles, that is an unnecessary expense. Even with dead worms, the contents are harmless,' said her Step-Mother, who had come to investigate the report of trouble in the kitchen. 'Ella has already agreed to do the job. Make sure there is a bath for her, and burn whatever she is wearing to do the job.'

'Yes, Ma'am,' said the Cook and Chantelle as they bobbed a curtsey. Mr. Bottle bobbed his head in acknowledgement, putting his virtual mask back on.

'Well, get on with it girl,' said the Cook. 'There are some old clothes in the scullery cupboard that you can wear. I'll light the boiler while you are doing it, after you've finished bundle the rags into a sack so they can be burned in the boiler later.'

'Yes Cook,' said Chantelle. She knew the miserable old woman thought she was currying favour. No, that was a pointless task; the Cook was one of her Step-Mother's old family retainers. Despite being a roaring snob to everyone else, her Step-Mother treated the Cook like an old friend. This was probably the reward for a lifetime of unswerving loyalty to Livienne du Fauché.

The real reason Chantelle had volunteered for the thankless task was to get samples from the bin, some dead worms and the residual liquid at the bottom of the bin. Maybe whoever had killed her Father might have disposed of the poison there. She knew she had to be careful on two fronts. First, Chantelle did not want to be exposed to any poison in the bin. Second, she didn't want the Cook to see her take the samples. The old baggage would tell her Step-Mother, a possible suspect.

She found the clothes. A huge chemise and a voluminous blue kirtle that had belonged to Carlotta and was more than three of the new standardised sizes too large for Chantelle. Finally over a tight fitting coif she pinned on of Carlotta's billowing white veils.

'Girl, take the veil off, and put this old wimple of mine on before putting the veil back on. Cover as much of your skin as you can,' said the Cook. 'Plus these old tar coated gardening gloves will protect your 'ands.'

She also had big rubber boots on under the ensemble. She doubted they added much to the protection as there was a crack in the sole of the left boot, that let in a small amount of water.

Chantelle was now certain she looked as stupid as she possibly could.

'Before yous start,' said the Cook, 'Lizzie 'as just said to fill these bottles wi' the liquid in the bottom of the bin and a sample of the worms. She says that them busy-bodies from Castello del Filippo will wanna know what killed them blessed worms.'

The Cook handed al set of sample bottle identical to the ones her Aunt had given her. Great thought Chantelle, I can legitimately take the samples she wanted, without anyone batting an eyelid. Aunty Bronwen could get the results from her friend at the Coroners at the same time as her step-mother.

'Right then girl, of you go, but remember to be careful out there.'

'Don't worry, I will be.'

J t was a quick but deeply unpleasant job. The undigested plastic went into one plain paper sack, the very dirty clothes went into another and the worms and residual liquid went into a wax lined sack. All three went into the old bin. The air holes for the worms made it a perfect brazier. The whole thing burnt with a ferocious heat, leaving almost no residue, nor much of the brazier. As promised, Chantelle had the luxury of a warm bath with clean water and soap.

'First you soap yourself and wash in that shower, wash all that muck off, Ella. Then you can relax in that tub. You've earned the luxury,' said the Cook.

'Thank you, Cook.' This was the first time that the older woman had called her anything other than "Girl". Chantelle was too tired to argue and did as she was told. The shower was hot and stung as it removed anything that might have stuck to her skin and hair. Then she climbed into the warm velvet like spiced water of the bath. After a ten minute soak, she climbed out, dried herself, pulled her maid's uniform back on and trudged to the kitchen.

'You look done in Ella, you can have the rest of the day off,' said the Cook.

'Won't the Mistress object?' asked Chantelle.

'Leuk, Ella, ay don't know er care wa' 'appened betweun de two o' yous. ay don't know why yous 'as been demoted ter de servant's 'all. and ay don't care,' said the Cook in the thick Elizaburg accent she used with friends. 'De fact is, you're e'yer now and yous 'av provun yoself ter be an 'ard worker, who follows orders without argu'n. Ay terld Lizzie yous wuz one o' me people, so she can't pull any dull stunts like thisavvy again'

Chantelle looked at the older woman in a state of amazement. This was very strange. Was Cook the only person left alive who could stand up to her step-mother and win.

'Ay know wa' yer think'n. Ay 'uv beun work'n fer er wi' Lizzie fe thirty years, ay am de only one she listens ter. She knows ay know far tew much about 'er ter sack me.'

'So, we're friends now?' asked Chantelle.

'Nope, but we ay colleagues' said Cook, reminding Chantelle who was boss.

A definite step forward, Chantelle thought to herself. Maybe the Cook would be more civil with her now. She left the kitchen before the Cook had time to change her mind. She was feeling so cold that she laid a fire in the grate in her room, despite the fact it was warm and sunny outside. She felt like ice, so she climbed into her bed and pulled the blankets tightly around herself and fell into a deep sleep.

She heard female voices. Her sister, the Cook and her Step-Mother. They seem to be arguing about her.

'Why does she need to be moved?' asked her Step-Mother.

'You can feel how hot it is in here Lizzie. The girl's burning up. She needs to be somewhere cooler,' the Cook said.

'So we move her back to her old room until she gets better,'

'All this fuss over a housemaid,' said her Step-Mother.

'This woman is my sister, and I will nurse her until she gets better,' said Madeleine.

'You will do what you are told, Missy,' said Lady Livienne.

'Yes, whatever.'

'Lady Madeleine is right, Ella needs to be moved now!' the Cook said to her employer. 'Ella, child. You need to get up now.'

'But I'm so comfortable here. I can feel my self getting more comfortable. Sinking to a deeper level.'

'Oh Angels, she's losing it. Quick, get her up and out into the cooler night air,' said the Cook.

Chantelle felt herself being lifted out of her bed and walked through the door, down the stairs and out of the servant's quarters.

'Where am I going?'

'Back to your old room, back to your old life,' said Madeleine.

'Don't push it Missy,' said her Step-Mother, 'this is only until she gets better.'

'Oh well, I tried,' said Maddy. 'But it will happen sooner or later.'

Doctor Sanders was at a meeting in Ponte di Carla and would be gone all day. Bronwen quickly set to work on the jobs she was supposed to do that day, it did not take long.

Then she started work on the jobs she wanted to do. As she had hoped, samples from the Baron's body were still in storage in the evidence freezer. His death had been unusual, so samples taken from his body would be kept for three years, for comparison in the case of anyone else who died under similar circumstances. A vile of his blood, another of the liquid in his stomach, plus other samples of body tissue were present. While her tests were running, she sat down to read the autopsy report.

'Gotcha!' said Dr. Sanders. I knew you would want to dig deeper into the death of your late sister's husband.'

'You did, Doctor,' said Bronwen, acting innocent.

'I did,' he replied. 'So did I, but I couldn't find anything. Although I didn't really know where to look.'

'Palpadino poisoning,' said Bronwen. 'It killed the worms in the plastic film recycling bin at his house. Fortunately it had degraded to below the fatal level for humans, by the time my niece went looking to see what had killed them. It made her really ill.'

'No, I didn't even think to look for such an unusual toxin. Your niece was very lucky,' he said. 'Unlike you, caught doing unauthorised tests during working hours,' Dr. Sanders smiled. 'Although I'm not going to report you, as I shouldn't be here either. Also sacking you would make the next bit difficult.'

'Yes, why aren't you in Ponte di Carlo?'

'The meeting was cancelled at the eleventh hour.'

'Oh, I see. So why are you here?'

'To give you some good news. Now the University Health Board know who you really are, they have decided to give you a job that matches your qualifations. They have been talking about creating this new post for years, but they only wanted, and you were out in Pendragon, boss.'

'Without an interview?' asked Bronwen.

'Yes, as you are already on the payroll.'

An alarm pinged, showing the blood test had finished.

'Anyhow, so you're looking for traces of Palpadino in Baron Gilbert's blood and stomach fluids.'

'Positive, in all samples' said Bronwen as a second timer pinged. 'Palpadino is such a rare toxin these days, testing other sources for its presence made sense to me.'

'That should be enough to re-open the case,' said Dr. Sanders, as he read a positive result from the stomach content test. He began typing into his computer. 'Now that's odd.'

'What's odd Dr. Sanders?' Bronwen asked.

'The case of Baron Gilbert du Fauché's death has been closed with a security seal that should be obsolete.'

'Who on Anseris would do that, and why?' asked Bronwen 'Old poison, old codes. This is getting silly.'

'**S**he's waking up,' said Clementine. 'Go tell the temporary housemaid the permanent housemaid is awake.'

'Why should I do it. You go,' said Citronella.

'Somebody has to stay with her, that's going to be me.'

'Why, because you're the older one. That is so unfair Clemmie It's only a ten minute difference.'

'No, it is because I have done volunteering in hospital, sitting with sick people. You haven't.'

'Both of you, disappear!' said Madeleine as she breezed in.

'What are you doing here? Maman has forbidden you access to this room,' said Clementine.

'She's my Sister, do you think I won't nurse her whilst she's ill you stupid women.'

'Don't speak to us like that,' said Citronella.

'Just go, will you. Or I'll go and tell Maman you've been bickering like eight year olds again.'

That seemed to do the trick as the Twins exited the room as quickly as they could.

'**C**hantelle thought she was dreaming. She could not possibly be lying in her old bed in her old room. She had heard Madeleine argue with the Ugly Sisters. Madeleine had brought a large mug with her, and put it on the table beside the bed.

'Hilde told me you had to drink all of this, while it was still hot,' said Madeleine.

Chantelle was now fully awake. This wasn't a dream. She was back in her old room. Madeleine expertly propped her up on the pillows.

'Hilde?' Chantelle asked her younger sister.

'It appears that she has known Aunty Bron as long as she has known my Maman. You'll have less of a hard time with her from now on. Her husband though, that's a different story.'

'Maddy, I can deal with Dave Bottles. He's a sweety. So, I take it, this is a temporary reprieve.'

'Yes and no. Yes, Mama still insists you're a servant, but you won't be going back to the Servant's Quarters. You're to be our Lady's Maid, and move to the attic room in this half of the house.'

'So, any news on the samples?' asked Chantelle.

'Aunty Bron is not pleased with you, putting yourself in danger.'

'So?'

'So the poison has been identified and there were significant levels of it in Papa's body. This should be treated as a murder case, but the medical examiner can't get passed some sort of old Interdiction Code.'

'Oh, so still nobody is investigating.'

'Don't worry, it's only a matter of time.' Madeleine gently kissed her sister's forehead. 'Now, enough excitement. You so need some sleep.'

'OK,' said Chantelle, who was quickly asleep.

She dreamt the strangest of dreams. Not a bizarre cheese fueled fantasy, instead she saw her memories, the memories of the last time she had seen her Father strong and healthy. He had been in a good mood, things must have gone well with the Commander at Castello del Filippo.

'Livienne, I've brought some guests home for Lunch.'

'Really Gilbert, I wish you would give me more warning. How many more should I tell Cook to cater for?' asked his wife.

'Two more, dear, Hans and Ray. Business over for the day, we are going out on water to do a spot of fishing.'

'Very well, lunch will be served in twenty minutes. You'll have to wait for that before you can do any fishing.'

Chantelle could tell by the older woman's body language she was annoyed. As usual. However her Step-Mother tried to sound happy about the changing arrangements.

'Ah, Chantelle my dear, I have been thinking about what you said last night,' said her Father, 'Come with me, we have much to discuss.' Then turning to Hans and Ray, who were filling their pipes. 'It would be wise if you smoked them in the garden, must keep Livienne happy. I'll catch up with you in a few minutes.'

She followed her father out of the house, then up the stairs to the fortified tower at the centre of the building. This was the Solar, the part of the manor the family would evacuate to if the house ever came under attack. At the moment, it was exclusively the Baron and Chantelle's offices.

'Chantelle my dear, I know that as a father, I have failed you miserably,' he said, as he sat at his desk.

'Papa, I have always loved you, and do not begrudge your absence during my childhood.'

'But you should, Daughter. You should.' He opened a drawer in his desk. 'You are twenty four years old and have never been further than school in Ponte di Carla, but your younger sister goes to school in Elizaburg.'

'I chose to go to school at the Ponte di Carla Academy, Papa.'

'But you want more. You think your life is passing you by. My estate office barely provides enough challenge for a mind like yours. I know you spend more time researching and writing your articles for the local history society magazine.'

'I am contented with my lot. Working with you here. Where would you find another secretary who knows the estate so well.'

'No, my daughter, you are not. Which is why I have written to my old friend and fellow political prisoner Maurice Mendelsohn, the Admissions Tutor at Elizaburg University. He entered your name into the Mature Student Selection process. You approve?'

'Oh, Papa yes, more than you could know.' This was a dream of hers, one which could never come true, to many real barriers in its way. 'But Papa, I left school early, after my Secondary Certificate to work as your secretary. How can I go to University without the Tertiary Certificate from the final year at school?

'Staff in Dr. Mendelsohn's department read all you have written for the Local History Society. They said it is of a quality in excess of what is required for a Tertiary Certificate. That you will have no problem studying as an undergraduate and passed your name onto the History Department.'

'They're not just saying that, because I'm the daughter their boss's friend? I would hate to deny a worthy student a place at University, just to return a favour owed.'

'As honest as ever,' said the Baron. 'That's not how the system works. The History Department offered you a place at the University, based on merit.'

'Yes papa, I shall accept the offer. How can I refuse.'

'Very well. In September, when Madeleine travels back to the Planetary Capital, to study for her Tertiary Certificate, you shall accompany her. You'll share a house I've rented with three good families for their daughters, whilst they are at school or college. There will be a staff of two, so you won't have to worry about domestic distractions from your studies.'

'Thank you, Papa, thank you. How can I ever repay you?'

'Chantelle my dear, I don't want repayment. A parent never wants repayment. We only want our children to go forward and honour us with their own success. Our immortality lies in the achievement of our children.'

'Bellé-mére will not be happy. She was expecting Madeleine to come home, so she could match make for her as she is match-making for the twins.'

'Well, she might have been successful with Madeleine, but now she won't have to bother,' said her Father enigmatically. 'She has such silly ideas. It gives my old radical heart a buzz that there is more to life than marriage and children for young women these days. She should get with the programme.'

'Come on Gilbert, the day is wasting away,' said the Commander. 'I need to cross swords with Old Rameses again, while the Ansersol is still shining.'

Chantelle and her Father had arrived at the steps to what was now a wine cellar connected by a tunnel to the Boathouse. The wine cellar had been a defensive position where guards protected the only way into Cenerentola House if the drawbridge was raised.

'Commender, may I ask you a question?'

'Of course, Chantelle,' said the older man.

'You run a fishing business, you spend a lot of your time on your ships, fishing for a living. Why do you spend your spare time on a boat on Cenerentola House's moat, trying to catch another fish?'

'Ah, I can see why you ask that. It is all to do with the difference between fishing and angling.'

'Do enlighten me, Commander, I assume they are the same thing.'

'Not at all. In my line of work I harvest stupid creatures from the sea, who seem willing to throw themselves into a trawler's nets, that is mere fishing. When I come here, I am rejoining a battle of wits with a worthy opponent. Old Rameses is a perch I have been trying to catch for a number of years, that is angling. Whilst he is still a fish and destined to lose, he is a genius compared to the sad creatures of the deep.'

'You see, Chantelle, it's the thrill of the chase,' said her father's friend Ray Payntor.

'Three dimensional chess,' said her father.

'An excuse to sit in a boat and drink cold beer, chilled by the moat's water,' countered Lady Livienne.

'That, madame,' said the Commander, 'is a bonus.'

'Gilbert, on the subject of beer, you had better have one of these,' someone said. Her memory failed as her mind started wandering, right at the most important point. She could not remember who had said that. Neither could she remember who had handed her father a small purple fruit. All she could see was a statue of an Angel which had a small toy fishing rod in its hand where a sword should be. It was a copy of one of the statues on the Grand Basilica in Elizaburg. She secretly called it "Brilly Bobbery" a secret shared with her childhood playmate, Len Simples, who had difficulty saying the statues title 'Brilliantly Robed in Glory" and regularly referred to the statue by the silly name.

When perfect clarity returned she was looking at her Father's face. He had dropped the fruit whole into his mouth and began to chew. Almost immediately, the smile faded.

'You've given me one that isn't ripe. It's too bitter.'

'They're all bitter, Gilbert, stop complaining,' said Payntor.

'How would you know Ray, you're allergic to them.'

'Do you expect something that miraculous to have a pleasant taste as well. You really are expecting the moon on a stick, Gilbert,' Lady Livienne added. She knew her Father had just eaten a maletbon fruit. Uniquely Anserian, they prevented hangovers the morning after a heavy nights drinking.

'I know, but that one was particularly loathsome,' her Father said.

'Then it will be particularly effective. Look on the bright-side Gilbert,' said Ray, as he climbed into the boat.

'I'm going back to the house with Belle-Mama,' said Chantelle. 'I've so many things to do now. So much to prepare for.'

'And I know you shall enjoy every second of those tasks, ma chère fille,' said her father as she kissed him on the cheek.

'You are determined to follow through with that monumental waste of money then. Educating girls,' said the Lady Livienne, with a note of disgust. 'I told you yesterday, what does a woman need an advanced education for?'

'Yes, Livienne,' said the Baron, rolling his eyes heavenward, 'I'm determined to educate our girls to the level of their ability. That includes your twins. If that means them joining the Ugly Sisters, so be it. Only the grave can stop me, and my new Will shall trump even that.'

So that was what they had been arguing about the pervious night. School fees for Madeleine and college fees for me.

'Are you sure about this?' asked Aunty Bronwen, who had been allowed to visit Chantelle during her illness.

'Yes, positive,' said Chantelle, recounting her dream from the previous night. 'Somebody gave Papa a poisoned Maletbon fruit in the boathouse. The fruit must have contained the poison that killed my Father, then the worms in the recycling bin, where the killer disposed of the evidence We now have three suspects.'

'Indeed, my Mother and the Commander,' said Madeleine.

'And two of the three sides of the magic triangle. We know the method and the opportunity, all we have to do is work out the motive.'

'However, Chantelle needs to rest, so we will have to discuss that later,' said Madeleine.

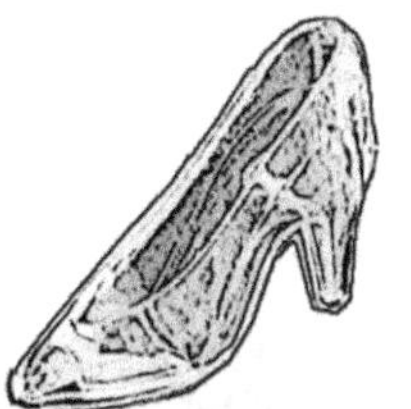
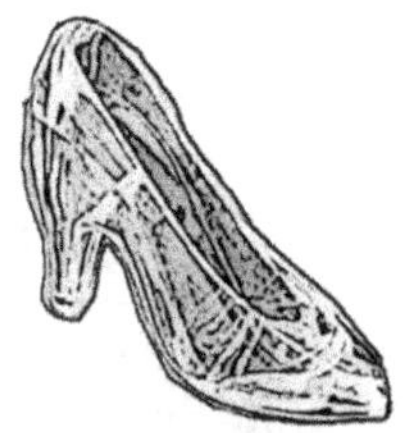

12

Now, that's interesting, thought Jadwiga. She was supposed to be filing away the firms outstanding paperwork on a dreary Tuesday morning.

Jadwiga had been fascinated by lock mechanisms since childhood. If I was not going to be a lawyer, she thought, I would be either an top notch locksmith or safe-cracker. Except the Locksmiths Guild still refused to accept female apprentices. Neither, she imagined did the underworld.

The locks in this place were pathetically easy for her to pick. So the mysterious Room#3 had been unlocked all morning, and she had not been able to resist taking a quick look inside. This firm was not as incompetent and dull as they pretended to be. It had a number of investments opportunities set up, all of dubious legality, which Mr. Nouveauté was either a partner in or managing for other clients.

Back in Room#2 she opened the envelope on the top of the pile. It contained a letter from G. F. Barnard and Sons, a practice in Castello del Filippo. She knew she should file it away with out reading it, but she could not help herself. The letter informed Mr. Nouveauté that as their client, the late Baron du Fauché had not created a new Last Will and Testament with them, so Mr. Nouveauté could go ahead and apply for probate on the Will in this firm's files. They also said that as the Baron was now dead, they would no longer be perusing his divorce petition. She wanted to take a photocopy of the letter, but she knew that was unethical, not a good way to start her legal career. Besides Chantelle would be able to get a copy of this letter, along with a copy of the divorce petition from the other law firm.

It was not surprising why the Baron had wanted a divorce. He had discovered his wife had also bought one thousand ordinary shares in

Commander Liepmann's fishing company. A file in Room#3 had instructions to hide the shares by transferring them to a company technically owned by Monsieur Nouveauté but was actually owned by Lady Livienne. The late Baron opposed the expansion of the Commander's company into the Mare di Napoli, and must have stumbled on this ruse. The straw that broke the camel's back.

'How's it going?' asked Miss Williams over the intercom.

'Better then I expected,' said Jadwiga, her voice steeped in irony.

'OK, then I'll send a cup of coffee up for you in the document lift. It's black with no sugar, isn't it?'

'That's right.'

'Thank you,' said Jadwiga politely over the intercom, as the steaming mug of hot black liquid appeared. 'I'm more than ready for this!'

'Our filing should have been computerised years ago,' said Miss Williams. 'I remember the old man wanted to modernise this place before he retired. I was surprised André was so against change.'

'Yeah, it's usually the younger partners who want the change.' Jadwiga was surprised that the older woman was speaking out against Monsieur Nouveauté. Normally she was his number one fan. She must have looked shocked.

'Sometimes I do disagree with André you know,' said Miss Williams.

She called him André, twice, thought Jadwiga. She had heard rumours about the boss and this woman. They must be true. If anyone else in the company called the boss André at work, they would be censured.

'Why don't you come down,' said a new and male voice over the intercom. 'I'm sure there is something less dusty Miss Williams can find for you to do. And it must be so hot up there.'

Well Monsieur Nouveauté, if you insist on me wearing a heavy traditional dress to work, with a gorgette in addition to a veil. Even her Mother didn't make me wear that. So, what do you expect?

The people downstairs were as invisible to Jadwiga as she was to them.

'Don't worry, Sir. It's a quarter of an hour until my lunch, I can carry on with the conveyancing reports until then.'

'You're in Room#2?' asked a shocked Monsieur Nouveauté.

'Of course, Sir, it had the most things to file in it.' Jadwiga replied. 'The Wills in Room#1 are up to date and I never go into Room#3, it's always locked.'

Eventually the clock crawled to 12.30pm. The last report fell into the filing cabinet and she headed downstairs.

'Are you going out for lunch today?' Monsieur Nouveauté asked as she reached the bottom.

'I always do on a Tuesday, Sir,' she replied.

He was a man who looked far older than his years. He had lost his hair early, what remained had been allowed to grow into a bushy carrot coloured ring around the bald scalp. His excessively bushy sideburns, goatee beard and a small toothbrush moustache sat below his narrow hooked nose stopped him looking like a monk.

'The day has improved greatly, hasn't it?'

'Yes sir, it was really dreary this morning.'

'You've earned yourself an extra half hour's lunch, the way you battled through that backlog this morning. We really should have been more vigilant with our filing.'

'Thank you, Sir,' she replied as she left the building.

Jadwiga walked down Zucca's main street. Each shop had the owner's name on a sign, plus a traditional carved symbol hanging above the door. As with ancient Earth, the symbols had been designed to direct illiterate people to the correct tradesman. Universal literacy had existed on Anseris for nearly two centuries now, but the symbols persisted. Some were obvious, like the shoe shop's exquisitely carved wooden shoes. Others were less so. Why did the chemists have a stubby cross painted green hanging outside? Also, what was the point of the big round bottles with narrow necks filled with coloured water in the window?

The townsfolk were going about their business, as they had for centuries. She had wondered why the town's main street had turned its back on the sea. Why didn't it have a wide esplanade looking out beyond the eastern tip of Cenerentola Island into the beautiful Mare di Napoli? After all, so much of the town's income came from the sea.

Her favourite cafe was at the edge of town, and had embraced its location. There was a nondescript entrance in the street at the front, but at the back was a terrace overlooking the wide arc of the Mare di Napoli. She ordered her Tuesday favourite at the counter and chose a table on the terrace, looking out to sea. The June sunshine sparkled off the surface of the smooth, deep dark waters of the Mare di Napoli. She could see small fishing boats bobbing up and down on the water. Then she spotted a modern naval vessels with its cylindrical wind turbines spinning in the gentle wind. Jadwiga remembered Janek joining the Naval Juvenile Reserve and attending their summer camps. She could appreciate the appeal of living and working on one of those ships in good weather like this. When the ship was up North in the stormy seas around the Lonely Islands things would be so different.

Janek was yet to enlist, his future was swathed in hypertheticals. Getting past father's emotional and legal blocks an Enlisting was the first hurdle. The Free Queen's Navy maintained the exact number of officers and enlisted sailors to replace retiring servicemen. There were always more applicants than places. The Army or Airforce absorbed those recruits the Navy did not want. Janek would rather return to civilian life than join the other services.

She had thought she wanted to practice law in a quiet country town, after being at the heart of government in Elizaburg. She knew now there were many beautiful and quiet places to visit, but after the bustle of Elizaburg, she really wouldn't want to live in any of them. Too quiet.

That quiet would not last. Her mother was coming to stay for a fortnight. Another, possibly final attempt, to heal the breach in her family. Her mother was so old fashioned. Jadwiga had long ago realised tradition made some women so prickly and hard to love.

The first attempt had been shortly after Princess Imogen had become Queen Johanna. Her Majesty had ordered her mother to take her daughter back and do nothing to stifle her ambitions. And her mother had said no, that she would not allow such a wilfully rebellious child back under her roof. The arch royalist had defied her new Queen.

Jadwiga had won a scholarship to the Castle Rock Academy, in the village outside the castle's main gate. The Queen's Council met in the Great Hall of Ellisford Castle. It was logical Jadwiga moved to the Castle. Jadwiga had expected to be billeted with a family in the tiny community of Bailesparc within the castle grounds, She had not expected a room in the Queen's Suite, at the heart of the castle. She had lived there for three years. Behind closed doors Imogen had been like the big sister Jadwiga had always wanted, but never had nor never could have. The Castle now felt more like home than the house in the Jewellers Quarter of Elizaburg.

ℌ penny for your thoughts?' said Madeleine.
'I'm afraid that would buy you a pennyworth of donkey poo,' Jadwiga said, hiding her real thoughts.'I'm a child in Orlof, I should be used to that smell,'

'Yes, it seems to be particularly bad this year,' said her younger friend. 'I didn't used to notice it when I was flitting between here and Elizaburg.'

'Glad it's not just me then,' she said. 'Doubly glad, I have news.'

'Indeed, do tell.'

'You're not going to like it, I think you had better sit down.'

'You're going to tell me my mother and father were going to get a divorce, aren't you?' Madeleine asked.

'Yes, how did you guess?'

'I've suspected their marriage was over, since after Jule, when I returned to Elizaburg' said Madeleine, 'didn't have any proof though.'

'Well you won't have any proof from Nouveauté and Company,' Jadwiga said. 'They know they left too much sensitive information on the pile for filing this morning. I suspect they are terrified I have seen something I shouldn't. I suspect they will spend this hour shredding anything incriminating I might have seen this morning. It doesn't matter what they shred, there are other ways to prove what they have been up to.'

'Anything that's not Maman's dodgy bussiness affairs. Anything that is actually incriminating.' Madeleine sat in the chair next to Jadwiga.

'Plenty, I'm afraid. Too much to say here and now.' Jadwiga laughed, 'however, Mr. Nouveauté, the boss has given me an extra half hour on my lunch. He'll deny when I return to the office and sack me for poor punctuality.' Jadwiga laughed. 'So I'll be back five minutes early.'

As this was rural Fiandre, both young women were wearing traditional long dresses. Jadwiga had always hated traditional clothes she thought they made her look dumpy. Madeleine on the other hand had an extra three inches to carry the long skirts perfectly. Jadwiga noticed the younger girl was wearing her hair down and head uncovered Disobeying her mother's standing orders.

'You have very little time for your Mother,' Jadwiga said.

'Not my fault. She has been pushing me away for years, just like yours. Our mothers are supposed to be the most important women in our lives, the ones we love above all others, who love us in the same way. Somehow, I don't think our mothers received the memo.'

'Sad but true,' Jadwigas said. then changing the subject, 'Still coming on Sunday?' Then she ordered two glasses of Arance di Fiandre juice from the passing waiter.

'Yeah, what are you planning?' Madeleine asked.

'A relaxing city Sunday afternoon sunbathing. Something you've been missing out here. Even though the climate is much better here than LizB. It will be good for Chantelle's recuperation.

'About Chantelle, she can be surprisingly old fashioned.'

'Not that old fashioned,' said Jadwiga, 'it will be a pleasant taste of what she can expect when she gets to Elizaburg. And your Aunt will be there to help us.'

The juice arrived. Jadwiga loved the locally grown Oranges, which refused to have anything to do with the colour Orange. Their skin remained green when the fruit was ripe and the flesh was tinted with a red pigment. It was the sweetest citrus fruit she had ever tasted. When squeezed, the dark red juice was like nectar.

'That is something I am going to miss back in Elizaburg,' she said, trying to move the subject away from their awful mothers.

'I know, I tried to find Arance delle Fiandre in Elizaburg. They don't grow enough to export out of the Archduchy.'

'That's a shame,' said the city girl, between taking sips.

'Not really, Jadwiga. Sometimes the old fashioned ways around here are a good thing.' Madeleine took a long sip of the juice. 'Mass cultivation would only reduce the quality, especially if the large orange plantations in Gingerwall and Holywall started growing the fruit, and undercut the local growers.'

'You sound like someone who really knows her stuff,' Jadwiga said.

'Oh! I do. All the farms are in the old Barony. Five of them rented from the estate. I was trying to get Papa to apply for Geographical Protection for the fruit and its juice. He died a few weeks later. I don't think he was as confident as me,' she said. 'It's now something Chantelle has to do when we win.'

It was no good, the truth was just too horrible for her friend, and she began crying. 'Oh Jadzie, I hate it that he is dead and she is still alive. I don't know how I would cope if we found out she had killed Papa.' Jadwiga noted the horrified look on the other girl's face. 'Oh Angels, do you think anyone heard me. We are trying to keep our suspicions so secret.'

'Well, the waiter and the cook are arguing like crazy inside, and we are the only customers on the terrace and the beach is deserted.'

'Oh, that's good,' said Madeleine, blowing her nose.

'Don't worry, Lady Madeleine,' said the waiter, when he arrived with Jadwiga's lunch, 'everybody here in Zucca thinks your Mama killed your Papa and hate her even more than they did before.'

Apparently the staff of the café had heard Maddy's outburst, but it would not get back to Cenerentola House.

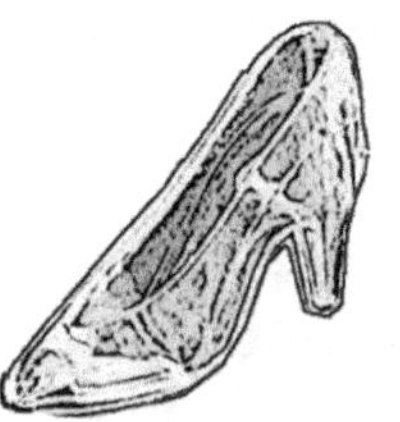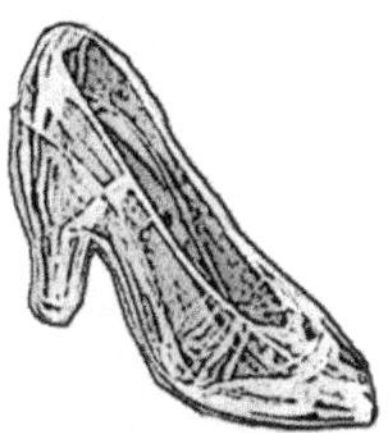

13

$\mathfrak{J}$t was a Sunday morning and everyone else was in church. Initially her Step-Mother had also insisted on Chantelle attendance every week. However, the priest, called a Caretaker, in the little church on the island declared that forcing an atheist to attend church was contrary to the Book of Care, the planet's holy book. Chantelle loved being in a silent house, where she could think without interuption.

Chantelle was examining what would be her room, when she was back to full strength. The lady's maid had to be instantly available to her mistress, so lived in that attic of the Family section of the house, with its spiral staircase down to stories to Lady Liviene's room. Next door was the long empty room where a governess would live, with its stairs down to the nursery.

Tomorrow, the two new housemaids would clean and tidy this room, today Chantelle knew, they had the time off after church and were visiting their families.

The room had been unoccupied for four years. Ever since Alexa, her step-mother's Lady's Maid had finally lost her patience with Lady Livienne, storming off in disgust at her ever increasing workload. In the meantime it had been used as makeshift stowage. There was a box of her Step-Mother's things on the bed. Chantelle moved it to sit down, and noticed that it contained two diaries, last year's and this. Her Step-Mother had been moaning about losing her current diary for weeks now. If the diary had belonged to anyone else, she would have returned it unread. However, her Step-Mother was a suspect, and it could include information useful in the investigation. Chantelle quickly hit gold

The Sea of Naples, is the largest and most profitable fishery on the Rift Sea. Her Father had worked hard to guarantee everyone had fair access to that fishery. This rankled with Commander Howard Liepmann who had worked just as hard to control the rest of the Rift Sea fisheries, and wanted exclusive control of all the waters that separated the Southern and Eastern Continents. Liepmann had be a friend of her father for years and could not understand why her father was not exploiting the fishery, or selling it to him, so he could. Obviously her step-mother also could not understand that sometimes there was more to life than making money.

Wednesday 21st Jenavieve

Off to Venezia, meeting with Cmdr L. He wants me to persuade G to sell the fishing rights to his FC. Says my investment in his FC will go through the roof if his FC buys them.

Monday 2nd Fevriona

G says a rare form of pearl has been found off the coast of the island. I told him G should definitely sell the Fishing Rights to Cmdr L. I said that the plebs wouldn't know what to do with all that money. Wealth belongs to the Gentry and above, it is their duty to let enough of it trickle down to the Plebs to keep them alive and working productively for the rich.

Monday 9th Fevriona

How the hell did G find out about my investments with Cmdr L. He says I should sell my shares or get a divorce. Me, a divorcee, it would ruin my social standing. I told G. that I would sell the shares. I didn't say that I would sell them to a company I own, which AN manages for me.

Wednesday 11th Fevriona

I've been served with divorce papers by G. How could he? Didn't use AN, he went to a firm in Castello.

Tuesday 10ᵗʰ Marcia

Argued with G. again about Mistake's education. He is becoming unbearable. No wonder the old order locked him up for his stupid radical ideas. A woman's place is in the home. They should not have careers other than the one the Angels designed them for.

Now he wants to send that bitch Ella. to university. What a waste of money. It's bad enough he is paying Mistake's school fees. Not that she was ever a proper daughter to me. Why couldn't I have normal girls who respect traditions. The Twits want to be Ugly Sisters. They may be embarrassing retards, but they are my embarrassing retards and they are not going to waste their lives mumbling prayers and looking after the children of plebs.

My wicked step-mother is so utterly selfish. It's the twins' life, not hers. Citronella and Clemantine should choose how they lived it. Being a Merciful Sister was not Chantelle's choice. She could not think of a single reason she would ever wear a brown habit.

Nobody would be surprised that Baroness Livienne Emily Saint-Claire du Fauché and former Royal Councillor Jadwiga Anna Orlof Smitz had declared war with each other the minute they had met. Lady Livienne had chosen to go to early morning prayers at the Church in Zucca, to see the new arrival in a socially neutral location.

'Did you see what she was wearing?' Lady Livienne asked her daughters after they returned home from church. Lady Livienne was flushed, not from the walk from the ferry, but with a self-righteous anger.

'Who, Mama?' Citronella asked.

'That dreadful social climber who has already done so much damage.' Lady Livienne sat heavily on the well padded chair. 'How much poison has she poured into the Queen's mind? They say the Queen calls her "My Little Sister"?'

'I thought she looked very pretty in that yellow kirtle and orange surcotte,' said the twins in unison.

'Yes, but it was silk. A few years ago someone that low born would not have been allowed to wear anything that fine.'

'The Sumptuary Laws were stupid,' said Madeleine, 'why should a person be banned from wearing good quality clothes because their father could not belong to a social club called either nobility or aristocracy?'

'I've no objection to good quality clothes worn by good quality people, our clothes are all good quality. They are however ma de of cotton, because one does not show off in church, and that is exactly what that girl was doing.'

'That is not in the Book of Care,' said Clementine. 'It is simply something done by the Gentry.'

'It is a form of snobbery,' continued Citronella, 'it is saying to the peasantry, look we can afford simple clothing for Sunday and fine clothes for the rest of the week, whilst you can only afford simple clothing. The Aristocracy find that sort of thing tacky.'

'And that voice,' said Lady Livienne, changing tack, as she realised she would never win an argument with the Twins on a religious topic. 'So fake, trying to sound like the Queen. But it didn't matter how good she looked in her flashy clothes, or how refined her diction is as soon as her Brother opened his mouth the River Ellis spewed out.

'Janek's accent is a good deal more cultured than the average Elizaburgers,' said Madeleine. 'Jadwiga and Janek are from the Eastern Continent, would you prefer they spoke with a Welsh accent?'

'Yes, at least that has music and poetry,' replied Lady Livienne. Then changing the subject she said to the twins, 'I suppose you two are going into the room you call the Chapel to mumble some more?'

'Yes, Maman,' replied the twins.

'You can be too pious you know. That won't help you when you're married. Fortunately, I'll soon be able to announce your betrothal,' Lady Livienne said as her daughters left the room. She knew that if they were legally betrothed, it would bar them from joining the Merciful Sisters for twelve months, during which time she would get them properly engaged and married to the two fools who would soon agree to take the twins off her hands.

H ave you heard the news, the Flying Scarves are doing a show at the Zucca Assembly Rooms on Summer Solstice,' said Madeleine like an avalanche. It was 10am and she had completed her traditional post church meal, known as the Full Angerlish Breakfast, the meal of fried bacon and eggs with sausage, black pudding, fried potatoes and fried tomatoes.

'That's nice, Miss,' said Chantelle, painfully aware that the Lady Livienne was in earshot.

'Jadwiga and her brother Janek are going. And now, so am I. Aunty Bron got tickets for Nye and me.'

'Congratulation, but why the fuss. They're only a pop band, Miss,' said Chantelle, winking at Madeleine. Her Step-Mother had no idea she was over acting.'

'Only a pop band? Ella, they are the hottest rock band in the Kingdom.'

'What about the Giant Clams, Miss?' asked Chantelle.

'They're good, but they're not the Scarves. How did Viscount Leonard manage it. And I'm going to see them on 28th June.'

'No your not, Madeleine. You will be with myself and the twins at the Black Masquerade at the Palace of Government Ballroom at Castello del Filippo. Where I will find your future husband.'

Madeleine looked like a child had been told Christmas had been cancelled. Rock music, the ancient music of protest from Earth had always existed on Anseris. No matter how much the authorities tried to suppress it. Nobody cared that for much of the planet's history it had been Acoustic Rock, as there had been no electric guitars. It was the music that mattered.

'You are a young noble lady. There is no way I would let you mix with all those grubby Plebeians, listening to that racket. Especially if that young upstart is going to be there.'

'But Mama, I hate the Black Masquerade, it is so very stupid,' said Madeline sounding closer to six than sixteen. 'That white make-up is a nightmare and my hair takes weeks to recover from that black dye.'

'It is an ancient Anserian Tradition, and you are going.' Then turning to Chantelle she said. 'Don't even start to think about having time off to go to that awful rock concert. On the night, once you have gotten us ready for the ball, you will stay here, Cook and the Butler are going to family in Genova, the housemaids will have night off as they cannot be responsible for the house, that leaves you in charge.

C hantelle knocked on her Step-mother's dressing room door. The woman was changing out of her horrible green church clothes into a more luxurious horrible green outfit.

'Enter,' said her step-mother. Who was at her dressing table. 'Ah, Ella, what is it.'

'Mistress,' said Chantelle as she curtsied. 'I have found your diary.'

'Excellent, where was it?'

'In a storage box with last years, Mistress.'

'I hope you haven't read it,' said her Step-Mother. 'No, you actually believe in honour and other idiocies, instead of pretending I used to belive in honour, then I grew up.'

Chantelle handed the awful woman her book and curtseyed again. Her step-mother had no social filter, she just said something as soon as it entered her head, not worrying about the consequences.

'You may go,' the older woman said. Chantelle curtseyed again and left the room. She had to get of the house on her afternoon off and be with sane people.

'T here's no point in trying to get a blood test next time your in town,' said Hilde Bottles, 'the Baroness has put a block on it.'

'She can't, can she?' asked Chantelle. 'Anyway, I couldn't anyway, it's Sunday.'

'I'm afraid she can,' said Citronella, who had just walked into the kitchen. Her twin could not be that far behind her. 'There is a group of clergy who do not believe Genetics is a real science. Maman is claiming to be one of their followers. She's using her new found religious beliefs to control what sort of medical treatments her employees receive. The Angels know why?'

The Caretaker Faith, the religion of Anseris, believed in progress and had always supported scientific research. The Church had preserved so much knowledge during the rule of the Benedictian Kings. Chantelle knew exactly why her Step-Mother was doing this. Chantelle needed genetic evidence that she was her Father's daughter in order to prove she was not a random orphan he had taken pity on. A throat swab did not produce a good enough sample for this. It had to be a blood test. Because she had stupidly signed Indenture Papers, she had no way of getting that blood test and proof through normal methods. The longer the lie was allowed to live, the more the truth was diminished.

'You read Maman's diary?' Madeleine was horrified and fascinated in equal measures. The two young women were sitting on the ferry, heading to Zucca. The Smitz had invited them to an afternoon of good food, good wine and relaxation in the lovely weather.

'Yes. It appears she has always called me Ella,' said her sister.

'But you read more than that?'

'Not really, my good manners won out in the end. And it was so boring. No juicy titbits and nothing incriminating,' said Chantelle, who then changed the subject. 'The Mistress, would have kittens if she knew you were fraternising with a servant. Her book of etiquette forbids it.'

'The bitch can swallow that book whole,' said Madeleine.

'Maddy dear, you should at least pretend there is some love between you and your Mother. For Papa's sake.'

'Papa would understand, especially if he knew what she was doing to you.'

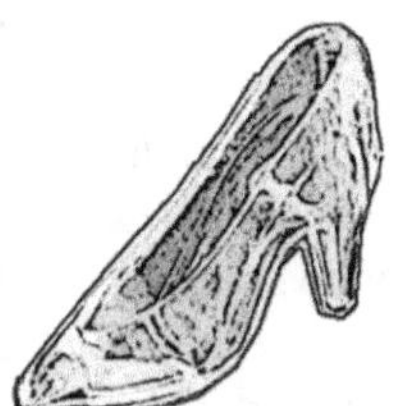 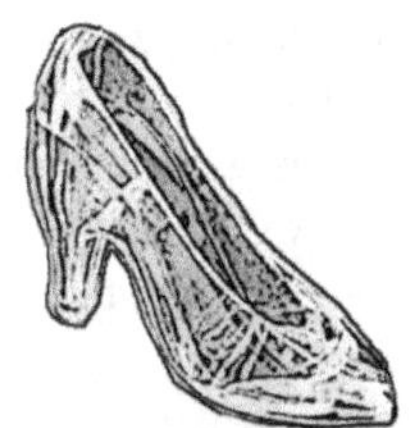

14

Madeleine. Filling the house's swimming pool had been the big surprise. Madeleine had changed from her kirtle into one of her long hidden one piece swimsuits, made from a blue and white plaid material. She was trying to persuade her sister to change as well, into Maddy's other swimsuit, a strapless one, with stripes in various shades of blue.

This sort of swimsuit had been re-introduced to Anseris during the brief period of galactic contact a century earlier, then banned for most of that time by the Benedictian Kings. Now they were starting to make a comeback in the more liberal parts of the kingdom.

'I'm not a frump. But it's so flimsy,' said Chantelle, 'I don't think it will fit me.' Chantelle held up the swimsuit selected for her to the light. It was tiny and seemed unlikely to fit any adult woman.

'Well this one fits me perfectly, and we've both got the same body shape,' said Madeleine.

'They're one size fits all,' said Jadwiga, who had also changed, 'and on this occasion, its true.' The three young women were in Jadwiga's spacious, modern bedroom.

'Oh very well,' said Chantelle, 'I'll give it a try.'

'And you better put the lotion on,' said Madeleine.

'What, to grease me into the garment?'

'No silly, to stop sunburn,' replied her sister.

'Oh, I see.'

Wealthy Anserian women had always striven to keep their skin as pale as possible. So the word sunburn meant any darkening of the skin exposure to the Ansersol caused, not just the painful redness caused by overexposure. The sunscreen she was applying to her naked body would allow for the production of Vitamin D, but stop them developing a suntan and other negative effects of the Ultra Violet radiation.

The garment might look like the twentieth century originals, but they were considerably more advanced. Both Chantelle and Madeleine were roughly three inches taller than Jadwiga, who had brought the three identically sized swimsuits from Elizaburg. They fitted all three women like second skins with no pinching or pulling. Cups inside stretched to support and covered their breasts, defying gravity on the garments that had no shoulder straps to support them. However it left a lot of flesh exposed. The net result was no hiding place for any imperfection.

'Will you wear that after your mother arrives?' Madeleine asked her friend sceptically.

'Angels no! It'll be hidden back in my suitcase before my parents get here. But, my sis... my friend Imogen let's me wear them in her pool.'

'I can't go outside, the boys are in the garden, I can't let them see me like this,' said Chantelle, who like Madeleine had not noticed the slip, and had idea who Imogen was, and did not really care.

'You're sounding like your wicked step-mother,' said Jadwiga 'These are nothing. They say that everywhere else in the galaxy having a natural tanned complexion is quite normal. Women wear a skimpier garment, the bikini, which is just a set of modern underwear for an all over tan,' said Jadwiga.

'You're joking,' said Madeleine, who thought her current swimsuit was daringly radical.

'According to the book on galactic history I read while passing the law to declassified it. They even had nudist beaches where naked men and women would share the same public space.'

'Now I know you are joking. Even the most liberal of planets would never allow that,' said Madeleine.

'It's true. Now I can show you the book.'

'Well having put this ridiculous thing on,' said Chantelle, 'let's go out and catch the rays.'

'Don't forget the sunglasses,' said Jadwiga, who had put a pair of dark glasses to rest in her hair just above her forehead.

They walked through the sliding French windows, onto the balcony and down onto the patio. Chantelle did feel a bit self-conscious at first about exposing so much skin, but was soon relaxed when she realised, nobody outside of the garden could see her.

On the patio, in the shade of a large parasol was a heavy glass and metal table with six matching chairs. In front there were four reclining deckchairs, then there as a large bubbling jacuzzi. At the bottom of the stairs, large glasses of iced lemonade were waiting for them.

'The Island doesn't seem like a large enough piece of land to warant a Barony,' said Janek. The ladies had been sitting comfortably on the deckchairs for forty minutes, while the boys had kicked a football around. Now they had returned to the patio for drinks. 'Even if you include Zucca.'

'The Barony of Cenerentola was the most important Barony on the Mare di Napoli. My family used to actually own Castello del Filippo and all the land in a fifty miles radius. Now we just have a title which only has meaning in the Barony. We used to be called Phillips-Forsythe. When the money from the Emerald mines was pouring in, we took the village next to an Archducal castle and made it what it is today. Cenerentola Village was once larger than Castello del Filippo. Its name means Castle of Phillip'. Chantelle loved telling people about history, and was so glad Janek had given her an excuse to lecture. 'The sad thing is money was also pouring out. We squandered all our money, and we became du Fauché, a Gentry Clan instead of an Aristocratic House. Nobody knows how much money went into building the palace at Castello del Filippo in the reign of Queen Helena VI and her daughter Queen Gertrude III, it is time some of that investment paid us back.'

'I don't understand,' said Jadwiga.

'You can explain it to us in the water.' said Madeleine, as she stood up and walked towards a jacuzzi. Turning to Janek and Aneurin, 'You two, shower! I don't want to boil in your sweat!'

Chantelle was reluctant to move. She had not realised how little physical work she used to do while she was her Father's secretary, until the unfortunate recent change in her circumstances. Even though she had been promoted to a Lady's Maid, she still did far more work than ever before, so she treasured moments like this, on a quiet Sunday, when she could lie doing absolutely nothing. Everyone was heading towards the jacuzzi. She had to join them.

'It's quite simple,' said Chantelle as she climbed into the tub. 'Ooh, bubbly. Um anyway, during the reign of Queen Gertrude III, my profligate ancestors imported a security system from the Lambour, it has a monitor that records a full genetic profile of anyone entering the building.'

'How do they manage that?' asked Nye, who was as always sitting next to Madeleine.

'I don't know, it's alien technology.'

'You talk like it's still working, is it?' asked Jadwiga.

'Last time I was there I got a buzz off it,' said Chantelle, 'so the equipment is still there. But I didn't have the ability to tell if it was working. If it is, I can now use the Psychic Interface to get information from it, without triggering any alarms on the jury rigged Anserian controls. I've been practising on the unused security control device at Cenerentola house.'

'Jadzie could ask Mr Franke if the Lambourian equipment is working. He has friends who would know.' said Madeleine.

'OK, I'll ask, said Jadwiga. 'But how are you going to get a chance to use it?'

'I think I will be able to get a profile for me and my father from the equipment at the Summer Solstice.'

'I get it,' said Janek, 'the two profiles will be proof that you are the late Baron's daughter. But that's the day of the Black Masquerade?'

'Which I will be going to disguised as Madeleine. As an added bonus, Maddy will be able to go to the Flying Scarves gig.'

'What does my Mam have to say about this?' asked Aneurin. Madeleine was lost for words.

'I'm impressed,' said an unmistakable voice. Its owner, Aunty Bronwen, was reclining in a chair, looking very elegant with her wide brimmed straw hat, sunglasses and a translucent blouse over her swimsuit. She obviously did not care about what people might say, as she had crossed the street from her house dressed like that.

The result of living in socially liberal Pendragon for so many years.

'Don't worry, Mr. Franke let me in,' she said.

'Afternoon, Mistress Tudor,' said the Smitz twins.

'Afternoon Janek,' said her Aunt. 'I can hear your sister, but not see her.'

'His sister is here, Mistress Tudor' replied Jadwiga as her head popped out of the water.

'You know, twins, I'd much prefer it if you called me Bronwen.'

'It is a mark of respect,' said Janek. 'Our Mother would have our guts for garters if we didn't show deference to someone older than us.'

'The girls call me Aunty Bron, but that's a family thing, why not call me Aunty Bronwen, that is much friendlier, while being polite.'

'OK, Aunty Bronwen, although I still don't think my Mother will approve,' said Jadwiga, who despite everything, still wanted her mother's approval.

'We are not related to Aunty Gill,' said Janek, 'she's just our neighbour, but we've always called her that.'

'So, back to business. you've come up with a solid plan Chantelle. I suspect there is more.'

'There will be at least half a dozen kids forced to go to the ball,' said Maddie, 'it's not as if I would be on my own.'

'Misery loves company.' said Jadwiga.

'There is a blessing though. The Masquerade drags on until 3am, but because I am fifteen years old, I will be sent home at midnight, with all the other "Children".' Madeleine had obviously not heard everything her sister had said.

'What, the standardisation of Majority Act set fifteen as the legal Age of Consent and Majority for all castes, classes and genders,' said Jadwiga.

'It is a tradition Jadzie that isn't going to change just yet.'

'Anyway,' said Chantelle, 'everyone will be in white-faces with their hair dyed deepest black. So Maddy gets to go to her concert, and I shall go to the Ball, as Madeleine.'

'I haven't returned the concert ticket yet,' said her Aunt. 'Maddy you shall go the gig. And Chantelle, you shall go to the ball.'

'All we need to work out now is how to make the swap,' said

Aneurin, dreaming up all sorts of plots and counterplots.

'The Twins and I will get dressed in the afternoon and take a ferry to Zucca to peruse the stalls of the Craft Market. That is when we make the switch,' said Madeleine as the penny dropped. 'Well, the twins will probably spend the afternoon praying while I peruse the stalls. I'm supposed to meet up with them after the market has closed. The Twins won't know the difference.'

'What about your Mother, Maddy?' asked Aunty Bronwen.

'Maman will go to a pre-ball reception in Castello del Filippo,' said Maddy, 'she is not interested in the craft market, and doesn't care how we get there, as long as we get there. Her carriage will pick her up at 3.00pm.'

'What time are the twins supposed to be meeting you?' asked Janek.

'Six in the evening,' replied Madeleine.

'There is no way I will be able to get to the Island, get Chantelle ready and get back to Zucca by six. Especially if I have to wait until Livienne has left before I can start.'

'I'm sure the twins are expecting Maddy to do a bunk,' said Chantelle, 'and happily go without her.'

'So I'll drop you off in the old town of Castello at 7.30pm.'

'That's not really a problem, Aunty Bron. It's more important for you to get me onto the last ferry of the evening, at 12.30am. So it looks as if I have been home all night.'

𝕹o offence, Jadwiga, dear, but. I've been wondering what a man like Erik doing acting as a baby-sitter for someone like you.'

'No offence taken. You're thinking why isn't such a well read, well connected policeman out catching criminals?'

'And what makes you think I'm not?' said a male voice in the room next door.

'In a small town in Fiandre, miles from anywhere?'

'Mistress Tudor, your son will tell you, with fast broadband being miles from anywhere is not a problem.' Erik walked into the room and sat on a comfortable chair. I can keep in contact with the half dozen investigations my department is running, while still being an effective bodyguard for the ex-councillor.'

'Why do I need a bodyguard anyway?' asked Jadwiga, 'I'm not in politics any more.'

'Let's not forget, you have been responsible in part, or even in the whole, for a lot of changes to the way things are done. Some of those changes have offended the more hidebound, and they will never forgive you. It makes you a target for the nutters.'

'So what,' said Jadwiga.

'Her Majesty doesn't want people thinking they can use you to gain an advantage with her through you. Jadzie, you stopped being an ordinary plebeian girl from Elizaburg a long time ago. You don't just live with the Royal Family, you're part of it now. The only person who hasn't realised that is you. As far as Her Majesty is concerned, it stopped being a private joke. You are a sister to her, a princess. That means you need protecting like a princess.'

'Oh!' said Jadwiga, 'So it's that obvious.'

'You've quite an interesting history, Mr. Franke,' said Mistress Tudor. Thank the Angels she wanted to change the subject, as she recognised he had uncharactaristically said something that should perhaps have remained unsaid.

'Well, I've made a lot of enemies in my time on the beat. As a Chessman and as a detective.'

'You were a Chessman?' asked Jadwiga, still a little shocked.

Erik Franke was a mountain of a man. Six foot seven tall and four foot from shoulder to shoulder. He had been a policeman, in various capacities for four decades.

'Yes, because I am a big bloke, who apart from a bit of hay fever, has always been physically fit, the Political Police assumed I was a meathead. I was seconded to the Chessmen to break up opposition rallies, cracking skulls in the process.'

'Which you refused to do,' said Jadwiga.

'Which I refused to do. You see, I believe in the inconvenient concept of the Rule of Law. I wanted to be a policeman when I was a child above all else. I saw it as a duty to protect the law-abiding from the criminals and to punish those criminals justly.'

'That must have made you popular with your bosses in the Political Police.'

'Yes, for the two years I was seconded to the Chessmen, I spent eighteen months suspended. I used the time studying the sort of political theories that were prohibited to ordinary people.'

'So much for being a meathead,' said Bronwen.

'Yes, my wide knowledge of the Laws of Anseris, and my wide network of contacts, saw me snapped up by the Criminal Detection Directorate when I was sent back to the Crown Police Service.'

'So you ended up in the Royal Protection Squad?' asked Bronwen.

'Sure, in the investigative branch. Although everyone thinks I'm cruising to retirement, working as Jadwiga's minder. Nobody sees what I really do.'

'Right,' said Jadwiga.

'And if you two ladies didn't already have the security clearance you have, I would never have told you.'

'We won't spill the beans, Uncle Erik.'

Erik knew young Jadwiga only called him Uncle Erik if she really wanted him to do something for her. He had never married and had never, as far as he knew, fathered any children. He had four nephews, but would much rather replace them with this bright girl and her Navy mad brother.

'So what do you want me to do?' he asked.

'Chantelle has come up with a plan to get a genetic profile of herself and her late Father. One that will prove she is his daughter.'

'Yes, so what's the plan?' asked Erik, who then sat in rapt silence as it was explained. He believed Lady Livienne du Fauché was doing was illegal, and would normally be more than happy in assisting young Lady Chantelle in any means he possibly could.

'So you want me to ask around, find out if the Lambourian security devices at the Palace of Government are in working order and still being used these days?' he asked.

Hell yeah, thought Erik, I wish there was more old Lambourian kit lying around the place. Not that he would tell anyone one that. In fact, Erik found himself in a difficult position.

'You ladies have the correct level of clearance, but I don't think anyone else in your group does. That's my problem.'

'So you aren't going to help us, Uncle Erik?'

'I will do what I can, within limits, but I'm not promising anything.'

'Well maybe you can help us with something else, which doesn't have security implications.'

Erik knew some people called female Fenzrians "Witch Women" as an insult, but there was something bewitching about this elegant and sophisticated woman he had never experienced before. He knew she had once had a liaison with that nutter Ned Jenkins, who was her boy Aneurin's Father. He could see why she would want her son to have nothing to do with his dad. Jenkins was a major figure in the True Anseris group, one of the groups who opposed the reforms of Queen Johanna. He was the sort of Gwenerian who gave the rest a bad name.

'Certainly, Mistress Tudor,' he replied.

'The case regarding the death of Baron du Fauché is covered by an administrative block called an Omega Matrix code and permanently closed. What exactly is that?'

'Brozhnik! Ay 'aven't 'eard dat one fer years,' said Erik, shock temporarily knocking all the polish of his Elizaburg accent. 'It's what the Chessmen used to cover the assassinations they never officially carried out. As we all know, they were supposed to stay within the law. They didn't.'

'But the Chessmen were abolished two years ago. Why would this code be used to close a recent investigation?'

'Unfortunately, their malignant influence refuses to fade away. Somebody is putting the frighteners on the local coppers,' he said. 'It doesn't frighten me, I know someone who can get it lifted.'

'Imogen,' said Jadwiga.

'Imogen?' asked Mistress Tudor.

'Now she is officially Queen Johanna, Her Majesty, has reverted back to using the name Imogen with her family and her close friends, like me.' said Erik.

'Why would the Queen do this?' Bronwen asked.

'She's very keen to root out all the abuses of power from the previous regime that still exist. Too many former Chessmen now control the organised crime groups in this part of the Kingdom and are expanding their operations, Her Majesty wants to nip that in the bud.

'Also she was a friend of the late Baron,' said Jadwiga. 'The birth to Princess Marion, stopped her beeing at his funeral.'

'And she's obviously a good friend to you also, Mr. Franke,' said Mistress Tudor. 'Have you seen young Princess Marion yet?'

'Lovely child. The image of her Mother.'

With that Erik left the room, to his office, to do his real job.

Aneurin knew his mother was still an attractive woman and the effect she had on men. As was painfully visible by the way Mr Franke acted in her presence earlier that evening. Now everyone back in mediaeval garb, the effect was still obvious.

'Is there a problem, Mam?' he could see his mother looking at her own back in a mirror.

In reply his mother asked the worse question a woman can ask a man, the answer is always wrong 'Does my bum look big in this?'

So Aneurin gave the worse possible answer. 'But you're a woman. It's the way your body is put together, your natural shape. You're supposed have a big bum. There's no point denying it.'

The room went very quiet. His mother went whiter than usual. Before she could explode Erik stepped in.

'Young Master Aneurin, if ever you want a serious relationship with a woman, never ever say that again.'

'But it's true, Mr Franke. Female anatomy is different from male.'

'Women know that, and don't care because they are taught to hate their bodies from birth,' he said, quoting one of Jadwiga's sayings. 'They want reassurance, but can't accept it because they are programmed not to. It's so sad, because the human female body is awesome. I know, I grew up in a household full of women.'

'Why, thank you, Mr. Franke,' said his Mother. Then turning to him she said, 'Right then Aneurin, time to go home.'

'One more thing, Mistress Tudor,' he said. 'All the Lambourian security equipment at the Palace of Government is up and running, but you never heard this from me, OK'

'Heard what, Mr. Franke?' she asked.

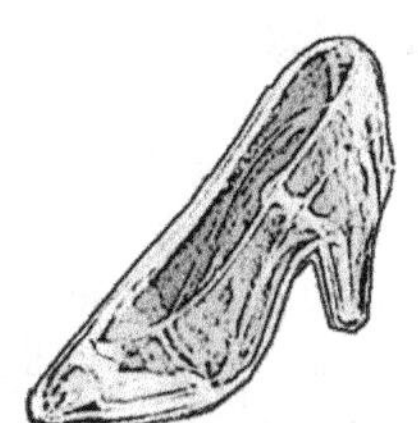 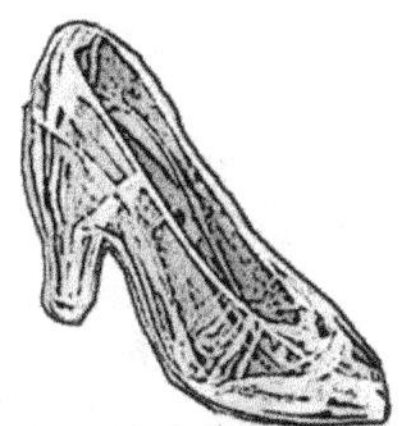

15

Anseris is one of the few worlds inhabited by humans that takes twenty four hours to rotate each day and three hundred and sixty five days and six hours to orbit Ansersol, the system's orange central star. So the Anserian seasons followed the Earth calender, of course with one local variations. At the end of June it is the Southern Hemisphere, not the Northern, that points directly at the Ansersol. From space it looks like the Anserian Northern hemisphere has all the Oceans, and the Southern Hemisphere has all the land. Naturally they settled in the South.

'The Bottles had departed for Genova, where they will be celebrating Solstice with their daughter and her family,' Chantelle told her sister. 'The coast is almost clear.'

The Night of the Solstice had arrived. Chantelle had spent the afternoon preparing her Step-Mother and her three daughters for the night's festivities. In addition, she had to do her share of the work Hilde and her husband Dave normally did as Cook and Butler.

'You look lovely,' said Chantelle to Madeleine.

'You're having a laugh, aren't you?' Madeleine's skin was perfect, unblemished and as white as milk. Her normal ginger locks were dyed a dull black.

'You do. You've really blossomed over the past few months,' said her sister.

'Oh this is so unfair, this is your dress, made for you. It doesn't even fit me. You should be wearing it to the Black Masquerade. I know Papa would let me go to the Flying Scarf's concert instead.'

'I know,' replied Chantelle. 'When I'm pretending to be you, I'll tell everyone I'm to ill to attend this year.'

'Do you know how crazy that sounds?' asked Madeleine, but she never heard her sister's reply.

There was no way they could have talked like this if her Step-Mother had still been in the house. Obviously suspicious that Madeleine and Chantelle might swap, she remained in the house until Madeleine had finished putting on all the make-up and the heavy black velvet dress, before leaving for Castello del Filippo, with Commander Liepmann. To make sure that nothing changed, the Twins were supposed to stay with their sister.

'Madeleine, hurry up dear,' one of the Twins shouted up the stairs. 'The coach has arrived.'

All motor vehicles were forbidden on Cenerentola Island. Lady Livienne was in no hurry to change that. The carriage had been hired for the night from the local livery stable. It had already made the trip once with Lady Livienne and returned to pick up her daughters. It looked historically accurate, basically a shed on wheels, but it had a much better sprung suspension and far more comfortable seats.

'I don't know,' said Citronella as the coach arrived at the bridge, 'just because Zucca is a word for pumpkin in an old Earth language, does the coach have to look like one.'

'What are you talking about?' asked her twin sister.

'Well look at it. The canopy is ribbed and painted orange, the undercarriage is painted green. Have you never noticed that?'

'No, you're being stupid as usual. All private hire coaches look like that, anywhere in the Archduchy. It's part of their operating licence,' said Clementine.

'Don't call me stupid, I didn't know that.'

'Well you should have!'

'Will you two put a sock in it? If Maman heard you squabbling she wouldn't be happy. You're twenty not eight years old,' said Madeleine, who knew how much their Mother hated the twins bickering like children.

e have three hours before the coach picks us up again, to take us to the Masquerade. We will spend that time in the Priory, praying with the Sisters.'

'Won't you look out of place, with that white make-up and those black dresses?' Madeleine asked the twins.

'Of course not. It is Summer Solstice, so they will have white faces and black ceremonial habits. If we weren't going to the Ball, so would not change into our usual brown tunics, we would wear black ones instead.'

'Which is the closest you'll ever get to being Ugly Sisters,' said Madeleine.

'Not true,' said Citronella, 'on the twenty first of September, we are travelling to the Abbey at Ponti di Carla to begin our postulancy, the start of our new lives as Merciful Sisters.'

'You're not going to tell Maman, are you?' Madeleine asked, knowing the answer. 'She won't find out until you arrive at Ponti.'

'No, we're not, and please don't call the Merciful Sisters that.'

'Everybody else does. The Sisterhood of the Merciful Charity of the Angels wear such an ugly brown habit.'

'Everybody else is wrong,' said Citronella, 'and to a Merciful Sister it is a thing of great beauty. A sign that they have abandoned the vanities of life. We give up all possessions.'

'Come off it, you know that's not true. My cousin, Sister Vera has lots of possessions.'

'None of them actually belong to her, they belong to the Order, who let her use them.'

'You're not supposed to tell anyone, Ronnie,' said Clementine with a hiss. 'She'll tell Maman, who will find a way to stop us going. We're slavishly following all her orders, so she will never suspect we are going to rebel.'

'She can't stop you Clemmy. Or you Ronnie. You're both over seventeen years old, both adults. Under the new law you have been for a year. You should tell her.'

'Beau-père supported our choice and was helping us. Maman hated it. She has said if she discovers the merest whisper of us joining the Order, she will announce our betrothal,' said Citronella.

'Even though it's not true, it will legally stop us joining for twelve months, in which time she will find someone to marry us.'

'She can't force you to marry anyone,' said Madeleine.

'She has always found a way to control us. It's why in so many ways we're still like children. Especially when she is around. So our last action with her will be childish. To leave her without telling her where we are going.'

'So, I won't tell her a thing. She is so determined to ruin our lives. We must all rebel.'

'Thank you, dear,' they said in unison.

Madeleine walked in silence with the twins. She had always known they were religious, but many women talked about childhood plans to enter a convent, and they were that deeply religious. Before Papa's death, normally sensible Chantelle had started calling them the Ugly Sisters. She thought it was a joke that triggered her Maman. Madeleine remembered coming with them, when they first started volunteering here at Zucca's orphanage. With those poor children, the twins were completely different people. No bitching and bickering, their only concern was the youngsters in their care.

'Look at those tarts in their City clothes. Don't they know that Zucca is still a Traditional town?' said Clementine. The bubble seemed to have been broken and the lofty ideals put on hold. The girls in question were wearing denim jeans and looked stunning. This was pure jealousy.

'Not for much longer,' replied Citronella, 'but the constables really should deal with those who flout the old law while it still stands.'

'The constables have better things to do, like catching the real criminals,' said Madeleine. 'Chasing after a handful of early adopters is a waste of police resources.'

'This place will soon be as bad as Elizaburg. Do you know that girls there are wearing really short skirts, six inches above their ankles.'

And the rest, thought Madeleine, most of her city skirts were twelve inches above her ankles.

'I hope you never did anything that scandalous when you were there, Maddy?' the twins asked in unison.

'Of course not, I'm a good girl,' Madeleine said with a totally straight face. She had even worn trousers, and would be tonight, when she had switched places with Chantelle. 'Don't worry, this place will stay as trad as trad can be. Even Nye, who is from out in Pendragon, is going to continue wearing trad clothing. He says that he wants to fit in with his new home.'

'He's Fenzrian, of course he does,' said Clementine.

'Your horrible cousin. What about his dreadful mother?' asked Citronella.

'I think Aunty Bron will wear what she wants, when she wants. After all, Zucca will be a Free Zone.'

Madeleine, watched as her sister rang the bell on the door of the small priory attached to the orphanage. She knew she would never choose that route to escape her mother's plans. She loved life and all its varieties too much to be enclosed within the rules and regulations of the three female religious orders. Once a week, on Sunday, was enough to demonstrate her faith.

Anyway, she had to go straight to the Tudor's house. Chantelle would need this dress if she was to successfully carry out all the things she wanted to do under cover of the Black Masquerade.

adeleine looked at herself in the mirror. The city clothes she was wearing were as black as the velvet dress, but much more her style. They had been sent by courier from Elizaburg to Aunty Bronwen's house especially for tonight. She had luxuriated in a hot shower as Aunty Bronwen's awesome shampoo and shower gel washed all the gunk off her skin and out of her hair.

Madeleine knew the jeans and top she had chosen would have scandalized her Mother, who believed that a woman's legs should remain hidden at all times. If dear Mama had known she had been wearing this sort of thing in Elizaburg for months now, she would have dragged Madeleine back to the Island in a flash. It wasn't that Madeleine didn't like the traditional, or Country Style clothing, but she wanted to have a choice.

'If you want to do some shopping before the show,' Aneurin

shouted up the stairs, 'we'll have to be leaving now.'

'OK, don't freak out,' said Madeleine as she skipped down the stairs.

'Why, I know you've got legs, I've seen you in a swimsuit.'

'I'm wearing more than that tonight,' she replied.

'Wow, Maddie, you're right. You looked about twenty years older in that horrible black outfit.'

'I'm glad you approve, Nye,' Madeleine replied. 'I feel twenty years younger. Whoever invented the Black Masquerade deserves to rot in the lowest level of the twenty hells.'

'It was invented by the Immortal Empress, so don't worry, she probably is,' said Aunty Bronwen.

'And you look twenty years younger as well, Aunty Bron.'

'Oh nonsense, dear. They're only trousers,' the older woman laughed. 'I have too much to do, to be encumbered by a trad dress.'

Bronwen removed the tickets from her bag. 'These are valuable, so look after them. Leo is a very dear boy and his mother is an old friend, they would be so disappointed if you were to lose them.'

Madeleine took the tickets and put them in the inside pocket of the black jacket she had just put on. Everyone left the house and got into the car.

'You know, Aunty Bronwen,' said Jadwiga, 'you are like a Fairy Godmother of old, granting everyone's wishes. Perhaps you should have wings.'

'Well, I might not be a Fairy Godmother,' replied Aunty Bronwen, 'but I'm definitely a Fenzrian Godmother.'

T he bottle of white make-up that Aunty Bronwen had brought with her looked as repulsive as the bottle sitting in her Step-Mother's room.

Chantelle had spent hours that afternoon painting the face and the upper body of that woman and her two horrible daughters in the thick white paint traditionally worn by both men and women at a masked ball. As this was also the annual Black Masquerade, she had also applied temporary dye to their hair, making it as black as her own.

Madeleine had used a modern spray to do her own whitening, but used the traditional black shampoo for her hair.

'Why on Anseris have you brought this bottle with you?' asked Chantelle.

'Because that woman will know exactly how much is in her bottle of white make-ups and wonder where the amount you would need for tonight has gone.'

'Maddy said I could use her spray?'

'Thank the Angels, it will save us so much time,' replied Aunty Bronwen, taking a spray bottle from Chantelle, 'but your face has to be done the traditional way. Otherwise they won't be tricked into thinking you're Madeleine without the magic ingredient.'

'Well, at least this one smells better,' Chantelle said as she removed the cork.

'Of course, this is good quality stuff, none of the unnecessary sulphur compounds to bulk it out.

The make-up not only contained silver, it contained Lunavaporon. In its purest form this mineral forms into the gemstone unique to Anseris called Moonglow. In any form, Lunavaporon reacts to a person's electrochemical system. Within the make-up it allows the person wearing it, to broadcast an emotion over a short distance. This was usually the desire to confuse identity, for complete anonymity.

'At least I don't have to dye my hair,' Chantelle said when she finished dressing. Looking at herself in the mirror, in the black velvet dress and white make-up, she was ready for the Black Masquerade.

'Your hair has to look dyed,' said Aunty Bron, who had rubber gloves on and was massaging something into Chantelle's hair. 'Maddy's a natural redhead and even the wash in wash out black dye she used looked really fake. Although the "wash out" is a bit of a lie, Maddy said she was twenty minutes under the shower before any red could be seen in her hair, and another ten to get back to anything approaching normal. She says it will need to be washed at least three more washes to get rid of all the dye.'

'That's why people hate Black Masquerade so much.'

'Well, I've taken the gloss away, your hair looks suitably dull and fake now,' said Aunty Bronwen. 'Dear Angels, this might just work, even her Mother would think you are Madeleine.'

'This was originally made for me, it never quite looked right on Maddy, about an inch too long. 'I'm still about an inch taller.'

Chantelle's half sister had left Cenerentola House earlier, in this stunning to look at but hell to wear black velvet dress. It included a velvet laced bodice. Now it was her turn. Thank the Angels old Queen Kathyren had been obsessed by simple mediaeval clothing that pre-dated excessive corsets.

'The Immortal Empress only ordered the black clothes,' Chantelle explained. 'One of the Free Queens ordered the sweltering velvet clothing on what was usually the warmest night of the year. However, the sadistic old bitch would have approved of the change.'

Chantelle could feel herself beginning to boil already. Dear Angels, she was supposed to dance in this.

'Prey that these green contact lenses don't come out when she is looking at me.'

'If she thinks your Maddy, once she gives you a dressing down for separating from the Twins during the afternoon, I doubt if Livienne will pay much attention.'

'True, she will be more interested in finding husbands for the ugly sisters.'

'Why do you call them the Ugly Sisters?' asked Aunty Bronwen.

'Because they want to join the Merciful Sisters, but they are too weak to stand up to their mother,' said Chantelle.

'But they love their luxuries too much to be nuns,' said Aunty Bronwen.

'The Merciful Sisters look like they are nuns and everyone calls them nuns, but they aren't really. They don't make vows, they only sign contracts. They could break the contract and leave at any time, but rarely do. The contracts cover chastity and obedience, they are all for that. Technically they live in poverty, as they claim they give all their property to the Order, who then lets them use their things. I remember visiting one of my cousins, who trains women how to be Merciful Sisters at their headquarters in Tintagel. She lives in what they call the Mother-house, but her room was not very monastic.'

'Did Maddy get off to the Flying Scarves concert?' Chantelle asked as she took the seat facing her aunt in in the coach.

'Yes, they met up with the Smitz and are having a high old time. Maddy will be back home by the time you get to Zucca tonight. You'll be on the same ferry back to the island.'

'Good, we can co-ordinate our cover stories.'

'Now pay attention. You will need these toys. Aunty Bron first took Madeleine's mobile phone from her purse. These were a common sight in Guild Towns in the more liberal Archduchies. Conservative old Fiandre had just upgraded the network, because more and more people owned these newer phones. Chantelle's mobile phone was like a brick in comparison.

'Won't that thing's bright screen draw attention to me?' asked Chantelle, 'I'm supposed to be blending into the shadows.'

'I said toys. The mobile phone will remain in your purse at all times,' replied Aunty Bron, 'because you also have these.'

She had taken a small square box from her purse.

'Nye's Earbuds!'

'Yes, fully charged and switched on. You can explain away the mobile in your purse, you're claiming to be someone who has spent years in Elizaburg. Of course she'll have the latest mobile phone. You'll have to hide the earbuds when you are in the ballroom. They are high frontier tech, which is still too nerdy, even for early adopters like Maddie. Remember to take it out before you return to the Ballroom.'

'So not true, earbuds might be so last month out in Pendragon, but it's bleeding edge cool for the fashonistas in the Capital,' said Chantelle, perfectly imitating her sister, 'who use them with no idea how they work. With earbuds there's no need for an ugly microphone arm to reach my mouth, the sound of my voice as it echoes up the middle ear is captured with clear precision. All I have to do is whisper and still be understood.'

'OK, so back to business. When you've left the reception area you head to the video surveillance archives,' said Aunty Bronwen. 'Which naturally is the other side of the building to the video surveillance suite and will be totally ignored tonight.'

'Of course, everybody at the masquerade tonight has impeccable security clearance and normally wouldn't even think of leaving either the Ballroom or the Supper Room.'

'No dear, the equipment inside the building will be on standby, the external cameras will still be running,' said Aunty Bronwen. 'They are not totally stupid, they will still be worried about people who aren't on the invite list breaking in.' She fumbled around in her bag. 'But just to be on the safe side, try this on.' It was a piece of black silk that could hook over Chantelle's ears and covered her face from mid-nose down to her neck. 'When it the ballroom it will sit in your purse looking like a black handkerchief.'

'Then once I have uploaded the DNA scan data of the day Papa last visited Castello del Filippo, I have to go to the Wills Library and insert this request slip from Nouveauté and Company into the clerk's diary, so they send a copy of Papa's will to you. I have to remember to stamp it with yesterday's date and copy the clerk's initial to authorise it.'

'Jadwiga says there will be at least two other requests slips there. When the clerk sees this in his diary tomorrow, he will just process it without checking.' Aunty Bronwen smiled. 'Then you return to the party, remembering you are supposed to be a juvenile who has to leave at midnight.'

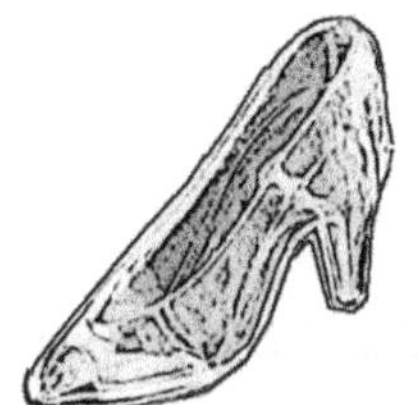 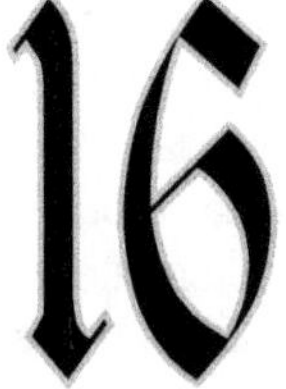 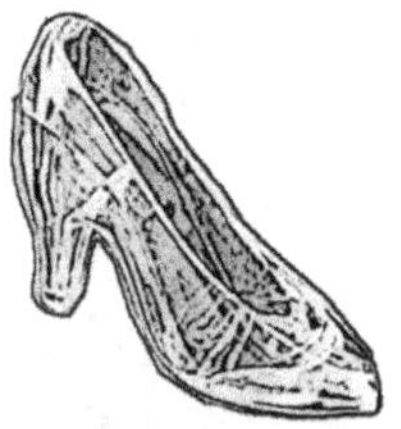

16

The palace at Castello del Filippo had been financed
by an economic bubble and when it burst, the Monarch
had claimed it in lieu of taxes. Most of the palace at
Castello del Filippo had been converted into government
offices. Only the Grand Ballroom, its dining room and the
terraced lawn in front retained its former glory.

Chantelle's carriage arrived outside the palace and its door was
opened by a liveried footman, who helped her down, and
escorted her to the entrance of the Grand Ballroom. She was then
passed onto another footman, in an even flashier livery. She
handed Madeleine's invite to the man, who escorted her to the
top of the stairs, where she was introduced under her pseudonym
for the night.

'The Lady Adele Phillips-Forsythe,' the Master of
Ceremony's voice boomed across the Ballroom.

Chantelle was not surprised at how she had been introduced.
Black Masquerade Names should not have any direct link to a
person's real name. It had to be subtle bordering on the obscure.
The du Fauché family was a notable exception. This was the
only place and time they were allowed to use their original name,
so use it they did. By following the family tradition, Madeleine
was infuriating her Mother. Sure enough, Chantelle could see the
older woman was walking towards her with a face like thunder.

'I told you to stay with the Twins,' the older woman said.

'Did you tell them to stay with me,' said Chantelle, perfectly
imitating the tone her sister uses to annoy her Mother.

'They say they were looking for you all afternoon.'

'And I was looking for them. They're pretty hard to miss,'
was Chantelle's retort, 'like a pair of giant black olives.'

'And why did you not use the agreed name for this party, like every other member of Clan Carrefour here tonight, you should have been introduced as "Megan Mortimer".'

'Because I'm not Clan Carrefour, I am Clan du Fauché.' This was doubly true as it was Chantelle pretending to be Madeleine.'

'You spend too much time with that maid,' said Lady Livienne, 'and your so-called Aunt.'

'Because she's not a maid, she's my half-sister. Also, Aunty Bron is my aunt, by marriage.'

'How many times do I have to tell you, there is no evidence that she is your Father's daughter. Now, go to the dining room and have something to eat with your real family.'

'If there is anything left.' Chantelle wondered if that was a barb too far.

'**W**hy didn't you meet us outside the Priory, like we arranged?'
'Oh just go, I have a dance partner waiting for me.'
Citronella asked her as soon as Chantelle had sat down.

'Yes, Maddy, we left you with your Aunt, then went to pray and make preparations for when we become Sisters in Religion, as well. You were supposed to meet us outside the Priory, so we could travel here together.'

'I'm sorry, I forgot the time,' said Chantelle, having a idea what they had told Madeleine. Lady Livienne had forbidden them to visit the orphanage and priory, in the same haughty way she had forbidden Madeleine visiting her relatives. It look as if they were ignoring the maternal command as well.

'Anyway, we're heading back to the Ballroom. Maman says we must dance with as many young aristocrats as possible,' Citronella said. 'To guarantee we make a good match.'

'We are really doing it so we have the pleasant memory. There will be no balls for us from September, when we turn our backs on the vanities of the World,' said Clementine.

So they were actually going to do it, thought Chantelle, and they had confided in Madeleine. I must not act surprised, so she turned to look at the buffet table.

'May theAngels bless you Maddy dear. Thank you for keeping our secret,' said Citronella.

'Both of them,' said Clementine. 'Maman would hit the roof if she knew where we had been this afternoon, and why.'

Chantelle studied the Twins, all in black, she tried to imagine them all in brown instead. It was all too easy. They honestly thought she was Madeleine. Now she had fooled all the members of her own family here tonight. Angels, her crazy scheme was working.

C hantelle finished the plate of goodies she had selected from the buffet She was not going to miss a chance to eat something prepared by the second best chef in the Archduchy. She knew her step-mother would be waiting for her at the door from the Dining Room to the Ballroom with a full dance card that would keep her glued to the dance-floor until Midnight. Sooner or later, her Step-Mother would get tired of waiting at the door, so Chantelle stationed herself by the entrance to the terrace, so she could make a bolt outside when she saw her step-mother coming. To Chantelle's horror, Lady Livienne was standing on the Terrace and Citronella and Clementine guarding the door to the ballroom.

'Ah, Lady Adele, may I have this dance?' asked the man to her right.

'Of course,' she said. It meant she could get past Citronella at the door, who would not stop her as she had a dance partner. Then she noticed who had asked her, Viscount Leonard, organiser of this, and every other major event here in Fiandre, while his parents and grandfather attended the Queen's Ball at Ellisford Castle.

'I had heard how much you had grown over the past year, whilst you have been in Elizaburg,' said the Viscount.

'I had a bit of a late spurt, it is true, my Lord. Nobody was more surprised than I.'

'You must have been. Tell me, was it something in the water in the West?'

'No, my Lord. I went to a doctor in LizB with excruciating back pain. He found my blood was lacking in a particular protein. This was stunting my growth and causing the pain. I had series of injections of that protein. It caused a growth spurt. I'm taller now but I should have been as tall as Chantelle.'

'I have to say, when I first saw you, Lady Adele, I thought you were your half-sister.'

'Yes, my Lord. Many people have pointed out how similar we have become. This is much more her sort of thing. I would have preferred to be at the concert and Midsummer Supper in Zucca tonight. Mama insisted I come here, make contacts, help her find a suitable husband when the time is right.'

'At Black Masquerade, where identities are hidden?' The Viscount was chortling.

'I told her that, but she refused to listen.'

'Is Lady Chantelle not here tonight?', asked the Viscount.

'I'm afraid she is still too ill to leave the house, even on a warm Summer night like tonight,' said Chantelle, mimicking her sister.

'Such a pity, I've known her all my life.' The Viscount had a faraway look in his eyes, as if he was remembering earlier times.

Chantelle could feel her heart racing. He had been plain Len Simples, Granny Glad's illegitimate grandson, when they had been young children. Granny Glad or her daughters had always been her family, not servants. Granny Glad had taken her home to the Island with the rest of the Simples to maintain her emotional continuity. Things had changed again when Aunty Jackie married Earl Edwin, Len Simples became Viscount Leonard and went to live in the castle in the old town of Castello del Filippo. She had made regular weekend trips to the Castle until they were both twelve years old, Leo had been sent to Tintagel Naval Academy and she went to a boarding school in Ponte di Carla. Now he was back in Castello del Filippo and she was stuck in the manor house on Cenerentola Island. He might as well still be in the Navy.

'You share the same birthday, don't you?'

'Yes, Lady Adele,' said Viscount Leon, 'she was like a Sister to me for so many years. I was surprised how much I missed her when I was first sent to Tintagel when I was twelve. They say absence makes the heart grow fonder, my dear Chantelle.'

'My Lord, she is too ill to attend tonight. I am Lady Madeleine.'

'Bravo, Lady Chantelle, what an excellent actress you are,' said the Viscount. 'Did you really think you could fool me, Ellabella.Even in a room choking in a hallucinogenic fog.'

'So, how did you know then?' she asked. When he called her Ellabella she melted slightly.

'Who else has known you for so long?' The Viscount then pulled a data pad from a pocket. 'I have just had confirmation. This place has features that pre-date King Benedict I's stupid ban on genetics, it goes all the way back to the reign of Queen Gertrude III. Everyone who enters the building at some point touches one of the sensors that reads their DNA profile. We can check the identity of everyone in the building by cross-matching our data with the government's records.'

'The government's DNA scans were carried out for health reasons, using it for anything else is a ghastly breech of privacy,' said a horrified Chantelle.

'Yes, I know, but this palace was built in the days of the dictatorial monarchy. It's next to impossible to change. I didn't check anyone else, and I do apologise for using the system on you. I had to check I wasn't going mad. Everyone thinks you are your half-sister.'

'Please, my Lord, don't tell my step-mother. I wanted to help my sister, she would be so utterly bored here tonight. A pop concert followed by a Midsummer Supper really is more her cup of tea.'

'I would not dream of it, my Ellabella. But please don't be such a stranger. Now that I am home from the sea permanently, I hope we can see more of each other,' the Viscount bowed, 'and please, we are childhood friends, call me Len.'

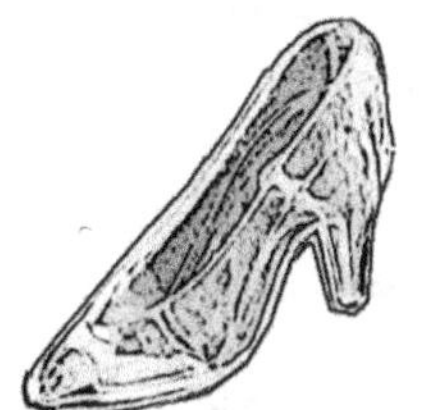 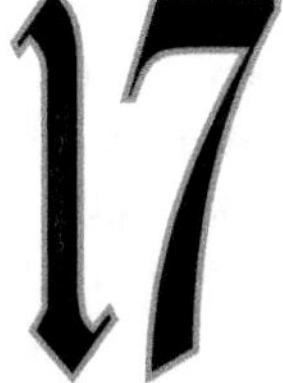 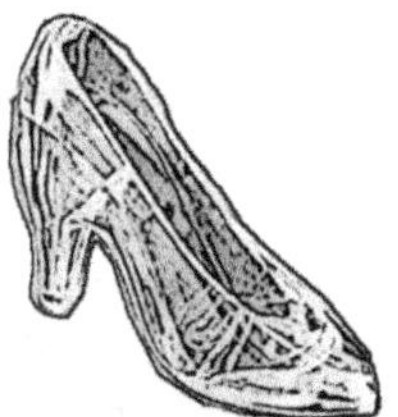

he music ended, and the coast was clear. Her Ugly Sisters had dance partners, while Chantelle Step-Mother was deep in conversation with Baroness Reydmondson. from Ponte di Carla, too engrossed in the gossip to pay any attention to her daughters.

'May I have this dance?' asked a spotty teenager. Even under all the white make-up his acne was painfully obvious.

'Of course,' said Chantelle, who knew if her step-mother saw someone who she thought was Madeleine dancing with anyone eligible, then she would not interfere. At the end of the current dance, Chantelle would slip quietly away.

'Lady Adele, you have been in the capital for over a year. I know my sister and her friends would love to talk to you about it.'

Oh hell Chantelle thought, how could she deflect the queries of these youngsters. Madeleine could easily answer their questions, Chantelle probably knew less about Elizaburg than these teenagers. She cursed herself for becoming so parochial.

'I don't doubt it,' said Chantelle, 'but they'll quickly find out how dull it really is. Grass is always greener, as they say.'

It was time to change the subject, give her time to think. 'So how many people our age have been dragged here tonight?'

'There are at least eight of us, four boys, and three girls, four now you've arrived, who would all much rather be at the Flying Scarves concert tonight, or at least watching it with friends on the television.'

'Like the massive 3D set with surround sound in the conference room down the hall,' said Chantelle.'

'How do you know about the TV?' asked one of the boys.

'Advance research. Do you think I want to be here tonight?' If they were watching the concert, they could not ask awkward questions.

The music stopped, and another young man asked her to dance. She had not realised that there were three other couples, who were all in their teens dancing next to her.

'Safety in numbers, said one of the girls. 'It stops our mother's making us dance with boring old farts, or even worse, eligible bachelors in their twenties.'

'Yes,' said the girl's former partner, who had moved on to a different girl. 'If they were so eligible, why are they still single?'

'Some of them are in their thirties and creepy,' said the new partner, 'why would they want to marry a teenager.'

'Not as creepy as the widower my mother is trying to marry me off to,' said the third girl. 'Oh I'm Amelia, by the way. Real name, not the silly pseudonym. You have been dancing with my brother Brett.'

'Pleased to meet you, I'm Madeleine.' Oh Angel's this is so embarrassing thought Chantelle. Lying to these youngsters. If they knew she was really twenty four, passing as sixteen, would they think she was creepy as well?

'Pleased to meet you, Madeleine. That's Therese, her pushy parents have worked their way up into the Gentry. They are determined to get her married into the aristocracy.'

'I'm seventeen next month, I want a career in the Inter-planetary Merchant Fleet, based out in Pendragon,' said Therese, 'not get married to some stuffy titled land owner on the Home-world.'

'Aneurin, my Fenzrian cousin is from Pendragon. He recently moved with his Mother to Zucca, to study.'

'Pendragon and Fenzrian, he sounds cool! But why does he want to come here?'

'There aren't many oceans on the space habitats. He wants to be an Oceanographer and has got a place at the Institute.'

'Fair enough,' said Brett.

'That's Claire,' said Amelia, 'and the other guys are Edward, Michael and Patrick.'

'Hello, and I bet you boys prefer Ted, Mike and Pat?'

'Almost, I prefer Paddy. You said there was a television in a room around here?'

'Sure,' said Chantelle.

'Thank the Angels, Madeleine. We'll go get the nibbles and the drinks, if you go and switch the TV on.'

Did the teenagers actually think Chantelle was one of them. Then she remember with all the Lunavaporon in the room, she had to remind herself she was not a teenager. When Madeleine finally met any of these seven youngsters they would think she was the new friend they had met at the Black Masquerade, but she would be a stranger to them. She had to tell them the truth during the next commercial break.

'You know, I've been ill recently. I really shouldn't be here, but I'm helping my half-sister out. She really didn't want to be here tonight, and the doctor says I'm too ill to be here. We look almost identical, we could be twins, despite me being eight years older and having different mothers. I'm really Chantelle du Fauché.'

'That's so cool,' said Amy. 'So where did she want to be?'

'My Aunt Bronwen scored two tickets for the Flying Scarves concert tonight, we swapped places. I've been lying to you for hours, and I've hated it.'

'Don't stress, Chantelle,' said Brett, 'we assumed Madeleine had a metropolitan sophistication because she'd been to school in Liz-B.'

'Now we know its because your technically an adult, but you genuinely don't act like one' Therese said. 'You've sneaked out of your sick-bed to go to a party, even if it is dire. You've stopped a real teenager suffering a night of torture in that ballroom. In doing so you arrived here late, which annoyed your step-mother. You found a way for us to see the Scarves's gig on television and in doing so you annoyed all our parents.'

'Yes, so?' asked a very confused Chantelle.

'You've been irresponsible and annoying to parents all night,' said Amy. 'Which means despite your actual age, you're still a teenager.'

'So you don't hate me for being a weirdo?' Chantelle asked.

'Hells no,' Amy said, 'I hope I'm that cool in my twenties.'

The break ended, and the band started the the next five songs, before another break. Conversation stopped. Much to Chantelle's relief her revelation had been accepted by her new friends.

he concert came to an end at about 10pm, and the teenagers went back to the Ballroom. She slipped unobtrusively in the other direction, down a darkened corridor and into the labyrinth of functional offices beyond the splendour of the front of the building. Making sure no-one was watching, she lifted her dress and found the secret pocket sown into her chemise. It contained the small silver earbuds.

'About time,' said Bronwen. 'You're there to work, not pleasure.

'Just because you didn't get an invite,' Chantelle said, still in the teenager mindset of her new friends. She mimicked the world-wearing mocking tone of Madeleine at her most annoying.

'And you're only pretending to be a teenager in the ballroom.'

'Come on, Control, I had to wait until I could get away without it being obvious.' Chantelle knew not to use Aunty Bronwen's name over the air. Someone might be listening. If they could break through the paranoid level of encryption on the signal.

The room she was looking for was at the back of the building, on the third floor, in what had once been a nursery dining-room. The door was protected by a push-button lock. Chantelle closed her eyes and concentrated on a pair of glass charms on her charm bracelet, the way Aunty Bronwen had taught her. The five columns of ever-changing numbers appeared above the lock as soon as she re-opened her eyes. The secret was not to be surprised by the illusion, that would break the link between herself and the lock.

'I'm in,' she said as the door swung open.

'Good, and is the PC on?'

'Yes, and logged in. Viscount Leonard told me that the DNA scanner was being used tonight.'

'Angel's the old man has been at death's door since he became Archduke. Young Leon should be the Earl by now.'

'And an Earl needs his Countess,' said Chantelle.

Chantelle was horrified. She had fought the massive crush on Viscount Leo that developed when she had been a teenager. It was wrong, he had been a brother she had told herself. It was why she had considered the celibate life of a Merciful Sister. After a week as a guest in a convent she knew that her crush was down to teenage hormones focusing on the nearest boy and the Merciful Sisters had thown a bucket of cold water the crush, which made the siren voice stop singing about Leo. Only this facts was incorrect. Now they were singing sweetly about Viscount Leonard. Chantelle desperately wanted to hear that song again.

'Oh please, this is no time for daydreams,' said Aunty Bronwen sharply, bringing Chantelle to her senses.

'As if he would marry me, I'm currently a plebeian,' said Chantelle.

'And will remain one if you don't get a move on. You're channelling Madeleine too well.'

'Here we go, found the file I'm looking for. Oh brozhnik, it's embedded in a video file, I can't extract it here. I'll have to send you the footage as well. Oh Angels, it's huge. Somebody's bound to notice.'

'Government moves huge files around all the time, especially at night, and no-one notices.Upload it, we can extract the DNA print at our leisure.'

'Finally, that's the last of it,' said Chantelle as the file finished transferring.

I'll cut the link for now. Contact me when you reach the next target.'

The Legal Archive was down in the basement and the entrance to the stairway was closer to the party than Chantelle liked. She held onto the bannister as she went down. There were the strangest of dancing lights making a net pattern at the bottom.

'Oops,' Chantelle told her Aunt. 'There is at least one piece of the security system still active.' She spotted a spot of light on the bannister.

'Don't worry, wait a couple of minute and the system will assume it was a false alarm and switch the bigger trap off,' said a young man.

'Nye, did you enjoy the concert?'

'Who?' the voice asked without waiting for a reply, the link was cut.

Chantelle cursed herself. When the trap disarmed itself as she bypassed the security system to pop the lock on the door open.

Her Father's Will was one of the newer documents deposited in the Archive. It was not hard to find. She took it out of the filing cabinet, unfolded it on the clerk's desk to make sure the number on her authorisation chit matched the number on the document. This was her chance to finally read her Father's Last Will and Testament written in Latin. Of course it was. Anserian civilisation was modelled on Mediaeval Europe, where the language of the Church was also the language of the Law. All the services of the Church of the Undying Queen had been held in Latin and Lawyers had all been clergy. The secular legal profession still insisted the master copy of all historically important documents be written in the long dead Roman tongue. The late Baron du Fauché's Will was an important document. However the Latin and fancy calligraphy were for show. The typewritter Official Translation was used in courts.

The Will had been written and signed by the Baron himself, in his flowing hand. It was not a surprise that a third rate solicitors like André Nouveauté had problems on the day of the Funeral. The Lawyer had been reading what he thought the document said on the day, not what it actually said. She noted the Certified Translation was dated three days after the funeral, it should have been created while he was still alive. This was why her Father had insisted she studied Latin, so she would never, either by malice or incompetence be bamboozled by lawyers. Fat lot of good t't had been, Chantelle thought to herself. Her Papa had not predicted the malice of her step mother, who had stopped Chantelle seeing the document at the funeral.

'Here it is,' Chantelle said, "Uxoris mee et meorum filiorum inspiciantur Estate", or "My wife and my children are to be looked after by my Estate." On the day he read that as "My wife and her children," and then written that in the official translation withou rechecking the original source.'

'If Awful André wasn't so crooked, he would have had someone else check his translation, before it was certified. What he says is there would have been "Uxori et liberis meis sinat Estate," completely and utterly different,' said Aunty Bronwen.

'The brozhnik ratfink!' said Chantelle angrily.

'What?' asked her Aunt.

'"Non est necesse appellare a successore meo. Lex communis, et obtinebit." Is what is written here,' said Chantelle.

'It's not neccessary to name my successor. Common law will prevail?" So what?'

'So, Common Law states issue take precedence. Papa didn't nominate his successor because he knew I should have been named Baroness. Nouveauté deliberately misinterpreted this.'

'OK, Baroness. Should we even be discussing legal niceties over this link? Just do what you came there to do,' Aunty Bronwen said. 'Then we'll have plenty of time to properly study that Will.'

'OK, job done. let's go and party.'

'Don't forget, dear Baroness, I will be waiting for you at five to twelve.'

'Yes Control. Over and out.'

A few minutes later, Chantelle was dancing with Brett. Her friends did not ask her where she had been. Then it struck her, apart from Aunty Bronwen who was unique, the people she spent her free time with were all teenager. No wonder these kids had accepted her as a teenager. And she still dressed like one. An old sumptuary laws, now long repealed, had limited translucent gauze veils to the upper classes. Now girls from all classes wore gauze veils until they married or their twentieth birthday, when they "abandoned the girl's veil" as a right of passage. Chantelle regarded this a silly custom. Being the Baron's daughter meant nobody questioned here when she flouted it locally.

'Viscount Dishy is looking at you, again' said Amy. 'You lucky thing. That's twice since you came back from wherever you went.'

'That's because he knows the truth, how could he not, we grew up together until we were eight, then I visited him every weekend until he went to the naval academy just before our twelfth birthday. Haven't seen him for years.'

'So you are just catching up?' asked Gretchen.

'Yes,' said Chantelle, heading in the Viscount's direction.

'Then go for it girlfriend.'

'What do you mean?' Chantelle stopped dead in her tracks.

'It's obvious you love him, and not as a brother. He feels the same about you.'

'Yes, something has been different between us tonight.'

'Go and dance with him, before you're dragged off early by the Midnight curfew.'

C hantelle' second dance since her return finished and she returned to her friends. A new youngster had joined the group. Chantelle would never have fooled this newcomer. Despite the make up and beautiful black velvet dress, Greta Protts, Cenerentola House's former scullery maid, remained unique. Everything about her was almost but not quite finished or properly tied down. Greta had been brought up by her excentric father in a tiny cottage on the western tip of the island that had been filled with books. After leaving Cenerentola House, she had worked with Carlotta and Gio in the village tavern. Then one morning, a di Propizio passenger ship had called in unexpectedly at Zucca. Greta had left with it. Now she returning as Signorina Margherita Adelaide Windscale di Propizio.

'Evening, Lady Chantelle. Bloody good joke, you swapping with your sister,' she said in a gentrified accent. 'I bet you're wondering what I'm doing here as a guest, not one of the staff? Well, tonight with my family. Tonight I'm Sorrisi Perlata, here with Pio Enzo and Nonna Lulu, aka Signore Vincenze Propozio and Dama Luisella di Propizio.'

Chantelle knew the family, they were successful merchants from Venezia. 'Carlota said you had moved to north, and you were living with relatives. She didn't say who they were.'

'I asked her not to. My crazy dad was hiding from a now defunct crime family. So sad he died just weeks before he could come out of hiding.

'I remember the ship that collected you, it caused a stir.'

'My family were aboard,' said Amy. 'That's how we met Greta.'

'Dad was fuming about the delay,' said his sister. 'Especially as they brought Margherita aboard and gave her the best suite. He moaned for the rest of the trip about the urchin getting the berth he couldn't book.'

'It took me up north to my family. Nonna wanted to know what had happened to her son Paolo di Prozzi. She sent some men to investigate and they found me. They checked me out, did DNA tests and the like. Next thing I know, a ship has been diverted to Zucca, to take me to Venezia. I knew they were Gentry because dad taught me French and Italian. Didn't realise how rich they were.'

They had paid for some serious dentistry by the looks of things. It was not just the rural accent that had been replaced. Greta's ruinous smile had been rebuilt in gleaming white.

'Is this your first trip home?' asked Chantelle.

'Yes, Nonna has been invited to this bash for years, this is the first time she's attended. She said it was an excuse to see where I grew up.'

'Have you seen my step-mother?' asked Chantelle.

'Hell yes. That's why I'm here, not at the concert. I knew she would try to suck up to my family. Lady Liv moaned about staff especially Carlotta and me. So the look on Lady Liv's stupid face when Nonna told her I am her ex-scullery-maid was priceless.'

Before the band started to play another anachronistic waltz Chantelle and the girl exchanged cards. 'It's Madeleine's mobile she'll be pleased to hear from you.'

C hantelle completed her third dance with Viscount Leonard. They were about to start the fourth, when the bells started playing an ancient tune before the hour was struck.

'Oh Angel's it's Midnight. Leo I should have left five minutes ago,' said Chantelle.

'You had better dash then,' replied the Viscount. 'You must keep up the pretence.'

Chantelle was already gone.

'Wait, you've dropped some jewellery!' he shouted after her, but she was long gone. In his hand was a charm, a glass shoe, small and extremely intricate. No, it wasn't glass, his own psychic interface identified it as some sort of scanning device. He had never been trained to use his psychic interface, so identifying the charm's real function was as far as he could go. Chantelle with her Fenzrian mother would be able to use many devices instinctively, no training required. She was at the head of a wave. The Queen wanted everyone in the kingdom to be able to use this fascinating technology. 'Well, well, well, it looks like I have an excuse to go over to the Island and see Chantelle when I return from Elizaburg.'

'Five to Midnight I said, not five past,' said Aunty Bronwen. 'Not to worry, mission accomplished, and I will be able to get you to the ferry in time. It's a good job there is is a short cut dead ahead, to get us past all the coaches.

'Evening, Chantelle,' said Madeleine. 'So, spill the beans who did you dance with?'

'Mostly Viscount Leonard,' she said.

'Cool, he always did have a thing for you.'

'Maddy, he's like a brother!'

'Used to be a brother, now not so much,' said Madeleine.

'Oh alright, I've been in love since he was sent to Tintagel.'

'So how many dances and with whom?' asked Aunty Bronwen. 'We need to co-ordinate information not go all gooey about young Len.'

'Spoilsport,' said Madeleine.

'There were two before I went on my bug hunt and then three afterwards. It could have been lots more. I had to come running.'

'Damn it, people will think I had five dances with dishy Viscount Leonard, and I never experienced that waking dream.'

'Again, let's stick to the details,' Aunty Bronwen said.

'So, I arrived, met with your mother and then went to supper...'

'Sorry, I did say about the short-cut coming up. Do continue.' Aunty Bronwen had taken a sharp left turn and driven them onto a country lane. She continued driving like someone possessed, and it seemed like minutes later, Chantelle and Madeleine where getting out of the car at the ferry jetty.

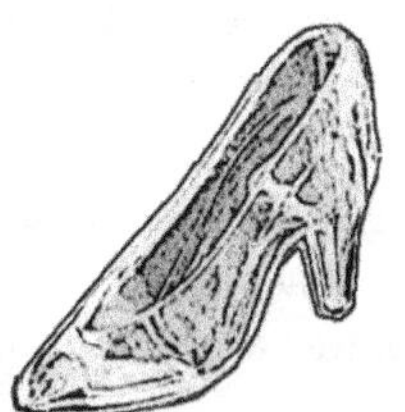 **18** 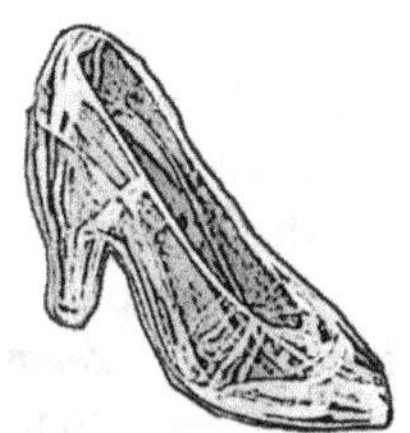

ronwen honestly could not believe what she had just seen, and in her long career as a pathologist she had seen a lot. When she had first played the file, it showed three men having the same genetic profile. She had worried that the Lambourian equipment was not working properly. That this would invalidate the profiles of Chantelle and her Father. Fortunately, or unfortunately, depending on how squeamish you are, she had seen something amazing. One of the men with the matching profiles had removed the front of his skull via his mouth and replaced it with a new one. With the application of some fake tan and hair dye, he became someone who walked, talked and dressed differently. Then after a short meeting he had done it again. She was sure she knew the person he had finally morphed into, but wasn't sure from where. However, this was all a secondary concern, she had proof that Chantelle Angharad was the child of the marriage of her late sister Angharad Myfanwy and the late Baron Gilbert du Fauché. That cow Livienne could no longer deny Chantelle that which was rightfully hers.

Bronwen once again marvelled at the foreign technology which was far older than anything else in use on Anseris. Sadly, nothing is perfect, as there was a fault on the audio track, ranging from making it completely absent to losing every fifth word. Naturally the part that she wanted to hear was missing. What was Face#2 saying to Commander Liepmann. Why had he bothered using Face #2? Did the Commander know the identity of Faces #1 and #3?

'Nye, can you come in here?' she said through the open door.

'What's up Mam?' asked Aneurin.

'I want you to see something amazing.'

'Ach y fi, that was gross Mam,' Aneurin said as the video had finished 'but cool at the same time. I think the dude is trying to hide something.'

'What do you mean?' asked his mother.

'There's something about the way he is acting Mam,' her son said 'I will have to think about it. What I can say is that Face#3 is Ray Payntor, the creepy guy who Madeleine says was a friend of the Baron years ago in Elizaburg.

'Ray Payntor! I hate that man. He left my sister to die in tha dreadful hospital...'

Aneurin quietly left the room. Normally when his Mother lost he temper, she would become very calm, precise and excessively polite. She had never exploded like that before. About half a hour later, he saw his Mother come sheepishly into the living room.

'I'm sorry, son, I really lost it there, didn't I?' his mother said nervously in a very apologetic tone.

'Obviously touched a raw nerve.'

'Yes, your Aunt's death was completely unnecessary. Thank the Angels that Mistress Simples came in when she did, otherwise Chantelle would not be here now.'

'Which is why you're so angry about what's happening to Chantelle?'

'Exactly. Her personality is so much like her Mother's. Which is strange as death permanently separated them.'

The Ansersol was hanging over horizon, both mother and son walked to the beach, greeting the Smitz who were also watching the local star set. The light had an end of day orange tone to it. Fishing boats were racing back to the ports, catching the remaining daylight and favourable tide.

'I really think Face#1 wanted the Commander to hire him,' said Aneurin. 'Obviously he doesn't want the Commander to know who he really is, so he uses Face#2, who is supposed to be a middle man for Face#3, aka PetePayntor.' Aneurin had said the name quietly, not wanting to light the blue touch paper again.

'Yes I can see that,' said his mother, 'if whatever Commander Liepmann wants Mystery Man to do is illegal. He also wants no direct trail back to the Mystery Man.'

Gansler Prime, the brightest object in the night became visible as the sky darkened. Half the heavens sparkled and fizzed as it was filled by a huge gaseous cloud called the Transom Nebula. Its wildly eliptical orbit of Gansler Prime brought it close to the Ansersol every eight years, causing the celestial fireworks known as Silent Night.

'I think Mr. Franke should see this. Perhaps he knows who our Mystery Man is?' said Aneurin. He walked towards the Smitz's front door, wondering what Erik the minder would say.

Erik watched the video and shuddered. He knew exactly who the mystery man was. Like most of his colleagues he thought this man had died years ago. There was certainly no trace of him when the Crown Police had arrested all the Chessmen's other black operatives two years earlier.

'The man in question is Stanley Silvermann,' Erik said calmly as he dropped his well upholstered body into a well upholstered chair. 'He was born without a properly formed upper jaw and nasal bone. It is a' Therese said,mazing that he lived for more than a few minutes after birth. His mother had abandoned him as soon as she saw his face, she said he would be better off dying quickly. Nobody would let her kill the child.'

'What happened to him next?' asked Bronwen.

'Well, Mistress Tudor, one of the doctors in the hospital where he was born wanted to experiment with his facial reconstruction techniques. He fitted the baby with one of his doll sized prototypes. This created a face of sorts for the child, allowing him to breath unaided'

'The surgeon brought him up?' asked Aneurin.

'No, he was adopted by a Chessman Sergeant and his wife. As he grew he needed to be able to easily change the implants to larger ones. A senior officer in the Political Police saw him do this and the boy was recruited into the Black Ops department. Silvermann became one of the Chessmen's best spies. He could adopt so many disguises easily, and he was an excellent actor.'

'He disappeared before the Queen dissolved the Political Police, with a bucket ofsecurity codes and access protocols. Not surprising his criminality has never appeared on the police radar,' said Erik.

'Could he have put the block on any investigation into Baron du Fauché's death?' asked Bronwen.

'Indeed he could,' replied Erik.

'Thank you Mr. Franke, you have been so very helpful. Is there anything I can do for you in return?'

'Just get enough evidence to lock that joker up, this video just proves he's still alive. If we prove he killed your Baron, who knows what other crimes we might finally solve.'

'Yes, I used to be a lot more radical in my youth.' Ray Payntor was in full flow. 'I still believe in some radical ideas, universal male suffrage, social security and a decent minimum wage, for example. Though on the whole I have moved a lot to the right.'

Considerably to the right, thought Madeleine. How her father had ever been friends with this man was a mystery to her. Why had her Mother invited this dreadful old bore to dinner again? Cook had shown a rare flash of humour by serving a roast boar's head, with an apple in its mouth. Madeleine wondered if Payntor had noticed the insult, as he had complimented Hilde Bottle's culinary skills.

'For instance,' Payntor continued, 'there was a time I would never have eaten this. My young head was chocked full of vegetarian nonsense. Yes, I know pigs are cleverer than dogs, but that is still pretty stupid, and pork products taste so damn good. You know, a boar's head prepared like this is a rarity in Elizaburg.'

Something we agree on, thought Madeleine as she tucked into the meat. Chefs in Elizaburg are obsessed with hiding the animal origins of meat dishes.

'What, Mr. Payntor, is your position on fish?' her mother asked.

'I love it. A nice battered piece of Neapolitan Cald with chips and mushy peas. You can't beat it.' He took a sip of his wine. 'Although the price and quality would improve no end if the Fishing Conglomerate controlled the whole of the Rift Sea. Economies of scale and all that.'

'I plan to dissolve the Commune at their annual meeting in November, then sell all the family's shares to Commander Liepmann. They tie up so much of the Estate's assets for no benefit to me.'

'What about the fishermen?' asked Madeleine.

'What about them? They would be much better off working for somebody. Plebeians being their own boss is just wrong.'

Even the twins found that hard to swallow, but said nothing. They had enough sense to keep out of this. Clementine gave Madeleine an evil look, as if warning her to drop the subject.

'I suppose they would be better off without the expense and responsibility of owning their own boats,' Madeleine concluded, believing the irony would fly over her mother's head.

'Indeed Madeleine. You can see what your poor Father could not,' said her mother.

No, amazingly her Mother had spotted the irony, and returned it with a far lower blow.'

'Could you pass me the apple sauce please?' Madeleine asked Citronella, she was not going to descend to that level.

They had to get Chantelle reinstated into the family before the Commune's meeting in November. The Baron, her Father, had equally distributed his five shares to his wife and children. Chantelle's legal status remained in dispute, her vote was null. Lady Livienne, would use her vote and Madeleine's for the sale, and bully the twins to do the same. Enough of the Commune member would also vote for the sale, giving appoval a win by one vote. The Merciful Sisters opposed the sale and with taking over Celmentine and Citronella's votes when they became postulants in September, and Madeleine voting against, then there would be a draw. Unfortunately, Lady Livienne had a casting vote in this case, and the sale would be approved. If Chantelle was reinstated, then there would be roundly defeated. by one vote.

'I didn't expect to find this place so attractive. I am planning on buying a house here, and then retiring.'

'In the new development, like Maddy's Aunt Bronwen?' asked Clementine. 'They're very stylish and really modern.'

'Angels no. They are all modern and hideous. No, on the edge of the old town, something traditional in appearance, but with all the modern amenities built in.'

'Oh, I see, well, I wish you well in your search. Ah, dessert.' said Lady Livienne.

Chantelle was bringing in a tray with five cups of ice cream on it. Madeleine's Mother insisted the two girls from the village were not refined enough to serve meals to guests, so Chantelle ended up doing that job. The situation was wrong. Chantelle's place was here, being served at the head of the table, not doing the serving.

'Ah maid, tell the Cook that she did an awesome job again,' said Payntor, just to annoy both Chantelle and Madeleine.

'Yes sir, certainly sir,' said Chantelle with a bobbing curtsey that miraculously did not disturb the ice cream.

'I don't know where Gilbert found that girl, but she has sponged off him for far too long. Good to see she's adapted back to her proper place so quickly,' Payntor said. 'Of course, whilst I am not a genocidal nutter, like the White Hand members, I do feel that those Fenzrians should not be citizens. They are after all descended from people who wanted to enslave us. We should have enslaved them. Added them to the ranks of the Serfs, who should never have been emancipated.'

'That attitude will not make you popular with many of your new neighbours,' said Madeleine.

'I don't care,' Payntor replied sullenly. 'I will have nothing to do with the witches and warlocks and they will have nothing to do with me.'

That was it, Madeleine had had enough of this stupid old man's appalling attitudes.

'Where do you think you are going?' asked her Mother. 'I have not given you permission to leave the table.'

'I do not like the table you keep. I am going to fetch my coat and leave this house for the last time. Aunty Bron has offered me a home. A cosmopolitan home that does not welcome bigots.'

'Go on, go and live with your witch-woman aunt,' said her Mother, who had stood up and was walking towards her daughter. 'But don't think you can take Ella with you. She signed indenture papers, and I will never release her. Tomorrow she goes back to being a lowly housemaid.'

'You are not my mother any more. I will take my inheritance and go. I formally repudiate you, from now on I am Madeleine Angharad Cenerentola du Fauché.'

'What? You're only sixteen, you have to wait a year until you're an adult, before you can repudiate me!

'No, you stupid woman, the law has changed. I became an adult on my fifteenth birthday! So I will take my inheritance, which includes a voting share in the Fishing Commune. Chantelle will be restored to her rightful place by then, so we will both be blocking you.'

'Go, I never wanted you anyway. You were a mistake,' her Mother screamed.

'Newsflash, I already know that, Lady Livienne,' she spat back.

The clock on the wall said 9.43pm, the ferry would be running for another three hours. She went up to her room and put some essentials into a pilgrim's satchel, took a cape from the wardrobe and went back down stairs.

Yes, I used to be a lot more radical in my youth.' Ray Payntor was

'Madeleine, please don't go,' said Chantelle, who had followed her sister up to her room. 'it's what your Mama wants, you know that.'

'She wants you to leave, so she can find a way to disinherit you,' said Citronella.

'I'm sorry, but let her enjoy her one and only victory,' said Madeleine. 'Disinherance requires a legal repudiation of a child. That requires both parents to disown their offspring. Something Papa would never have done when he was alive. However, I can still repudiate her. Her crimes are heinous enough.'

'And we'll miss you, even if she doesn't,' said Clementine.

'Remember, September is only a couple of months away now,' said Chantelle.

'How do you know about that?' asked Citronella.

'Maddy, you promised never to tell a living soul,' squealed Clementine.

'You told me, at the buffet table in the dining room at the Masquerade. You were piling your plate high with king prawns,' said Chantelle, 'I swapped places with Madeleine, so she could go to the concert.'

'I thought Madeleine was acting oddly,' said Citronella, 'and that explains why the Viscount danced with you, or rather her, so often.'

'No, you didn't. You're just trying to be clever,' said Clementine. 'I did too.'

'Girls! Stop!' said Chantelle. 'The most important person here is Madeleine. And I wouldn't betray your confidence either.'

'Praise be to the Angels,' the twins said in unison.

'Can't you at least wait until morning, Maddy dear,' said Citronella as she followed Madeleine down the stairs.

'No Citronella, this ungrateful child must leave now,' said her Mother, who was waiting in the hallway.

'At least let us accompany her to the village?' asked Clementine

'What on Anseris for?' asked her Mother. 'She's done the trip thousands of times. It's not as if there are any wolves on the island.'

'Thank you, girls and may the Angels bless you,' said Madeleine as she walked through the door. 'I'll do this on my own.'

As she walked, she started regretting her hasty decision. The road to the village from Cenerentola House was partially illuminated. Islands of light in the deep oceans of darkness. Madeleine heard a noise behind her, turned but could see nothing. It was probably just an animal in the undergrowth. Then an owl taking off from a branch startled her. Pull yourself together, she thought as the twig snapped. Like a shot she turned and shone the light of her torch into Erik Franke's eyes.

'Oh, Mr Franke, I'm so sorry.'

'No harm done, your Ladyship,' said the big man affably. 'Your sister, the Lady Citronella decided you should not walk to the ferry on your own. Not in the state you were in. She telephoned your aunt, Mistress Tudor, who then phoned me. Fortunately, I was in the tavern here on the Island, playing Darts and enjoy the beer.'

'Oh nonsense, I'm not in a state now, and I have done this journey thousands of times at night.'

'That is what your Aunt initially said, until Lady Citronella told her that Ray Payntor was at Cenerentola House. She asked me to come and escort you to Zucca post haste,' Erik explained.

'What has that old bigot Mr. Payntor got to do with anything?' Madeleine asked.

'All will be revealed in greater detail, when I deliver you to your destination in Zucca.'

The Baroness was wrong. There was one wolf on the Island. He was that wolf. He had excused himself from the dinner table, and gone on the hunt. It would be so easy to kill that bitch Madeleine du Fauché, send her to a watery death in one of the deep pools on the way into town or the stream. Nobody would suspect foul play, they would say the hysterical girl had rushed without thinking into the water. In his line of work, he was rarely accepted contracts to kill women professionally. No, he did that for pleasure, especially if the woman in question refused to accept her inferiority to any man.

Ah Brozhnik! That stupid brozhnik rent-a-cop had just turned up. NowPaynter had lost his chance.

Far more worrying was the fact that mention of this persona's name had triggered the arrival of the brozhnik rent-a-cop. Perhaps he was not as stupid as he looked. Maybe he should pay a visit to Mr. Erik Franke in a professional capacity, as he had obviously found a link between the Payntor persona and one of his kills. Then he remembered the big man, who had been seconded into the Chessmen to smash heads and refused to do so. A plod with a conscience who was quickly sent back to the Crown Police. Yes, Erik Franke definitely had to go before the Ray Payntor persona was permanently retired.

Anserian law defined a person's five loyalties. The first loyalty is to the Monarch. The second loyalty is to an Archduke. The third is to a family. The fourth is to the clan, a group of ten or more families in a district. The fifth and final loyalty to their home town. Loyalty to the Crown never changed, even if the person wearing it did. The other were more fluid. A person could ask an Archduke's permission to move to another part of the kingdom, changing their town and feudal loyalties. Marriage and divorce altered family loyalties, and usually it was the bride who joined her new husband's family, but not always. Men moving up the social ladder would often join the more powerful family of their new wife. Also if a widower remarried, his daughters sometimes adopted their step-mother's first name as their second name.

Relationships in a family could deteriorate so badly parents or child could repudiate each other. The clan could expel members. To be fully repudiated by family and clan was the greatest disgrace of all.

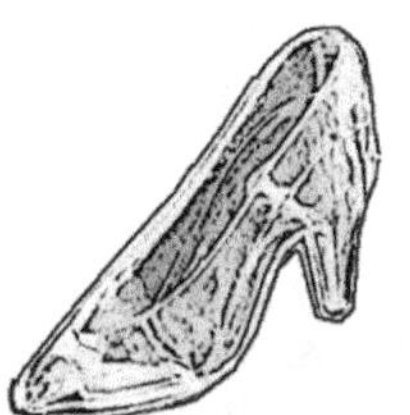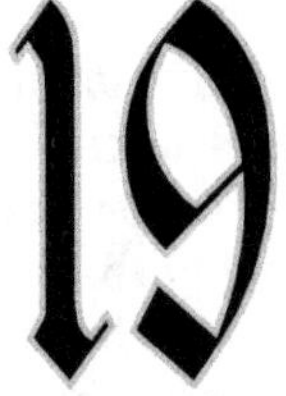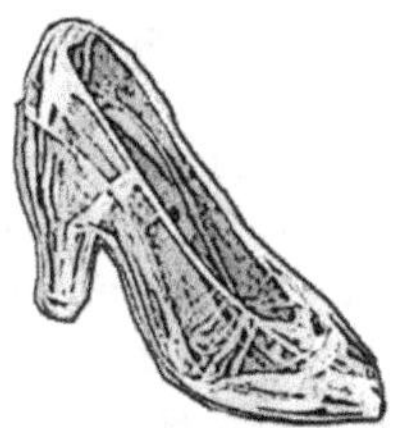

A nother Wednesday, another day off and Chantelle was on the road to the village and then Zucca when she ran into her step-mother coming in the opposite direction.

'I 've decided that from this week, you shall not leave the island on your day off. You may be needed here at a moment's notice,' her Step-Mother said. Chantelle's demotion back to housemaid had been short lived. Her step-mother valued the luxury of a lady's maid more than she imagined.

'Mistress?' Chantelle said pleadingly. Although there was no way the witch could enforce this order.

'I have made my mind up. I'll not change it.' The older woman sniffed, 'still pretending you are a daughter of the gentry, with clothes borrowed from your betters. I miss the days when someone like you would not be allowed to wear such fine clothes.'

Why, Chantelle thought as she trudged wearily into the village, all pleasure drained from the day. I am a daughter of the gentry, and would have been allowed to wear this under the old sumptuary laws. Her outfit consisted of a silken red and blue particoloured kirtle with a matching sidless silk surcotte and huge baggy sleeves attached. Topped of with a fine white gauze veil. It had been taken from her by her step-mother. Madeleine had returned to her.

Oh great, and here come the Ugly Sisters, she thought, spotting the twins coming from the village.

'Ah, Chantelle,' they said, 'we thought we had missed you.'

That's odd, thought Chantelle. Ever since the funeral, the twins had been slavishly following their Mother's order that she should always be addressed as Ella.

'Why do you want to see me?' she asked. What evil plan had her Step-Mother dreamed up, that the Ugly Sisters were helping her carry out. Hang on, what were the twins wearing? She had helped them put their plain orange or yellow outfits that morning. Now they were both wearing identical dark brown floor length woollen tunics which formed the base of a Merciful Sister's habit. Their hair had been cut to their shoulders barely poking out from beneath white headscarves.

'We have received instructions from our Prioress, Sister Grace, to take you straight to our new home in the Priory. Where she will explain everything.'

'As you can see, we have followed Madeleine's example and left home,' they said in unison. 'We are now postulants under Sister Grace's authority. She said it would stop Mama's match-making interfering with our vocation,' said Citronella.

'She was planning to announce our betrothal to the Reydmondson brothers,' said Clementine.

'Reynald for me and Donald for Emily,' said Citronella. 'Even if we didn't have our calling, we would never marry them.'

'And it appears, neither would anyone else,' said Chantelle, noticing they had already chosen new names 'their mother is as desperate as your mother to get them married off.'

'Well, our pledges are legally binding according to Canon and Regal Law. She's now Clementine Allison Tintagel, from our late Papa's mother. I'm now Clementine Emily Tintagel, from Mama's mother. We couldn't both be Livienne, so we went back a generation. Mama can't do anything to stop us. We've just told her, on the ferry,' said Clementine.

The Twins could have done this two years ago, but they let their Mother thwart their ambitions. They were followers, not leaders. Once Madeleine had shown them how to stand up to their Mother, using a new law, they had quickly followed suit with an old one.

'Well she could hardly miss us, could she?' said Citronella, in the twins verbal relay. 'We've been saying goodbye to our friends on the Island.'

'That didn't take long,' said Chantelle, 'you don't have any.'

'We do have friends here,' said Clementine.

'Not many, because we used to be beastly, but that has changed, as we have changed,' said Citronella. 'It is a pity our Mother can't change.'

So that is why your Mother was so salty, when I passed her on her way to the house earlier thought Chantelle. Lady Livienne was used to changing the facts to fit her opinions whenever she could, facing a fact she could not change had brought out her nasty streak.

'Well, we do feel sorry for her, if only just a little bit,' said Citronella, 'all alone in that big house. But she has brought that about by her actions. We must forgive her for that.'

They had arrived at the ferry. Chantelle was about to hand her five pfennig fare for her ticket, when Citronella stopped her.

'Your fare has been paid, Chantelle, you don't have to worry about money where we are taking you.'

The Sisters of the Merciful Charity of the Angels to All Children Priory in Zucca stood next door their Orphanage. It had been there since Queen Anne I created the Order four centuries earlier. Chantelle had visited the Orphanage next door, where the Sisters worked, to help with the annual Juletide Party, but never here, where the Sisters lived. It had the smell of incense, beeswax candles and highly polished woodwork that is unique to a religious institutions.

'What are you doing here, Mr. Franke?' she asked as soon as she spotted the man in a place men rarely visit.

'Lady Chantelle, I have been informed of your dreadful plight by my good friend Erik Franke,' said a Merciful Sister, who Chantelle recognised as Sister Grace.

'Sister Grace asked me here. I've known her since the day when she was still Lady Charmaine Grace Sancler, and being robbed at knife-point in Elizaburg. A perp thought he could take the money she had collected for the Order's good works. That perp regretted that thought. After that, I ran security for all the Order's charitable collections in the city of Elizaburg for years afterwards.'

'Mr. Franke, you never cease to amaze me,' said Chantelle.

'Anyway,' said Sister Grace. 'Erik asked me for my assistance. I contacted your Cousin in Tintagel, who came up with this plan.'

'You are not returning to Cenerentola House tonight,' he said 'We're taking you out of the Archduchy.'

'But I can't leave Zucca, let alone leave Fiandre. That stupid Indenture she made me sign when I wasn't thinking straight.'

'Exactly,' Erik agreed. 'When you fail to return home tonight Lady Livienne will report you as missing. The Crown Police will be looking for you, but you will be invisible. I really should arrest myself by assisting an indentured servant to abscond I'm commiting a class three felony. Sister Grace as well, who is about to do some magic.'

'Nobody would impede the journey of a car full of my Sisters, she said. 'The Crown Police would positively assist it, and they definitely would not check the Sister's ID papers.'

Chantelle and the twins followed Sister Grace into a side room. She was confused by what Mr. Franke and Sister Grace had said. Normally she understood them perfectly, why were they speaking in riddles today?

'A car with three passengers was about to leave for the Mother House in Tintagel,' said Sister Grace. 'Their departure has been delayed as they are now waiting for a fourth passenger. You have been granted special dispensation to wear this. You will be the fourth passenger. The twins will help you change.'

This turned out to be the habit of a novice of the Order. Brown clothes in a brown basket, the white wimple and veil seemed to sparkle in comparison.

'You are now under the protection of the Order, Lady Chantelle. I is called Sanctuary. Whilst you wear these robes you're our Novice Myfanwy. I believe it was your Grandmother's name. Using your Mother's name, as is our normal practice would be too obvious.'

'Yes Sister, my maternal Grandmother. She was a very devout lady said Chantelle. 'My aunt says that she might officially have been Myfanwy, but she was always known as Blodwen.'

'Which adds an extra layer to your alias,' said the older woman.

'But I'm atheist. Chantelle protested weakly.

'Oh!' said Sister Grace, 'but you can pretend to still be faithful. The Angels will not object, our cause is just. On arrival in Carlton, one of Mr. Franke's associates will meet you for the rest of your journey

'Yes, Sister. I can pretend.'

Five minutes later the twins were pinning a thick white veil in place. My word, I'm an Ugly Sister now, she thought. My face is the only part of me people can see but they will look strait past it, because of this habit. Since her fourteenth birthday, she had worn some sort of veil in public. None had been this heavy, two layers of cotton. No wonder the Sisters' skin always looked so red, they were slowly cooking themselves. This was hotter than the black velvet dress she had worn at the Black Masquerade.

'Are you ready, Novice Myfanwy?' asked Sister Grace.

'Yes Sister Grace,' Chantelle replied.

Chantelle could see how envious the Twins were. For the next few days she would be what they so desperately wanted to be.

'Girls, go to the chapel and sing Cycle #12, calling on the Angel's to bless your half-sister's journey.' The twins left without question.

'If looks could kill you'd be dead now. Cycle #12 should throw some water on that envy, it's rarely sung, because it's two hours long, dull and very repetitive.'

To Chantelle's surprise, Sister Grace unlocked a cupboard and rolled a full length mirror out. Why did a building full of women who did not give a damn about their appearances have a full length mirror?

'I can see you're wondering about the mirror. While we don't care about our individual appearance, the Order want us to leave a good impression with the public. This helps new Sisters learn, until they instinctively dress properly.'

If she had gone down a different path a decade earlier, after a year as a postustulant, she would have celebrated her seventeenth birthday by becoming a novice, and by now she would be a full Merciful Sister, teaching in a school somewhere far away. This would be normal for her.

'Good,' said the older woman as she inspected Chantelle. 'Before you leave, I will give you a quick lesson in how to pass as a novice Merciful Sister for the next few days. I don't doubt you will receive more lessons during your journey.

'There is, of course, one last thing you need for your disguise.' Sister Grace removed a brown carved wooden Avatar, an elongated octagonal central body with angel's wings, on a chain from around her neck and placed it around Chantelle's. Every Anserian, whether man or woman wore an Avatar. Even a non-believer like Chantelle would not be seen in public without this piece of jewellery which was like a signature. The Merciful Sisters wore mass produced wooden Avatars removing all outward individuality.

'I'll get a replacement after you've left.'

Twenty minutes later, Chantelle found herself sitting bolt upright in an ugly brown car. All vehicles belonging to the Order were painted the same dull colour with matching brown interior trim. The car was powered by Brown Olive Oil. For centuries the oil taken from larger and oilier brown fruit, grown on trees genetically enhanced by the Aggelii, had been used in lamps. Now all homes had electric lights, so it became an ideal fuel for cars on a planet with no oil or gas reserves.

'We shall sing hymn #26,' said Sister Maude, who was sitting in the front passenger seat. She was the oldest and most senior Merciful Sister present, a Cardinal Sister with a black veil, the same rank as Chantelle's cousin. 'Then we shall observe a half hour of silence as we leave the Barony.'

Chantelle was glad she recognised the hymn but was not sure of the lyrics. She had been so wrapped up, she did not see her Aunty Bron, Madeleine and Aneurin walking along Zucca's main street. If she had, she could not wave to them or show any signs of recognition. Merciful Sisters didn't do that sort of thing. Also her family was not supposed to know how she got to the Safe House.

Dear Angels, these women were dull. Most of the journey was in silence except for regular prayers every few hours. Chantelle knew most of them, as she had belonged to the Church of the Caretakers of the Soul most of her life, but some of the special addenda were new to her. On the hour tedious devotional hymns were sung. Occasionally, Sister Maude announced they would sing an additional hymn, for the strangest of reasons. Chantelle assumed that the old nun was dropping off to sleep and did not want to be caught napping.

Then there were all the silly little rituals, like not sitting on the scapular she was wearing, or raising her hand, like a child at school, if she wanted to speak to someone. When they did relax, they only talked shop, the children did this, the children did that or poor little Ivan wet the bed again.

Next to Sister Maude was Ordinal Sister Anne, the driver. Next to Chantelle on the back seat was the beige veiled Senior Novice Olivia. Chantelle remembered her from school, when she had been Freda Lambling, a Fenzrian who dyed her hair blonde. Two years older than Chantelle, she had not been particularly religious. Freda had been the most glamorous girl in school. As Novice Olivia she was far from glamorous now. She could have signed her final contract in Ponte di Carla. Making the pilgrimage to the Tintagel Mother-House marked her out as an obvious high flyer, destined to become a Cardinal Sister one day. Chantelle wondered what had caused this transformation in the intervening years.

'I know what you are thinking, Novice Myfanwy,' said Novice Olivia, after gaining permission to speak, 'I had a reputation for being a party girl, but I grew tired of endless partying. I became bored with being a clothes horse, tired of dye burning my scalp.So I broke away from the destructive circle friends the Curse had sucked me into. I began taking my studies seriously, enrolling in college to study Art and Education, so that I could become a teacher. Ironically at a party to celebrate my graduation, I decided to become a Merciful Sister. I had to prove my calling was genuine, before my entrance exam and then become a novice. It was my free choice, my life, my free will.'

'May the Angels be praised,' said Sister Maude. 'We know how strong the Fenzrian need to belong can be. So we guard against the Curse of the Great Machine in our Fenzrian sisters. Novice Olivia proved she was free of its malignant influnce.

'Now, we are due to stop for the night at the Abbey in Bardi. Because we are still within the Archduchy of Fiandre the Abbess there knows nothing of our subterfuge, she and her Sisters will take the situation at face value.'

Chantelle raised her hand.

'I know Novice Myfanwy, you fear you may give yourself away.'

'Yes, Sister,' said Chantelle, 'I've been worrying about that.'

'No need to worry Novice Myfanwy,' said Sister Maud. 'In the unlikely event anyone speaks to you, at the Abbey, tell them you became a Novice three weeks ago, and still have much to learn. That is all you need to say. Also as a Novice in her first year, you will be spending all your time in the Chapel praying with the one dozen first year novices of il Convento e la Chiesa Abbaziale di Bardi'

Oh joy, thought Chantelle, an evening kneeling and mumbling. Chantelle raised her hand, as did Novice Olivia. Beige outranked White so Sister Maude should have let Senior Novice Olivia speak first, but made a gesture allowing the lower ranking white veiled Chantelle the privilege.

'That's a relief,' Chantelle said before asking. 'Is this also a fast?'

'No, Novice Myfanwy. Why should it be? You will have your evening meal in the refectory, but meals are eaten in silence,' replied Sister Anne.

Chantelle was getting used to being addressed in this way, but still could not wait to return to being called Chantelle.

'Sister Maude, our temporary Sister would not know any of the Devotional Prayers,' said Senior Novice Olivia, when she was given permission to speak. 'They are never used in the other life.'

Chantelle could feel the bitterness in Senior Novice Olivia's voice. She had no doubt expected to make this journey in triumph, on the eve of her attaining something she had set her heart on and studied for over many years. Now she had to share the journey with an interloper, a fake who did not deserve it. Not all of her youngest travelling companion's old life had been prayed away.

'Then after we have sung Hymn #372, you will teach her while we travel, Novice Olivia,' said Sister Maude, 'and there is one demerit for referring to Novice Myfanwy as temporary. If it had been anywhere else, it might have given the game away. Plus a second demerit for your display of arrogance and pride. As penance you will spend the evening in chappel with the junior novices.'

'Yes Sister,' said the young woman, in a penitent tone of voice.

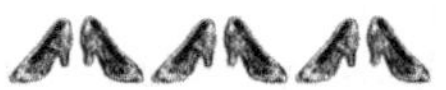

 adeleine had been expecting her mother to make a scene. She came storming in at 9pm, after Chantelle had been missing for an hour.

'I demand that you return my maid Ella to me straight away,' Lady Livienne screeched.

'Livienne, I don't know anyone called Ella, do you Maddy?' asked Aunty Bronwen in response.

'No Aunty Bron, I don't. What is that woman talking about,' said Madeleine, 'who is she anyway?'

'Oh very mature, Madeleine,' said her Mother. 'I am looking for my indentured maid, Ella, who has failed to return home after her afternoon off.' At this, point Lady Livienne noticed Madeleine's clothes, a pair of jeans, a white t-shirt and a brocade waistcoat. 'Madeleine, what on Anseris are you wearing?'

'The sort of thing I used to wear all the time back in Elizaburg. What does it matter to you, Lady Livienne, you're not my Mother any more. You made it very clear you never wanted me. Chantelle, bless her heart, has always been more like a mother to me than a sister. It's why I chose Chantelle to replace my original matronym.'

'Oh to the Hells with the lot of you. The Crown Police will help me track down Ella.'

'Best of luck, Livienne, I don't know anyone called Ella. There is my niece Chantelle, who you were illegally detaining and fraudulently denying her rightful inheritance.'

'That girl is not your niece, why do you continue with that lie? Unless you were going to benefit from her fraudulent claim to my late husband's estate.'

'I said when we met, I was there when the midwife cut the umbilical chord connecting Chantelle to my poor dead sister, and now I have evidence to prove what I say is true. She is the daughter of Gilbert du Fauché.'

'We shall see about that,' said Lady Livienne.

'Fair enough, Livienne. Fair enough. See you in an Archduke's Court,' said Bronwen.

This triggered something in Lady Livienne. 'I've not given you permission to use that name! And as Madeleine no longer consider me your Mother, you should both address me as Your Ladyship.'

Madeleine's reply was pure acid. 'Normally I would not be so disrespectful, using someone's given name without permission. But you don't deserve respect, Livienne. Now leave my Aunt's house!'

'Only when she tells me where my Lady's Maid is?'

Madeleine wondered if her mother had childishness lessons from the twins, as she had come within inches of stamping her foot in temper.

'I have no idea. Now, good day, Livienne,' said Bronwen as forcefully as Madeleine.

Madeleine watched her mother go, knowing that nobody in that household knew where Chantelle was, or who had arranged her escape. Madeleine suspected Mr. Franke had something to do with it. He was the Queen's personal policeman, so her Mother would have little joy there.

Madeleine, don't you thank that was a bit too harsh?' asked her, after Lady Livienne had left.

'Yes, I shall apologise tomorrow. Tonight I celebrate a definite victory for our cause.'

Madeleine noticed that like her mother, her Aunt was wearing a green and yellow kirtle with a veil and her hair up. It clashed with the architecture and interior design of her house. The last time Madeleine had seen her aunt wearing City Style had been at the Equinox. Since then she had exclusively been country style, even at work. There were very few Fiandrans who had taken advantage of the new Clothing Laws. Nye was not the only one going native.

'Yes, I know I have been exclusively country style. It's not a Fenzrian desire to fit in, its about the money I wasted on country style clothes before I arrived home,' said her Aunt, who must have read her mind. 'Aneurin said to wait until July. The delay wouldn't have helped Chantelle though.'

'So it's just Fenzrian meaness is it?'

'Maddy, that's not nice.'

'OK. I'm Sorry.'

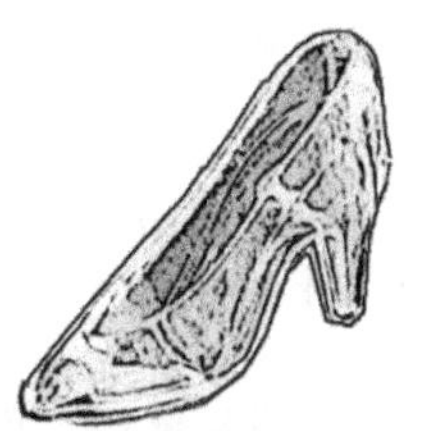 **20** 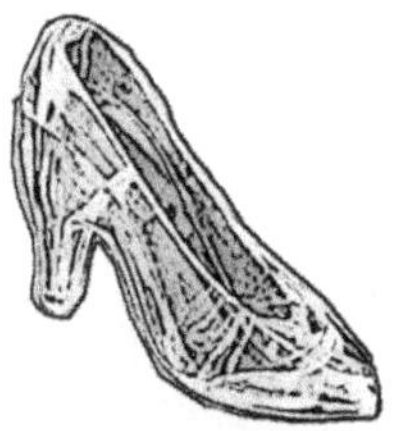

Saturday afternoon and the car carrying Chantelle into hiding had crossed the border half an hour earlier, heading to Taunton, a Guild Town in the Archduchy of Carlton. The change was obvious immediately, the mediaeval Italianate architecture had been replaced by black and white half-timbered buildings.

They would be spending the night in the Ivybridge Priory. The following day the four women would continue their journey to the Mother-house Convent at Tintagel.

They were now traveling along a branch of the Angels' Highway network, faster than the tortuous route along the man-made roads of Fiandre. Chantelle raised her hand.

'Yes, Novice Myfanwy?'

'The Angel's Highway from Ponte di Carla would have brought us here faster than the route we took. Why didn't we use it?'

'A novice would never question the decisions of a Sister,'or receive an answer,' said Sister Anne, 'but as we are no longer in Fiandre, and you are not a novice, I shall explain. The structure of the Angels' Highways themselves is virtually indestructible, but everything on it which makes it usable, like the road markings, the signposts, the crash barriers and the lights are maintained by humans. Each Archduchy has its own facilities company, who charge road users tolls. The one in Fiandre has two large shareholder, Andre Nouveauté and your step-mother, Lady Livienne du Fauché. We know from Sister Grace that your step-mother suspects the Order is helping you. If we used the Angels' Highway, she would have been able to find you by using her influence in that company. In Carlton, the facility company is owned by the Order of the Merciful Sisters of Charity. Road tolls helps pay for the Order's schools throught the Kingdom.'

Chantelle began to laugh, she suspected that nobody had ever laughed in this vehicle.

'You will be pleased to know,' Sister Maude said. 'When we arrive at Ivybridge Priory, you will collect a package of clothing suitable for a young woman in Carlton. You will be able shed the disguise and become Lady Chantelle again.'

Chantelle was surprised she felt some sadness at this news. She suspected it was her Fenzrian ancestry kicking in. Making her happier to be part of a group than as an individual.

'We need a break, so I am granting three hours in remissionis tempore,' said Sister Maude. In remissionis tempore was when rules were relaxed, but not by much. 'The people of Taunton, my home town, are used to seeing Merciful Sisters on long journeys taking a break in their town. While you wear that habit as a disguise, you remain Novice Myfannwy. The townsfolk will generally ignore you and they will ask to speak to you if they need anything.

Attracting the attention of a local and waiting until they had to asked for permission to speak, like naughty children in her classroom, made buying a bag of her favourite boiled sweets a herculean task. Fortunately, this rule did not apply to a child in distress, like the boy sitting on the pavement. The boy seemed so out of place, mumbling the Gwenerian Welsh and was dressed in traditional clothes.

'What's wrong, little person,' said Chantelle, getting into the role of Novice Myfanwy, using the Sister's greeting for young children. She switched to Gwenerian dialect of Welsh she used with Aunty Bron, asking again. 'Beth sy'n bod person bychan?'*

'I've lost my Mam,' the boy replied in Angerlish.

'I'm Novice Myfanwy,' Chantelle said in a Gwener accent.' This seemed to calm the child even further. 'I'm sure I can help you find your mam. Now what's your name?'

'I'm Gwilym,' the boy replied, 'people call me Billy now, Sister.'

'I moved here from Holywall last week. Everything is so different.' He began to cry again. The child was too young to understand the

---

*asking again. 'Beth seen bohd pearson bukhan?'

difference in ranks, but then again, nobody did when they spoke to a woman dressed the way Chantelle was.

'Well Billy, what colour kirtle was your Mam wearing?' Chantelle asked the boy, who had stopped crying. She guessed the mother would still be wearing traditional clothes, so it would make her easier to spot in a crowd of people dressed in City style.

'Her name is Elenud,' he replied, 'Elenud Maredydd. But she doesn't wear trad any more. We were buying new clothes for me. New clothes for my new life.'

Chantelle took the bag of boiled sweets from a pocket within her robes and offered it to the child, who took one, unwrapped it and popped it in his now smiling mouth in a blur.

Rats, thought Chantelle, it looks as if I'll have to take little Billy to the local constabulary.

'I know exactly where your Mam will have gone to get help finding you.' Chantelle used her psychic interface to activate the antique alien navigation device built into one of the charms on the bracelet, in a hidden pocket in her robes. It was so much better than the sat-nav app even the mobile phones so common in Carlton.

'OK Sister,' Billy replied.

'M adam,' said the bored desk sergeant at the nearest police station. 'I cannot speak your language, I shall fetch a colleague who can.'

'Sorry Officer, but as you can see, I am worried,' said a young woman dressed in denim dungarees and a blue top, looking every inch a Carltonian. Her voice however told a different story, as she spoke with an unmistakable heavy Gwenerian Welsh accent.

'Mam!' young Gwylim screamed as soon as he saw her, then continued in Welsh, 'I got lost, Sister Myfanwy brought me here.'

'Cariad, I was so worried about you. Don't ever frighten me like that again,' the woman said. Then she picked the boy up and hugged him, before turning to Chantelle. 'Sister, will you speak to me?'

Of course, with the Angel's blessing.' Chantelle replied.

'Sister, thank you so much. I thought I had young Billy's hand when I turned to look at some t-shirts for him, at a market stall. When I turned back he had gone.'

'It's easily done,' Chantelle replied, to put the mother at ease.

'Ladies, Welsh might be the official language most commonly used where you come from, but in Taunton, everything is done in Angerlish. I will have to get a Welsh speaking colleague.'

All the posters on the wall had a Welsh translation in small print at the bottom. Including the Wanted Poster with her picture.

'Yes, Sergeant, sorry Sergeant,' said Chantelle, not realising she had switched languages to speak with Billy's Mother. 'Now if you will excuse me, I have to return to my Sisters.'

'I'm afraid you will have to write a statement first,' said the Sergeant. 'Also, I will have to scan your papers. Our records have to be kept up to date.'

Everyone, including Merciful Sisters had to carry their plastic identities documents, so the Crown Police could keep a track on the movement of the population. A request was more likely in an urban area like this, and at the border of two archduchies, where they acted as internal passports. Chantelle's ID was still in Fiandre.

To Chantelle's surprise and relief, Sister Maude walked into the station's reception. Proving her identity had sped them into Carlton.

'I'm sure Novice Myfanwy can do that when we arrive the Mother-house in Tintagel. Our Order also appreciates well kept records, but we also appreciate punctuality, and we are already running late.

Sister Maude presented her ID Card. The sargeant scanned the barcode and shuddered when he read his monitor.

'Geoffrey Albrite, isn't? How many years has it been?'

'Too many, Sister.'

'It is always nice to see a pupil doing so well.

'Yes Sister. If your colleague fill in this in and post it to us,' the Sergeant said, handing the Sister Maude a pre-paid envelope containing a form.

'Thank you, Sergeant, May the Angels continue to bless you.'

'I didn't realise you were following me, Sister,' said Chantelle to the Merciful Sister walking by her side.

'Not initially, Chantelle, there are other reasons I sought you out.'

'Do you remember all your old pupils?'

'Some do. The size of the school is a factor. However, a naughty child like like Geoffry Albrite is hard to forget.' said Sister Maud. Hard to believe he is now a policeman.'

'I saw the way you dealt with little Billy and was impressed. Tell me, would you consider becoming a real novice then eventually Sister Angharad? Your mother had such a pretty name, and it would be yours as a Merciful Sister.'

'My half-sisters Clementine and Citronella are entering the Order. They show great empathy with children also.'

'But I am not asking about your remarkable half-sisters, Chantelle, accepted as novices already,' said Sister Maude, 'I'm asking about you.'

'No, Sister, I would not.' Wait a minute, thought Chantelle, did she just use my real name? 'Doesn't my atheism disqualify me?'

'Don't worry about your lack of faith. I know at least a dozen of my Sisters who have made the World a better place by being members of the Order. They know it is a way of achieving their goals. Unlike myself, they merely tolerating the rituals.'

The two woman walked into a church. They remained silent, until they had prayed at the altar at. Sister Maude then directed Chantelle to the vestry.

'The answer is still no,' said Chantelle eventually.

'As I thought. Now the need for dissembling has passed, you can be yourself again,' she handed Chantell her avatar and a bag of clothes. 'Lady Madeleine chose some of her Guild Style outfits for you'

Habits, like other traditional clothes were handmade. Chantelle's baggier traditional clothes fitted Madeleine. Sadly, her Elizaburg clothes were too small for Chantelle. Shops selling mass produced clothes were common in towns. Chantelle had been surprise, Sister Maude knew where to find one.

olly, how nice to see you again,' said the owner of the clothes shop they had just walked into.'What brings you home?'

'Home was a habedasherary, not this. However, I 'm here to buy some clothes.' said Sister Maude. 'Bree, is there anyone else in here?'

'Why no, Dolly, it's been a quiet day, and a funny week,' said a woman almost identical to Sister Maude's, but who looked years younger in City Style clothes and make-up. She must be closely related to Sister Maude. No-one else would dare call her Dolly.

'I would be grateful if you would close your shop and give us exclusivity,' said Sister Maude, 'and your complete confidentiality.'

'Why yes, of course.' The woman turned the sign on the door, pulled down the blinds then turned and examined Chantelle, who was removing her veil. 'So, you found the other Life not to your taste?'

'Um?' said Chantelle, unsure what to say.

'It's alright, Chantelle, you can trust my birth sister, Mistress Bridgi Poitiere. She is two years older than me and thought I was mad to join the Merciful Sisters. Didn't you, Bree?'

'Dolly there is deeply conservative, she likes things traditional and dull. Mother hated being called Maude, and would have hated the thought of her daughter Dorothy, changing her name to Maude' said the woman. 'She didn't have to. It's just the Merciful Sister's tradition. Which is why I still call her Dolly.'

'Our Mother died when you were five,' said Sister Maude, 'you can hardly remember her, I do not. And I prefer the name Maude, Dorothy sounds so prissy, and you know I hate being called Dolly.'

'Anyway, I have always loved modernity, which brought me into the fashion business.

'Oh, I see, Mistress Poitiere,' said Chantelle, who was now wearing only a knee-length white cotton chemise closest to her skin. 'You see, I'm not really a novice. The Order is helping me get away from a difficult situation in my home town in Fiandre. The clothes I was given for Carlton don't fit me.'

She had followed the older women into a side room, that looked as if it should be in a hospital, not a clothes shop.

OK dear, and call me Bree, everyone else does. Now strip down to your skin and hop on the scanner.' Mistress Potière was standing next to a narrow mirror and a raised platform. 'I need to know your right size. Don't worry, a curtain will protect your modesty.'

Chantelle noticed a little spot of light dancing over her body, as the platform slowly spun her around. Looking up she could see the source.

'Oh, and it's best not to stare at the laser dear, it might damage your eyes. Oh, and put the dressing gown on the hook on when we're finished with the scanner.'

'OK, Mistress Potière,' she replied.

'Thought so, Size 8C Long for everything,' said Mistress Potière from the other side of the computer.

'Is that good or bad?' asked Chantelle,

'You'd look knock-out in a Pendragon mini-skirt with legs like that, but as they are illegal everywhere else in the Kingdom, that is not an option.' said Bridgit Potière, as she slid a packet new city style underwear under the curtain.

'For which the Angels can be praised,' said Sister Maude, 'Those garments are shocking, but you would look nice in that dress with a pencil skirts you were staring at earlier.'

'She would Dolly. You see, you're not as out of touch as you pretend to be.'

The room was silent for a few minutes before Sister Maude asked, 'Chantelle are you decent?'

'Halfway.'

The curtain slid open and both Mistress Potière and Sister Maude gave Chantelle clothes.

After Chantelle had modelled dozens of outfits, she returned to the car with Sister Maude. Had she needed to try so many clothes, or had it just been an excuse for Bree and Dolly to have a longer chat?

Despite wearing unfamiliar City Style clothing, Chantelle was beginning to feel herself again. Especially as she was once more wearing her own avatar.

It was a good thing the Merciful Sisters travelled light, Chantelle though as the bags of new clothes filled most of the car's small boot.

Sister Maude lead a prayer thanking the Angels for the reunion of mother and child. As she was no longer dressed as a novice, Chantelle did not have to join in, but as she agreed with the sentiment, did anyway, letting the Curse have one tiny victory.

'Do you think it was wise, paying for your clothes with that card?' asked Sister Maude.

'My mother has no way of accessing my bank account. So the only people who know I have been on a minor shopping spree in Taunton work in the bank, and they would never divulge the information.'

'No, Chantelle,' replied Sister Maude, 'I was not worried about her finding out. My concern is about the lack of actual money in the transaction.'

'You prefer seeing an exchange of something for something?' asked Chantelle.

'Yes, I don't trust the security of those machines,' said the older woman. 'For centuries, coins were king. In some parts of the Kingdom, paper notes are still seen as the devil's toys.'

Senior Novice Olivia raised her hand, for permission to speak.

'My Father would only pay for things with cash, and refused cheques and electronic transactions,'

'Mine was the same,' said Chantelle, after raising her hand.

'Chantelle, you no longer need to raise your hand to speak,' said Sister Maude.

'It feels like the polite way to act in my present company,' said Chantelle.

'As you are a secular passenger, we no longer have to be as formal,' said Sister Maude. 'We are now in libertas tempore.'

'Thank you, D... um Sister Maude,' said Chantelle, quickly correcting herself.

The woman in the front seat had noticed and started laughing, something her colleagues rarely heard.

'I have met your half-sisters, they both have great empathy, but I am afraid that is because they are still children themselves. Their mother never let them grow up,' said Sister Ann,' who rarely talked. 'That will change when they join us. We will allow them space to grow. Of course, they cannot both be Sister Livienne, so each will adopt the names of a grandmother for their new life.'

Well they certainly need that, it was true that Lady Livienne hated it when Clementine and Citronella argued like children but then does nothing to stop them acting like children.

'Postulant Emily is a natural to work in one of our orphanages, and Postulant Alison, is destined to be a good teacher for the very young. However, times are changing,' said Sister Ann, 'we need young women with the management skills of the modern world to join us, to help us adapt to these changes.'

'My Father brought me up to be the manager of a large estate. I will have that estate to run, once my difficulties with my step-mother are resolved, I cannot abandon my duty to my people. I have a different vocation from my half-sisters.'

'I understand, Chantelle, my child,' said Sister Anne, as the car pulled off. 'During the in remissionis tempore we received a phone call from Reverend Mother Paula. It appears your aunt has been delayed for a few days, so you will travel with us to Tintagel, as our guest in the Secular Students' Quarters at the Mother-house until Mr. Franke makes new arrangements.'

'Ah! The reason I went to find you,' said Sister Maud apologetically, as this triggered her memory.

'Did she give you a reason?' Chantelle asked. 'Also, will I be expected to join in the prayers tonight?'

'I'm afraid not, Chantelle, we'll find out more when we arrive,' said Sister Maude. 'Our faith teaches respect for your sincere atheism. Tonight you shall sleep in a guest room, not the Novices Dormitory. When we are called to pray, you can turn around and go back to sleep.

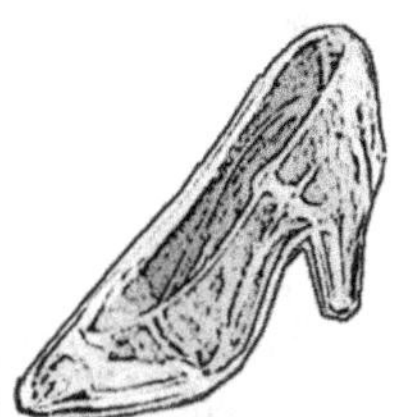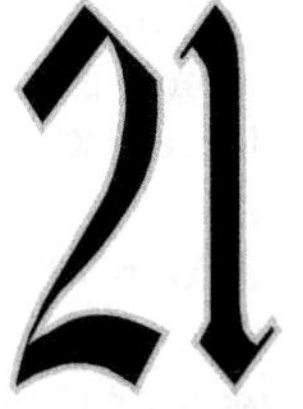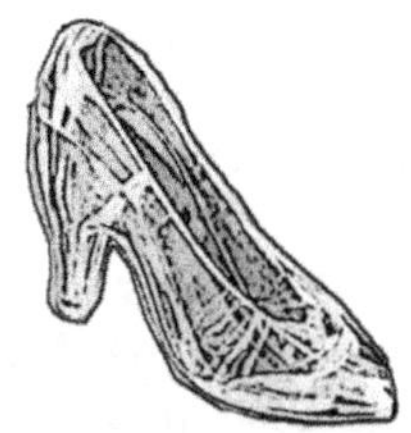

21

hilst Chantelle was praying in the priory in Bardi, drama was unfolding back at Zucca.

It was 5.20pm, the kids were shopping in Castelo, so she was the only person in the house and she was feeling dreadful. The knocking on the door, a continuous tapping was annoy her. She She suspected it was Livienne du Fauché so could not face that stupid woman again. I'm going to have to see a Doctor when I get to Belmont, she thought to herself.

She recognised the man in a tatty knee length tunic and hood with a ripped liripipe straight away. His beard was longer and peppered with grey, the years had not been kind to Ned Jenkins. Although considering his whacked out politics, he had probably been going out of his way to make the years as harsh as possible.

'Edward Jenkins. Now there's a face I hoped I would never see again,' she said, although common sense had forced her to keep track of his movements.

'Whore, child stealer and inferior creature, you have stolen my son from me. Denied my Angel given right to bring up my boy in the true ways of Anseris!' the man shouted at her.

'And a voice I never wanted to hear again. Get lost, you're not welcome in this house.'

'Whore, child stealer and inferior creature, by the Angels, you will make me welcome.' Edwin produced the knife, long and wicked sharp, which he pointed at Bronwen's liver.

'Oh, go away you stupid man.'

The knife slashed across Bronwen's midriff, slitting her tunic in half, but caused no bodily harm.

'Let me in, whore, or I will do more.'

'Will you stop calling me that,' said Bronwen as she took som
steps back letting the lunatic in at the same time.

'Well, you are wantonly displaying the shape of your body. Leavin
nothing to the imagination.'

Bronwen's outfit was a mixture of old and new, suitable for th
trip to Carlton. A pair of jeans and a tunic with flared sleeves tha
rich young men might have worn on Earth in fifteenth century Europ
but with minor anatomical adjustments, and no exposed skin or cleavag

'You always were an idiot, I used to wear trousers all the tim
when we were together on Pendragon Station, and dresses shorte
than your tunic. You didn't object then.'

'Sit there and shut up,' said Ned. She guessed he was losin
patiences, not good in his unstable condition, so she obeyed.

The house was fitted with the latest security system, one of th
first Anserian devices in over a century to be fitted with a psychi
interface. Bronwen tried to trigger an SOS.

'Now then, no witchcraft,' said Ned firmly, as he activated on
of the PI blocking devices that the superstitious were buying t
stop the march of progress.

'You're Fenzrian, you know it's not witchcraft.'

'I'm not, I'm Anserian, our people are now fully integrated,' sai
Ned, 'so I fully believe that the unnatural technology is the spawn c
the Twenty Hells. Once the False Queen is ousted and a true Anseria
Monarch placed on the throne, witchcraft will be outlawed again.'

'You know that is stupid, but you appear to have embraced th
stupid. And we are integrated, but old habits die hard.'

'Also, I don't want to be disturbed. We are not going to have a tal
I'm here to be listened to.' He sat down in a chair facing Bronwen.

'Well, I'm not listening so, you're wasting both time and oxygen.'

'You lied to me about my Son,' he said. 'I looked for him at the tim
he was born, records say he died at birth and you adopted an orphan.'

'What sort of fairy story is that, Ned?' Bronwen asked. 'The record
clearly show you are the biological father of my Son. You might hav
been a proper father if you had stayed on Pendragon Central and bee
part of his life. For the past fifteen years he has been exclusivel
"My Son" because you abandoned him.'

Thanks to Eileen there was no way anyone could retrieve the false record Ned had seen fifteen years earlier, any reference to it had been deleted. The much folded document Ned was shaking was worthless. When this was over, she would have to send her friend a big bunch of flowers to say thank you.

'I am his Father.'

'And you are just a buffoon. I carried him for nine months, I gave birth to him and protected him from his madman progenitor, who high-tailed it back to the Home-world to practice his insanity somewhere where it would not be interrupted. Only Holywall has that ridiculous law.'

'Holywall took our ancestors in. Allowed them to become Anserian, when we had only been components in the Devil's Machine. How dare you insult our Archduchy.'

'Because I've studied history. Queen Gertrude III gave us those freedoms. The Archduke of Holywall wanted us all killed. She forced him to accept us, and the Kingdom has benefited from our arrival.'

'You are trying to distract me. As an inferior woman, you should have handed my son over to me.'

Despite being bound in a chair by a madman with a knife, Bronwen had to laugh.

'Stop that at once, this is a serious matter!' Ned screamed at her.

'Shall we compare, oh superior one. I have a successful career as a Pathologist and have practised all over the Kingdom. You were struck off several years ago for gross incompetence and can't practice as a Dentist anywhere in the Kingdom. I was Professor of Pathology at Pendragon University for seven years. You are the leader of a fruitcake fringe political organisation. I have a steady income and own my own house.' She took a deep breath. 'You have no income and are dependent on the charity of your lunatic supporters. You live in the dilapidated ruin of the house you inherited from your parents, which you cannot afford to repair. Tell me now who is inferior?'

'You will always be inferior because you're female,' said Ned.

'You have beaten every woman you've known, except me, into submission. When I didn't help you form a perfect family back home, you finally did something about your daughter, who was five years old when we met. By the way, were you ever going to tell me about Elunud? She is Aneurin half-sister.'

'You didn't need to know about her,' said Ned.

'Of course not, she's just a woman who made a bad choice. Dumped by her boyfriend when she became pregnant. He was a bit like you, did a runner when parental responsiblities showed their face.'

'I took her back.'

'When you found out she had a baby boy. You got your Gwenerian thugs to steal her son and then turned her into a slave. Fortuntately she has escaped with little Billy, and is starting a new life in Carlton. You are barred by the courts from going within a mile of her or the child.'

'Shut your mouth, you lying whore!' he stood up and put the knife to Bronwen's throat. 'When the boy returns, he shall see me kill you, before I kill him.'

Aneurin walked into the kitchen and was horrified by what he saw. A wild eyed crazy man was standing with a knife to his mother's throat. He was carrying three bags of shopping, and was closely followed by Madeleine with two bags. The man turned to face Aneurin, taking the knife from his mother's throat and pointing it at him. Aneurin swung the bags upwards, knocking the weapon from the man's hands and it landed noisily on the floor. Dropping the bags, Aneurin took the advantage and punched into the man's stomach. The blow was fumbled, and the man caught Aneurin's arm and twisted him around.

'You know it is a sin to strike your Father, Boy,' said the madman.

'Well, I sin again,' said Aneurin, as he brought his right leg up, connecting with the man's groin, who tripped over a shopping bag as he stumbled backwards. On the floor, the man tried to grab the fallen knife. Madeleine kicked it away and stamped his hand.

'You'll pay for that, trollop,' said the man.

'I'd love to know how,' said Madeleine, as she kicked him in the belly. 'Nobody calls me trollop and gets away with it.'

She did not see the flailing arm coming towards her. A hand connected with Madeleine's ankle. Down she went, like a sack of spuds. Aneurin tried to catch her and both fell over, which gave

Ned the time to roll out of the way and pick up the knife, thus regaining the advantage.

Erik Franke did not know what made him cross the street to visit the the Tudor household, but he was glad that he had. Instead of finding the occupants busily packing for their trip to Belmont, he found Lady Madeleine and young Master Aneurin cowering in one corner of the living room, whilst a man was ranting in the middle of the room, holding Mistress Tudor firmly by the waist, with a knife sitting threateningly close to her throat.

'Dr. Edward Jenkins,' said Erik firmly, 'I advise you to release Mistress Bronwen immediately.

'Why should I release this bitch. She needs to be punished for her criminality,' said the man.

'At the moment, the only person acting with criminal intent is your good self,' replied Erik affably, then with more steel, 'An' if you try t' harm one hair on that lady's 'ead, I'll rip yer brozhnik 'ead off before ya can do anythin', ya piece of shite.' All pretence at civility had vanished. 'So chuck the knife and back off from the lady with your hands up.'

'I know you wouldn't do that. You respect the Fraud Queens fake laws to much.'

'Thank the Angels you're here, Mr. Franke,' said Bronwen. 'He burst in spouting all sorts of crazy stuff.'

'Shut up whore,' screamed Ned. 'Only a whore would wear such suggestive clothing and allow other whores to do the same in her house.'

'He keeps saying that as well. It was boring after the first half hour,' said Aneurin. 'Am I really that nutter's son.'

'You see, the bitch has turned my son against me.'

'E's been 'ere fer ova' alf an' 'our, an' not actually done 'owt?

'More or less,' replied Aneurin.

For such a large man, Erik had a remarkable turn of speed. In a blur, Bronwen was free and the man was holding Ned Jenkins in a neck brace. 'Which means e never wuz go'n ter do nowt. 'e's all bluster' Then more formally Erik said, 'Which means, by the powers vested in me, by her most Anserian Majesty, Queen Johanna III, I arrest you, Dr. Edward Gwylim Aberpumnant Jenkins, on the following charges. First, breaching the Queen's Peace and acting in a manner intended to cause injury to other human beings, to wit holding Mistress Bronwen Myfanwy Cenerentola Tudor with a blade to her neck. Second, the false imprisonment of Master Aneurin Edward Pendthree Tudor and Lady Madeleine Angharad Cenerentola du Fauché. Third, conspiring to murder the three above mentioned individuals. Fourth, trespass. You have the right to remain silent, but anything you do say will be taken down and may be used as evidence against you in a court of law.' The handcuffs appeared, as if by magic and clicked into place, as Erik showed his warrant card to Ned Jenkins.

'She stole my son from me. Filled his head with lies.'

'You didn't know he existed until today,' said Madeleine, 'you told us that enough times.'

'He is making his claim based on so called Gwenerian Law. It has no validity there or anywhere else in the Archduchy of Holywall, let alone the Kingdom.

'Gwenerian Law is based on natural law. No woman should have any rights because they don't have fully developed brains. They always need a male guardian to make decisions for them,' screamed Ned.

'Dear sweet Angels,' said Erik, 'even the late King Benedict III, a notorious misogynist thought they were over the top.'

'I have failed my son, by not going to Pendragon and removing him from that inferior creature,' Ned wailed.

Aneurin heard none of this, Erik could see the boy phoning the police, and not having much joy. 'Master Aneurin, tell the officer on the other end that, this is an OTH Code A5-2017. Then put the phone on speaker.'

The boy did so. Erik could hear well organised panic once the Duty Sergeant at the other end of the line looked up OTH Code A5-2017, 'and then, 'We have dispatched a police vehicle to your address, it will be there in five minutes.'

'Good,' said Erik said to the Duty Sergeant, 'and send a medic at the same time lad. The victim is a little shook up.'

our mother has had a bit of a shock,' said the Paramedics from a rapid response vehicle. 'I have given her a sedative and Lady Madeleine is sitting with her. I recommend she stays in bed for the next forty eight hours.

'But we're driving to Belmont tomorrow,' said Aneurin, in an unexpectedly high pitched voice.

'I wouldn't recommend travel for the next seventy two hours. Give your mother chance to rest. If she really must travel, I advise she takes the high speed sleeper train from Castello del Filippo to Tintagel and then a taxi to Belmont. The journey will be much quicker and a lot more comfortable.'

'Help! It's my Aunt, she's having a fit.' Madeleine shouted from the top of the stairs.

The two men ran back up to their patient. One applying a medical scanner, the other applying the medicinal patch, it recommended, to Bronwen's arm.

'Romeo Romeo Victor three niner, requesting an ambulance immediately. Priority A1.'

'Copy that Romeo Romeo Victor 3-9er, ambulance on its way,' said a calm voice on the radio.

The patch had stopped his mother shaking, but she was still breathing heavily. A Paramedic put an oxygen mask over her mouth and a normal rhythm was restored. Aneurin watched her, praying under his breath until he could hear a siren.

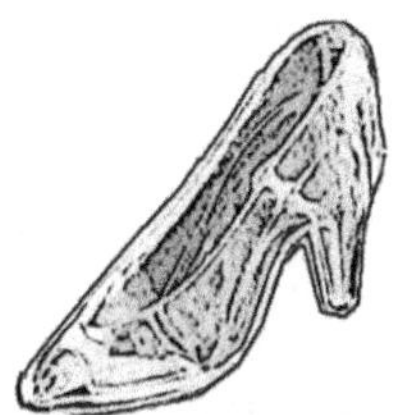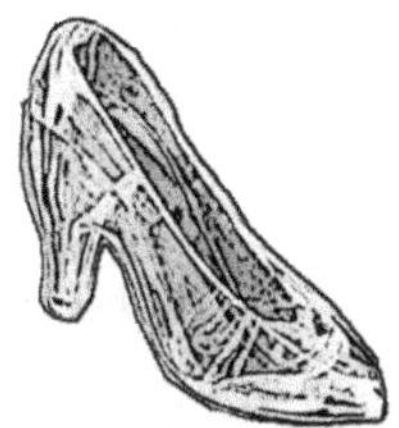

22

Infamous behaviour is remembered in different ways. Marcus Junius Brutus is the villain of a Shakespearean play. On Anseris, it is incorrectly believed Benedict Arnold, the turncoat in the American Revolution, created Eggs Benedict. Also on Anseris, the name of Otto Brozhnik survives in infamy as an expletive amongst all classes.

'I wonder what William Shakespeare would have made of Otto Brozhnik?' Aneurin asked Janek and Jadwiga. They had studied Macbeth as part of their Tertiary Certificate.

'I don't think he would pay the story much attention, he has covered that scenario in Julius Caesar,' said Janek.

'Do you think that the Immortal Empress preserved the works of Shakespeare to torture people in their final year in school?' Aneurin asked his friend, who had just sat the same examination.

'No, even she wasn't that evil,' said Janek.

'I like Shakespeare,' said Jadwiga.

'You would,' said her brother, staring out to sea.

'He was a genius. Shakespeare might have lived four thousand years ago but he has wise words to cover every situation. That's why Queen Kathyren preserved his works while junking so much of the rest of Earth's Literature.' She laughed, 'No, Queen Kathyren preserved Jane Austen to torture teenagers.'

The three youngsters were sitting on the edge of the ferry jetty at Zucca, on the continental side of the narrow strait and opposite the harbour were the Cenerentola fishing fleet lay at anchor.

Janek had hired Stefano Monteleone, a lobster fisherman to take them power-snorkelling. Janek had persuaded Aneurin to take a day off from his vigil at his Mother's bedside and Jadwiga had done the same with Madeleine. Aunt Bronwen was stable but unconscious and likely to remain that way for weeks. When she came around, she would be far from well and would need her Son and Niece's support.

Janek had heard about the species of oysters that lived in the water off the reef on the southern side of Cenerentola Island. None of the local fishermen could recognise them. Pearls had always been a favourite of his. Perhaps he could identify them and find a new source of interesting pearls for the Jewellers of Elizaburg.

'His story does have all the elements of a Shakespearian drama. Old Otto appeared to be the Earl Andrew Rushton-Browne's greatest ally, but he was recruited by the Immortal Empress to betray him. That would be the first act,' said Jadwiga, as the ferry left the island.

'The seduction and murder of Countess Rachel would make up the Second Act.' said Aneurin.

'Oh is it my turn?' asked Janek.

'Yes, hurry up, the ferry is halfway across the channel,' said his sister.

'So the Boatbuilder's exile and escape is the third act. With a nice soliloquy as he is sailing the boat he built back to Tintagel.'

'No Janek, your letting your obsession with the Navy cloud your thinking. This is about Otto, not the Boatbuilder,' Jadwiga said to her brother.

'Oh, I see. So Act 3 is the first betrayal, the trial and Otto working behind the scenes against the Boatbuilder.'

'Earl Andrew Rushton-Browne is universally known as The Boatbuilder, but I doubt he ever hammered a nail into a piece of wood,' said Aneurin, who was sceptical about the legend.

'But he knew about ship building, and united the exiles on the Lonely Islands, forming an army that would overthrow Queen Kathyren. He persuaded them to build the ship that got them back to Civilisation,' said Jadwiga. 'After he won, he just became another Archduke Rushton-Browne, he could have vanished into obscurity, but his legend lives on, as the Boatbuilder.'

'well Act four, the battle for Ellisford Castle, and the final fight between Brozhnik and the Boatbuilder. The the Final act to tie up all the loose ends,' said Aneurin.

'Except historically, Otto never met the Immortal Empress, and always was a spy,' said Jadwiga.

'Dramatic licence,' said her brother. 'It's why Otto Brozhnik was and still is regarded as the greatest traitor in Anserian history.'

'Rightly so, he wasn't just betraying the Boatbuilder, he was betraying the planet to death by starvation if he had succeeded,' said Jadwiga. 'Which is why his name is now a swear word.'

The ferry had arrived and the conversation stopped. Aneurin and Janek were fascinated by the mechanics of the ferry, so sat by Chief. Franchini, watching him operate the ferry.

'So what is the difference between a ship and a boat anyway,' asked Jadwiga, who had always lived a long way from the sea.

'A boat can be carried on a ship. A ship cannot be carried on a boat,' said Chief Franchini, 'its just a matter of size.'

'Well Rating Smitz, What are you doing here? You've signed the pledge. Why aren't you at a training base somewhere right now,' asked Chief Franchini.

Aneurin knew by spending so much time on the Island, every single detail of their life was becoming public knowledge in its small community.

'Not yet, my dad did two years in the Army when there was Compulsory Military Service, and hated every second of it. He did everything he could think of to stop me signing up. Now I'm too old for him to interfere.'

'I did my stint with the Navy, and then stayed on for another twelve years. It made a man of me. It'll make a man of you.'

The short trip on the ferry passed in silence. When it arrived at Cenerentola, Madeleine, who had been visiting friends on the Island, was waiting for them.

'Do you love a man in uniform?' Jadwiga asked her, 'apparently all girls do.'

'It's the codpiece,' Madeleine replied, 'such a shame its contents are so disappointing when it's removed.'

'Lady Madeleine, that is unbecoming for a young lady,' said Chief Franchini who was laughing, 'but funny as hell.'

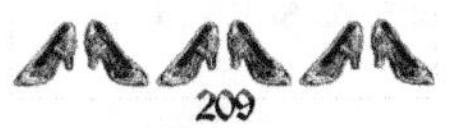

'𝔜ou don't think I take my diving parties out in my fishing boat, do you?' Stefano Monteleone's diving boat was a sleek and modern wind turbine driven vessel. Not what everyone was expecting.

'I didn't know what to expect. 'Rating Smitz over there arranged it,' said Aneurin.

'You'd better get used to it Rating Smitz,' said Stefano, 'I'm still known as Able Seaman Monteleone around here, even though I left the Navy ten years ago. You know news travels by telepathy. Apart from your sister, Rating Smitz, whose called you Janek or Master Smitz around here? Your social standing will go a-shootin' up when you properly start basic training. Not that you'll be here to notice it.'

'There's something you're not telling me, isn't there?' asked his sister as soon as she heard Monteleone's comment. It explained so much. 'Come on Janek, spill the beans.'

'Thanks Stefano, I was a-tryin' to keep it quiet,' said Janek.

'You mean you haven't told her Janek?' asked Stefano.

'Told me what? Tell me the truth. As Mother says, start at the begining and don't leave anything out. I will find out by other means.'

'Old man du Pré had a chat with me on Monday morning, he said my heart wasn't in this internship, and I explained why. He reminded me all Juvenile Reservists resident in Fiandre are still legally oblidged to report for enlistment within a month of their eighteenth birthday. It's the only Archduchy that still does this. Not that I need reminding. He even drove me to the recruiting centre outside Castello. Everyone is as obsessed with the Navy as I am in this Archduchy.'

'But your not from Zucca, or anywhere else in Fiandre,' she said.

'No, but I was in Fiandre on my birthday. As planned. Why do you think I agreed to the placement here? Then I apologised for using his company to get around my parents. But he said he approved of what I did.'

'You've not been on that field trip have you?' asked his sister.

'No. I've be with the other recruits at Castello. In my uniform I look like a proper sailor. I transfer to Gibralterra on Monday, to start proper basic training,' he said with a big smile on his face. 'They gave me a weekend pass, to say goodbye properly.'

'Don't you dare, Janek Axlbrandt Orlov Smitz, don't you dare,' he could see his sister had worked out the consequences. 'Don't leave me alone with our Mother for a fortnight. She arrives on Tuesday. Can't you wait until after she's gone home. It's only a fortnight.

'That's 47-D-62 Rating Smitz, Janek, Ma'am,' he said, a grin spreading across his face. 'I hadn't thought of that.'

'You're a sailor now, not a comedian,' said Jadwiga.

'Yes, I suppose I am.'

'No, he'll just look like one until he passes out after his basic training,' said Stefano, but nobody was paying him any attention.

'But two weeks alone with Mother.'

'Come on Sis, Dad will be there.'

'Rating Smitz, when has that ever stopped her,' Jadwiga said, an air of desperation in her voice. 'And dad will be mad too.'

'Sorry, Jadzie,' said Janek, 'it's a done deal. Nothing I can do about it, Ma'am. Duty Calls. Besides, Maddy and Nye aren't going anywhere, you don't have to spend much time with our parents.'

'You ratfink,' said Jadwiga.

'Anyway shipmates, lets get out there and do some diving,' said Stefano Monteleone, trying to avoid a family argument. 'You girls won't have been snorkelling before.'

'I have, with Imogen and Carlo, last year, in the High Tarn above Ellisford Castle. It was a lot colder there, but utterly fascinating,' said Jadwiga, unaware her answer should have been no. It had been one of the sports illegal for ordinary women just a week earlier.

'I haven't either,' said Aneurin, 'Born and raised on a Space Habitat.'

'Well, this is slightly more complicated than the old style of snorkelling, but a lot simpler than scuba diving. You'll have these tanks. It's quite simple, you fill and pressurise your tanks with these pumps. When you swim, you have this regulator in your mouth which you breath with. Don't go too deep, because it's compressed air not pure oxygen, and you only have ten minutes underwater time. Right, the new changing rooms on the left for the ladies, the one on right for us lads.'

The boat had arrived at the dive site. They had pressurised their tanks, and changed into swimming costumes. Stefano Monteleone's eyes bulged, when he saw the two women. He was used to the baggy female bathing suits with frilly hats, women wore on the rare occassions they went swimming in public. Once he got his composure back, they all jumped into the warm, crystal clear water of the Mare di Napoli.

Janek was not interested in the fish. He was fascinated by the imposibility of the oysters that grew in great numbers on the side of the reef devoid of all other aquatic life.

'They can't be what I think they are,' Janek signalled to Stefano using the naval diver's sign language he had learned as a child. 'They can't be Bolar Oysters.'

'So you do recognise them then?' Stefano signalled. They both knew that was not possible. Bolars are a fresh water species and as rare as hell.

Stefano knew Bolar Oysters produce the most beautiful blue pearls. Unlike normal pearls, their surface is made up of hundreds of irregular octagonal facets. They were really popular in expensive Avatars.

'There's thousands of the oysters there.'

The alarm sounded and they had to return to the surface.

The boat was bobbing gently up and down on the azure water of the Sea of Naples. Its single columnar turbine turning lazily in the breeze, charging the batteries that would power the journey back to Cenerentola. The diving gear had been cleaned and stowed away and now the boat's occupants were lying under a canopy on the deck drying themselves out after their dive.

'Of course,' said Stefano, 'diving up north in the waters of the Sunken Continent is fascinating.'

'You have to be properly certified with scuba equipment for that sort of diving,' said Janek, with a touch of envy in his voice.

'True. I did that in the Navy. For five years I was a diver.'

'In the Navy and paid to dive? Were you in God's pocket?'

'Just about Janek. Until the brass decided I was too old to do regular dives. They wanted to transfer me to a desk job on a shore base. So

I took the opportunity to retire and move here, to catch lobsters and dive.'

'I've never understood how you can sink a continent,' said Maddy. 'I mean, it's not as if they could put a big hole in the side and watch it go glugging down into the depth.

'There are two ways of looking at it,' said Nye. 'In the bad old days of Queen Kathyren, we were all taught that with the Angels she defeated the Demons by flooding the world. It drown the Demons City and made Anseris safe for humans.'

'Which is a load of old brozhnik,' said Stefano. 'Nobody believes the fairy story the Church of the Undying Queen told any more. Or their pathetic attempt to make us all forget how we really came to Anseris.'

'Which brings us to the second way of looking at it,' said Nye, continuing where he left off. 'The creatures, we now call the Angels discovered this world. Once it had an atmosphere and seas which over time it lost when the planet nearly stopped spinning.'

'With no gravity, there was nothing to stop it bubbling off into space,' said Stefano.

'Exactly. I don't know how they did it, but the Angels remelted the planetary core and started the world spinning again. Then set about restoring the Atmosphere.' Nye was now on a roll. 'But they got their sums wrong. The old atmosphere was Carbon Monoxide and Nitrogen, to get the perfect mix of Oxygen and Nitrogen, they needed to import more water, and so the old Northern Continents are on average twenty to sixty feet below Sea Level. The Lonely Islands were on a highland plateau cut in three by the new sea level and the Islands of the Sunken Continent were the tallest mountains on pre-Aggelii Anseris.'

'Which is what makes diving in those waters so fascinating,' said Stefano longingly. 'Imagining all the towns, villages and farms that could have been in the flooded valleys and larger areas of flat sea bed.'

'The Angels got a breathable atmosphere, but the weather was all over the shop,' said Nye, 'It still is in the North.'

'We rely on their weather control equipment, down South, to produce something we can live in,' said Madeleine.

'The weather up North isn't that bad,' said Janek

'Yes it is,' said Stefano, 'as you'll soon be finding out, Rating Smitz.'

'Please stop calling me that, I haven't earned the right.'

'Right ladies, you'd better get changed before we arrive back a Cenerentola Village.'

'This has been a great day, Stefano, Janek and all of you,' said Nye.

'So where do you think Chantelle is hiding?' Janek asked Madeleine, who had changed into a traditional dress when the women returned to the open deck.

'Well, she's not in the Priory, or the Orphanage,' she replied. 'Mother had the Crown Police search both buildings, because the Priory is the last place she was seen.'

'And the Merciful Sisters let them?' asked Stefano, who had been raised in the Orphanage.

'Oh yes, they were more than helpful,' said Madeleine.

'The Ugly Sisters know something. I mean the twins,' said Nye.

'They would have cracked under Mother's interrogation,' said Madeleine, 'but as the Twins no longer live at Cenerentola House the secret will be preserved.

'I'll tell you who does know, and isn't telling,' said Nye.

'Who?' he was asked in unison.

'Erik Franke.'

'Chief Inspector Erik Franke, of the Royal Bodyguard?' asked Stefano. 'I remember he tried to recruit me. To check for bombs and the like planted on bridges. I thought I saw him around and about.'

'No, Sergeant Franke, my minder,' said Jadwiga, trying to sound completely innocent, and not fooling anyone on board.

'He's no Sergeant,' said Stefano.

'OK, keep it under your hat. It's supposed to be a secret,' said Jadwiga

'A military secret?' asked Stefano.

'Yes, Able Seaman Monteleone, a military secret,' said Jadwiga. 'Classified by the Queen, herself.'

'OK, Ma'am, consider it firmly under my hat.'

'But I don't understand what freshwater oysters are doing growing in the sea?' asked Janek, after they had returned to dry land.

'That water be as sweet and salt free as you can have,' replied Stefano. 'The underwater cliffs where them oysters live ain't made of coral. It be exposed section of Island rock, full of salt extractors. Creates a pocket of fresh water big enough for them oysters to grow.'

It was a question Jadwiga had wanted to ask, but she was too busy climbing up the ladder on the jetty in an impractical skirt. She was going with her friends to see Stephano's collection of pearls.

'Why are there so many of them,' asked Madeleine a few minutes later. She had spotted an egg-shaped pearl.

'Them oysters are generally ignored by the fishermen,' said Stefano. 'The meat is poisonous because them oysters is full of the bacteria. And the fishermen reckon the pearls are worthless.'

'Worthless,' said Janek, after he had seen the rest of the collection of Bolar Pearls. Opulent blue in the square facets, blue with flashes of green and yellow lustre in the larger octagonal facets. 'Each spherical pearl is worth at least fifty krona. The three egg shaped ones about ten krona each.'

'How much? I used to be a-throwin' them oysters away, like everyone else does. It's only by accident I started a-collectin' them. Good job I didn't sell them to the Commander, when he did a couple of dives with me. He wanted to buy them all for seven shillings.'

'Did he indeed,' said Janek. 'Why didn't you sell them?'

'Regardless what that Commander said, they all legally belonged to the Commune. At the time Baron Gilbert had the Seigneur's shares which gave him three votes in the Commune. So he controlled what we can sell. He only wanted one vote, same as everyone else, when the Commune was set up. Like we was ever gonna let that happen.'

'I see,' said Jadwiga. How typically rural, she thought, letting centuries of feudal deference torpedo the late Baron's attempt at egalitarianism. 'Who controls what you sell now?'

'Baroness Chantelle. She inherited her dad's three votes.'

'Pardon?' said Madeleine, a question and exclamation in one word.'

'Yes, your Ladyship,' said Stefano, becoming strangely formal. 'She is the rightful holder of the title now, until her first born son reaches the age of seventeen.'

'Try telling my Mother that,' said Madeleine, 'she'll fight to the death to keep that title.'

'We heard what Mistress Bronwen, his mam, had to say about the genetic evidence,' said Stefano, 'We was ready to go a-stormin' Cenerentola House, to liberate our true Baroness and punish the usurper. Then our true Baroness did that vanishing act.'

'Well, it's a good job you didn't,' Jadwiga said. 'Chantelle might have appreciated your support, but it would have made her case in court so much harder.'

'Oh, I see. I'll tell the Lads to lay off, if Baroness Chantelle reappears.'

'Not if, Steffano, but when,' said Madeleine.

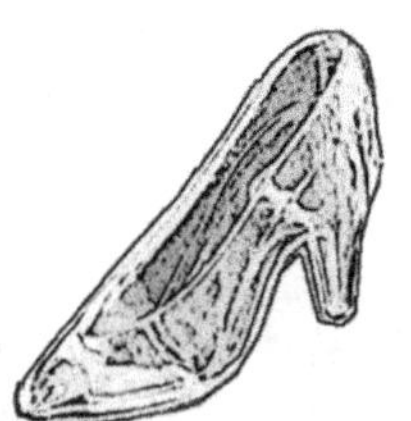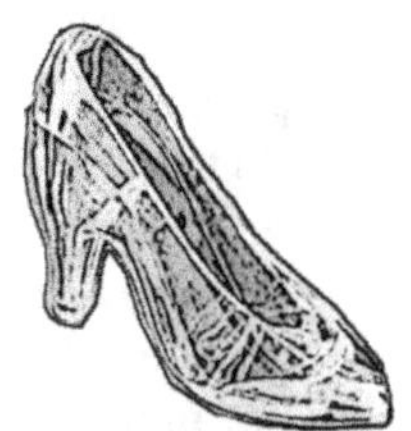

23

'**C**ousin Chantelle,' said the middle aged Merciful Sister who greeted Chantelle at the entrance to the Secundo Quartam building. Chantelle had said her goodbyes to her travelling companions. The two older Merciful Sisters were breaking their journey for a week, before they would would continue with their journey by, taking a plane to Baaden Spitz on the Northern Continent.

Senior Novice Olivia had just been introduced to her fellow final year novices in the Secundo Quartam building. She was now busy with them preparing for their big day.

'Sister Vera, it is nice to see you again. Is it really ten years?' Her cousin was Quartum Princep, the head of this building

'The years have flown. I remember your stay here as a fourteen year old banished any notions you might have had of joining the Order. Exactly what your Father, Angels give him rest, wanted. He didn't approve of the religious life.'

'He was never very keen on any aspect of religion. But he was open minded and allowed me to develop my own views on religion. Of course, adopting his atheist world-view pleased him, but it was my decision. I'm not sure how he would have reacted to my escape from Fiandre, pretending to be a novice.'

'Your Father was a man of principles, but he was also a pragmatist. He would have accepted it as a temporary measure.'

'Have you any news from Zucca?' asked Chantelle.

'I'm afraid your Aunt is currently in Hospital after being infected with Cuthbert's Syndrome. She is likely to remain for several weeks. Reverend Mother Paula has spoken with Mr. Franke and they agree it would be safer if you remained under our protection for a few more weeks. After Ellisford Castle and the Queen's Prisons, there is no safer place in the Kingdom. Getting in or out after sunset is impossible much to the annoyance of our secular students. You won't get bored so many lectures you can attend.

They walked across a courtyard into another buildingher own.

'This is Sister Monique, the Quartam Princeps here in Tertia Quartam, my equivalent. She runs teacher training for Secular Students and their accomodation here. She will be your host, if you stayed in my Quartam you would have to live as a novice in a dormitory.

'Sister Monique, so nice to see you again.' Chantelle recognised the other woman, who had been a secretary at the Angelbless Maternity Hospital when Chantelle was born. She was one of the few former colleagues from the hospital Granny Gladys had any time for, certainly the only one she called a friend. They had met during Chantelle's previous stay here at Tintagel.

'You'll probably see more of me than her,' said Sister Monique 'She is moving soon, Baaden Spitz to establish the new Continental Headquarters Convent there.'

'Like the ones at Paris, in Gingerwall,' said Chantelle.

'That's right.' Sister Monique took a long look at Chantelle.

'You were raised by my good friend Gladys Simples, I'm surprised you have not followed the family tradition? There is an excellent midwifery course at Tintagel General.'

'I have thought of it,' said Chantelle, 'bringing new life safely into this world is a noble profession, but one I happily to leave to others I'd rather be a teacher. However, I have to follow my real family's tradition, managing the family estates in Fiandre.'

'I thought Cousin Gilbert had arranged for you to study History at Elizaburg University?' asked her cousin.

'Yes, but when I graduated I would have returned to Cenerentola. An university education was designed to make me a more rounded individual and better manager,' said Chantelle.

'This might sound odd, coming from a nun, but don't let the tradition weigh you down,' said her Cousin, 'you should be yourself what you want to be, not what people expect you to be.'

'Happy Birthday, Cousin Stan,' Reverend Mother Paula said. 'It's not my Birthday, Cousin Felicia,' he replied, 'and you never ring me on my real birthday. In fact, you never ring me at all, let alone at Midnight. So what do you want?'

'I hear you're having difficulty locating someone called Chantelle du Fauché?'

'Yes, she disappeared of her own accord, before I could make her disappear along with her bothersome family,' said Silvermann morosely. He knew Chantelle's awful stepmother was looking for his Reg Payntor persona. It would be a fruitless search.'

'Well, she's here in Tintagel. Her cousin is Cardinal Sisters Vera, who arranged to smuggle her out of Fiandre under the protection of the Order. I know she did this because Sister Vera had to ask my permission first, as I am supreme head of the Order of the Merciful Sisters of Charity. I diverted her here. I knew you would want that.'

'Is this Sister Vera the colleague you're moving up north. The one who thinks you are cooking the books?'

'I'm not cooking the books,' said Reverend Mother Paula in disgust.

'No,' said Silvermann jokingly. 'It is high class cuisine. So, are you going to hand Chantelle over to me?'

'Everything I do is honest and above board. Sister Vera is ideally suited to establishing a new First-Daughter-House for the Northern Continent. Anyway, my loyalty to the Family has to be tempered by my loyalty to the Order. I said, she is under to Order's protection. I can't just hand her over to you, so you can kill her,' said Reverend Mother Paula.

'So you just phoned me to gloat,' said Silvermann as Reverend Mother Paula took a breath. 'As it happens, I'm not going to kill her. Cousin Alfred used to make people disappear if the Chessmen found them to valuable to kill. He will give her a new set of memories, a new identity and a new life, in one of my brothels on the new Jovian Barony on the seventh moon of Atlantis.'

'I'll be checking with Cousin Alfred. He's currently running an asylum for geriatric lunatics a few miles from the Order's Mother House,' said Reverend Mother Paula. 'If you are lying, I will not be happy. Don't forget, I can make your life difficult from in here, and you cannot reach me to do the same to mine.'

'I've just had a better idea,' said Silvermann. 'Forget Atlantis Seven. Leave her stew in your place.'

'No! I have tolerate filthy Fenzrians witches in this order, if they have a genuine vocation,' said Mother Paula, exposing her prejudice. 'I'm not accepting an atheist half-witch who as been brainwashed into thinking she has a calling.'

'A celibate Fenzrian, by definition, cannot reproduce.'

'Good point, well put. We're not the only female religious order. The Dutiful Sisters, the enclosed order, have a horrible windswept convent on the Lonely Islands. You make the arrangements for her to be collected and re-educated. I will persuade my sisters in religion from that Order to accept Chantelle du Fauché as a novice there,' said Mother Paula.

'So, she'll be collected from you by someone from the local Crown Police Station. The Family owns in those coppers. Thank you, Cousin,' said Silverman.

Chantelle woke up. She was in the warm comfortable bed she had been sleeping in for the past few weeks. She was regreting drinking so much tea with Sister Vera last night. Her cousin would be on a flight to Baaden-Spitz by now.

She swung her legs over the edge of the bed and used her toes to find her slippers.

'When I get my brown veil, I'm going to get a plush carpet,' she said as she sunk her feet into the carpet of her secular student's room. She was mimicking what Sister Vera said was a favourite saying amongst the Novices. A full Sisters had a room. The novices slept in servere dormitories. Chantelle had recently experienced three of them as Novice Myfanwy, and understood why novices said that.

Despite being able to furnish and decorate their cell, an ordinal sister's home remained modest. Even Cardinal Sister Vera's room just comfortable, her memory cheated. Of course, they were all far from the austere cell a Medieaval nun on ancient Earth.

Although anything was currently a more attractive career choice than mangaging the family estate. Sister Vera's words had revealed a truth that Chantelle had been denying.

'Angels, that stupid dream,' she said to herself, as she remembered her recurring nightmare's details. It began with her kneeling next to Sister Olivia, receiving a brown veil then cut to a schoolroom far away, where she was the elderly teacher, repeating over and over, 'They never came back for me.'

The details were clear, their meaning was opaque. What in all the twenty hells were Payntor and her step-mother were doing officiating at the ceremony. 'Oh Angels,' she said to herself, 'I hope the stupid women hasn't gone looking for Reg Payntor, who had started the lie about me not being the daughter of Gilbert du Fauché.' Despite everything bad that woman had done to her, Chantelle was now worried about her step-mother's safety.

The bell for Vigil rang in the Basilica Tower. It was just 1.50am. The Novices and one of the Quartem woke now. Soon they would start singing as they headed the first service of the day. The rest of the Merciful Sisters, were woken at 5.30am, for an hour silent meditation before Lauds. Chantelle returned to her comfortable bed. In her atheist opinion, going to church, to pray to aliens everyone now knew were not the messengers of the divine, was pointless. Going to church at 2am and 6am was ridiculous.

Bronwen had been awake for three minutes, finding herself in a bed surrounded by equipment. She hated being in hospital. She especially hated it when she did not know why she was there. She felt so weak.

The last thing she remembered was being in her kitchen, watching Erik Franke wrestle Ned Jenkins to the ground and handcuffing him.

'Don't move, Mistress Tudor,' said the nurse who came into the room. 'You're still extremely weak.'

Bronwen recognised the woman, Staff Nurse Dania Alfredson. Something was wrong. She was wearing the new dark blue scrubs the hospital board was buying for all its senior female nursing staff. A passing junior nurse was wearing light blue scrubs. Neither colour were being issued until the beginning of Augusta, but the outfits had all lost the initial starchiness of brand new clothing.

'How long was I unconscious? A Month, longer?' Bronwen asked.

Dear Angels, her voice was hoarse, it was also barely a whisper. Not surprising, a feeding tube had been inserted up her nose then down her throat. Bronwen could tell by the embarrassed way Nurse Dania had mumbled about fetching a doctor that she had been accurate about her guess.

'Mistress Tudor,' said Doctor Vincent who was wearing the purple scrubs for doctors instead of the old traditional outfit, 'you have been unconscious for six weeks. You had a severe attack of Cuthbert Syndrome, one of the worse we have ever encountered in someone born on the Home-world.'

'Cuthbert Syndrome? That normally only effects people born in space, who rarely come down into the gravity well,' Bronwen said, wishing she had the strength to lift herself off the bed. 'Oh Angel's, what about Aneurin, he's much more likely to get it than me. He was born in space.'

'Don't worry, he hasn't been affected. He wasn't deliberately infected,' said the familiar voice of Erik Franke. 'I'm afraid one of the White Hand nutters had a job at the Pendragon hospital. You got your pre-flight jabs at work, from her, Aneurin got his from a GP. This nutter messed with the 'flu' inoculations she processed for Fenzrians returning to Home-world. The jabs were laced with live Cuthbert Syndrome bacteria. At least two hundred and forty cases have been reported, twenty three of them fatal.'

'Why would anyone do that?' asked Doctor Vincent.

'There's a new law that abolishes the distinction between Earth origin Anserians and Fenzrian Asteroids origin Anserians. We're all plain Anserians now. They were making one last crazy gesture before the law takes affect. Anyway, the woman will be prosecuted and while I don't normally agree with the death penalty, I'm glad she will soon be taking a long walk out of a short airlock,' Erik said.

She did not hear the two men leave the room. Bronwen could not help herself, she let out a mighty yawn, and immediately dropped to sleep.

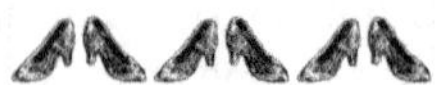

'Nice to see you awake, love. You gave us a real fright,' said Annie Bowen, standing at the bottom of Bronwen's bed. 'Young Maddy and Nye were doing their best, bless 'em. But they needed help. So the Island Women's Guild was happy to step in.'

The Island Women's Guild was the social group that all the older women of Cenerentola and many from Zucca belonged to. "Self-help and Solidarity" was its motto. Some saw it as community in action, others as a bunch of interfering busy-bodies. Bronwen's Mother had been a member, and if she had stayed at home she would be a member. After this she would definitely join.

'Aunty Annie, thank you.'

'Don't be silly, cariad, only to glad to help. Now, the doctor says you don't need that nasty old surgical gown any more. Although I couldn't find a clean nightdress for you in any of your cupboards. So I bought some for you in Zucca. The Guild will keep your nighties clean while your in here.'

'But Aunty Annie, I don't...' Bronwen didn't have chance to say she would be quite happy with the pyjamas she had slept in for years.

'Mammy!' said Aneurin as he entered the room. Bronwen had not heard him greet her that way, with a squeal of approval, since he was eight years old.

'Hello, darling boy.' She knew normally Aneurin hated being called that. Today he didn't care. 'I'm so glad to see you. Where's Maddy?'

'Maddy's here,' said a familiar voice, but not a familiar look. Her hair was considerably shorter, now. Shoulder length and worn down. She was wearing a city style dress, with a a mid-calf pencil skirt and a single breasted jacket.

'My Dad would've whipped me if I had shown that much flesh in public,' said Annie, dressed in hundred percent traditional style.

'I've brought your ebook reader, some actual books,' said Madeleine, ignoring Annie Bowen's comment, 'some toiletries and other things you will need. I don't think either Granma Annie or I have missed anything.'

'Maddy has been staying with me and Nye has been staying with the Hopkins. It didn't seem decent that they should be staying unchaperoned under the same roof.'

Obviously, Madeleine had been living with Annie Bowen and her family for a number of weeks, as the older woman talked about her as if she was one of her ever growing brood of grandchildren, not as Lady Madeleine, from the big house.

'Granma Annie has said I can stay with her until Chantelle returns home. Then I'll move back into Cenerentola House.' She laughed, 'Mama would be horrified at me living like a villager. But she's moved back to Elizaburg permanently.'

Horrified to hear you sounding like one too, thought Bronwen.

'The house is empty now the Twins are now Postulant Merciful Sisters, in the convent in Ponte di Carla,' said Aneurin.

'I really have been out for six weeks,' said Bronwen.

'I'm afraid so, cariad,' said Annie Bowen.

'I suppose the Smitz have gone home?'

'Yes mam. Well Jadwiga has, went back to Ellisford Castle on her own, after a monuemental blue with her parents. Janek is now halfway through basic training at Gibilterra Naval Base.'

'Granma Annie has some news, don't you,' said Madeleine.

'Don't you think we should let your Aunt sleep now, cariad?' asked Annie Bowen. 'We've given her more than enough news to be going on with.'

'Damn it, I've been asleep for six weeks,' Bronwen said.

'No, you've been in a coma, as someone with medical training you should know the difference,' said Annie Bowen.

'You know what I mean, Aunty Annie, you can't leave me on a cliffhanger.'

'Oh, all right. Will Francis's shop was broken into the week before Maddy's dad died. May the Angel's give him rest.'

'The previous morning Ray Payntor had been in, trying to buy a Palpadino based rat poison,'Madeleine said. 'He claimed he couldn't get it back home in Elizaburg.'

'Will refused to sell him it,' said Annie Bowen. 'He said that it was only sold to licenced Farmers and couldn't be carried between Archduchies. That chap Payntor seemed to accept it.'

'Three nights later, his shop gets burgled. Money taken from the till, some valuable items from the shop and the place messed up.'

'Anyway, when Will tidied up, to do a stock take he found two boxes of rat-poison had their contents removed and filled with sand,' said Annie, finishing her story.

'Why would Payntor steal rat-poison. Gilbert was killed by the pure stuff?' asked Bronwen, who despite herself was starting to doze.

'He used it to extract pure Palpadino without a manufacturer's molecular signature. Then he used it to poison my Father. 'The more I learn about that vile man, the more I hate him.'

Bronwen watched as Aneurin placed a supportive arm around Madeleine's shoulder, and Annie Bowen handed her a fresh paper handkerchief. Then gave in to tiredness and she nodded off.

After a second week as a guest at the Mother-house, Chantelle was summoned to Sister Vera's old office.

Now more accustommed to city clothes. With lightly curled shoulder length hair, she looked like a secular students. Especially when like today she was and wearing their unofficial uniform, a blue jacket, with jeans and long sleeve t-shirt.

'Reverend Mother Paula has been contacted by Mr. Franke this morning,' said Sister Monique, 'FPC Drake will take you to the local police station, from where, you will travel to Belmont, where you'll stay until your Aunt is fit to travel.'

'Thank you for having me, it has been an education,' said Chantelle politely.'

'Literally. You have spent more time in lecture theatres than any student, secular or religious,' said Sister Monique.

'The lectures have been fascinating. The Still Point Meditation training will be useful in my future career.'

'Chantelle, that is for novice sisters only.'

'I've got to apologise to Sister Petra. I still have my habit and permission to wear it, so I snuck in as "Novice Myfanwy". I've decided to let Maddy run the estate, it's what she wants. I'm going to be a teacher.'

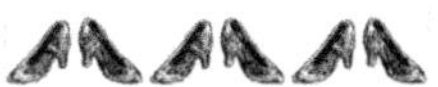

'Chantelle?' Bronwen screamed at 4am. She was sitting bolt upright in a strange bed, fully awake and trying to get her bearings in an unfamiliar room.

'Hush there, you don't want to be all hot and bothered,' said Nurse Dania, who was on night duty. 'You need your sleep.'

'To hell with sleep,' said Bronwen, now desperately trying to stay awake. 'I have to know what has happened to my niece, who left Fiandre the day before I passed out?'

'Mr. Franke, the policeman is due to visit you in the morning, he will explain everything,' said Dania as she administered the scheduled dose of sedative.

'So Erik, where is she?' Bronwen asked. The two were now "firm friends". It is hard to be stiff and formal to the man who saved her life.'

'I can't tell you,' he replied. 'Sorry Bronny.'

Bronwen had woken, to find Dania had been off duty for two hours, the Ansersol was well over the horizon and Erik Franke was sitting next to her bed, looking sheepish.

'Can't or won't, my dear?'

'I can't tell you, because I don't know. Chantelle arrived at her initial destination and one of my men should have picked her up and taken her to a safe house. In the meantime, my associates in this enterprise thought it would be better if she carried on to a secondary destination. This makes sense, considering where it is.'

'So where's the destination?' asked Bronwen, 'you must know by now?'

'Sorry Bron, I can't tell you.'

'Again, can't or won't?'

'Won't this time, because you are not supposed to know where your niece is, or how she got there,' said Erik. 'All I can say is that except for the prisons or Ellisford Castle, Lady Chantelle is in the most secure place on Anseris.

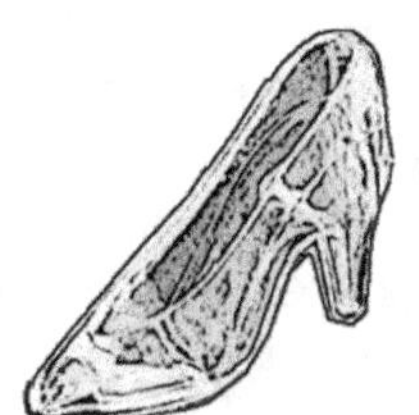 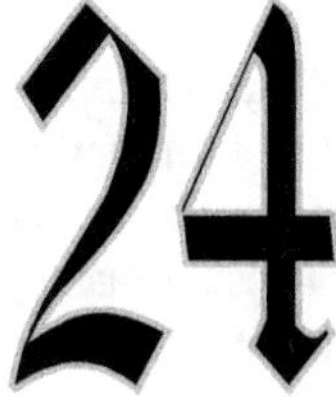 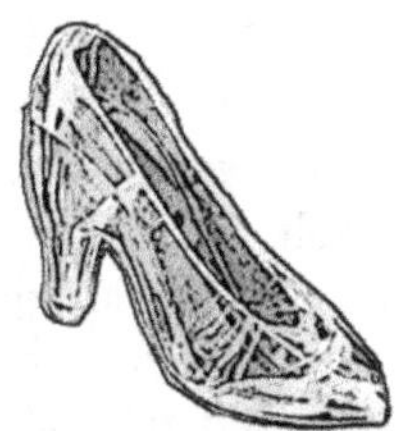

24

His grandfather Michael had passed away three weeks ago He had been buried and the week of mourning had passed. For anyone else, that would have been the end of the story. However Leo's grandfather had been the sixty fourth Archduke of Fiandre. A week of ceremonies followed the mourning. When they were over his father had become the sixty fifth Archduke of Fiandre and he was now the seventy second Earl of Fiandre. This all coincided with the hand-over of power from the old Feudal Government of the Kingdom and its Archduchies to the new Democratic Government. Everything was in uproar.

Leo had so much he wanted to say, but the woman he really wanted to say it to had vanished after the Black Masquerade. The night he had finally realised that he was in love with Lady Chantelle du Fauché, the woman he had shared his childhood with.

This morning he had gone to Cenerentola House and found it abandoned.

'Madam,' the young Earl said to a woman sweeping the front pavement of a large cottage on the outskirts of Cenerentola Village, 'What has happened to the residents of Cenerentola House?'

When she turned to face him, he recognised her instantly as Mrs Glanville. She had taught him and Chantelle as toddlers in the village school. At the time she had still been Sister Simone of the Order of the Sisters of the Angels' Merciful Charity and had looked set to remain that way. Then her life had changed as dramatically as his. He knew she remembered him, and despite the years and his new position in life he would always be Leonard Simples.

'Well, Leonard Benson Elizaburg Simples, I was sorry to hear about your granddad. He started my school, and funded it for twenty years. Now it will be funded by his legacy. Your one grandmother was a stuck up cow, but Gladys Simples was a good friend.'

If anyone else had called him that, it would have been a grave insult, Benson was the patronymic given to bastards. He had been Leonard Edwin Griffin-Phillips for many years now. Andrea Glanville remembered every person she had taught by the name they had first used in her classroom.

'Mrs Glanville, I came in search of Chantelle du Fauché, but she has disappeared,' he said, feeling like a five year old again. He had almost called her Sister Simone.

'I'm not surprised, Leonard, crazy things have been happening up in the big house since old Baron Gilbert, Angels give him rest, passed away. I'll explain it all, over a cup of tea. In you go.'

'Yes, Mrs Glanville,' he said, following the old lady into her kitchen, like a naughty schoolboy following a headteacher into her office.

'I in their right minds goes there in Augusta.' His old teacher was lifting a big metal kettle onto a fire in the range. 'And nobody in their right minds still boils water like this. I really should get a new electric kettle. She's apparently looking for someone called Payntor. Everything she has done was based on what he told her.' said Mrs Glanville, as she poured a cup of tea into her best china cup from her best china teapot. 'That's all turned out to be a pack of lies.'

'So that explains where she is, but why is the building empty of any of the family?'

'Well, young Leonard, the daughters of Lady Livienne's first marriages have signed the pledge at the Orphanage, they have been threatening to do that for months now. Afraid the law will get them for any minor misdemeanour they might have committed for their Mother. If they had done something serious, the Ugly Sisters would have handed them over to the police in a blink, pledged or not.'

A look of horror crossed Leo's face. Mrs Glanville had used that derogatory name for the Order without a blush.

'Somone who leaves the Order is called an Ugly Sister, I'm just repaying the compliment,' she said, offering him milk for his tea.

'So, Lady Madeleine, that's Lady Livienne's daughter with the late Baron Gilbert, had as much as she could take from her dreadful Mother and moved out months ago. Her Aunt, Mistress Bronwen Tudor, took her in. Well, she's not really Lady Madeleine's Aunt as she is the sister of Baron Gilbert's first wife, who was a saint and should never have died the way she did, but that is neither here nor there now. The Angels only know where Lady Chantelle had run away to, escaping the madness that had gripped the big house.'

'Run away?' asked Leo.

'Yes, the bitch made poor Chantelle sign indenture papers while he was still grieving. Lady Livienne said Chantelle wasn't really Baron Gilbert's daughter. Lady Chantelle had enough of being a Lady's Maid and has sneaked off somewhere. Now we all know different, she can come back home.'

'Oh, I didn't know that.'

'You always were easily distracted Leonard,' said the old teacher. 'However, now you have so much to be distracted by, here and at home. Anyway, everyone believes Mistress Bronwen knows where Lady Chantelle is, but wouldn't say, then couldn't say whilst unconscious in hospital. Go ask her, she might tell you now she's home.'

Leonard really wanted to get on, but knew there were rules and formalities. He would have to enquire after Mrs Glanville's health, finish a second cup of tea and a slice of cake. Normally, this was not a problem, he liked the older woman, and she seemed to know everything about everyone on Cenerentola and in Zucca, and would probably tell him in great detail.

'Although, she's off to Belmont to recuperate. She's taking her whole family with her.' Mrs Glanville drained her teacup. 'Chop chop young Leonard Benson Simples, you don't want to miss her, unless you fancy a trip to sunny Carlton.'

Released from the social niceties, he ran to the ferry, cursing every second it took to cross the narrow strait between Cenerentola and the mainland. Then into his red sports car, almost driving off without unplugging it from the charging unit.

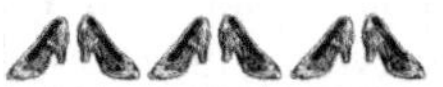

'𝔜our Grace,' said the young woman dressed in City clothes and what looked like a new shoulder length City hairstyle. She was almost Chantelle's twin. No she was slightly shorter and had a narrower chin. This had to be the real Lady Madeleine.

'Lady Madeleine, so nice to meet the real you,' he said to the curtseying young woman. 'Did you enjoy the Flying Scarves?'

'Oh yes, Your Grace. Chantelle told me you recognised our deception instantly, Your Grace. I'm afraid she isn't here, I don't know where she is.'

'I've come to visit your Aunt. I have been hearing some disquieting rumours. I believe she can clear everything up.'

'I'll tell her you're here, Your Grace,' Madeleine replied, 'I'm sure she will see you, but I can't say for how long. She has just returned home from hospital, Your Grace.'

'Do you know how much I hate being called that,' said Leo, 'I am a graceless sailor, who lost any social skills I might have had in Anseris's oceans.'

'I think you do yourself a disservice, Earl Leonard,' said Mistress Tudor as she descended on a recently fitted temporary chairlift. 'I heard you ringing the bell, I was on my way down anyway.'

'Mistress Tudor, I hope you are feeling better.'

'Yes, thank you, but we are friends, it's Bronwen, please. And do sit down you're making the place look untidy.'

Leo noticed that Bronwen Tudor still looked far from well. True it was a post-illness and now recovering sort of unwell, but it was still disquieting. The lady was a friend of his Mother, although she had not been back to the Home-world for years.

'As you wish Bronwen. When we last spoke face to face I had no title, let's pretend that is still the case,' said the Earl.

'Maddy, go fetch the box-files, the laptop and Aneurin.'

'𝔚e need to take a copy of everything here to the authorities,' said Leo after he read the files.

'There is not enough evidence yet,' said Bronwen. 'You can help us gain more evidence, so we have a water-tight case. Mr Franke will explain everything to you.'

'Chief Inspector Erik Franke?' asked Leo, who knew the man's reputation for thoroughness. Whatever was he doing here, why hadn't the Royal Protection Squad informed the Archduchy's authorities, as protocol demanded?

'Yes, him. He was on holiday here, but has now semi-officially taken over the case of Uncle Gilbert's murder,' said Aneurin.

'What more evidence does he need?' asked Leo. 'This dossier is very comprehensive.'

'The evidence is pointing towards Reg Payntor as the main suspect. A man who does not exist outside of the old Political Police's records. Chief Inspector Franke believes Payntor is really a former Chessman called Stanley Silvermann. Officially he was one of the casualties of the fall of the old order, dead for three years. We need to prove he is still alive and killed Baron Gilbert du Fauché.'

'The whole thing is connected to the fishing rights in the Sea of Naples,' said Leo. 'I know Baron Gilbert was refusing to sell them before he died. Look at that video again.'

'That is a very interesting theory, Your Grace,' said Erik, who had let himself in. 'Master Aneurin, please load the video file.'

The file showed Silvermann arriving at the Palace of Government early in the morning, and making his way to an office he had rented for the week, in the name of Charles Singleton, a wine merchant visiting the vineyards of Fiandre. There he touched up the Singleton disguise. Then he prepared a new one. It was Baron du Fauché's old friend Reg Painter, which he placed in a cupboard for use later. Silvermann took the other disguise into a side room, and returned with a different face. The Palace's DNA profiler confirmed it was the same man. He spotted the highly decorated mirror on the wall, and used it to adjust the disguise. Static hid what he was saying, but lip-reading revealed it was a string of expletives. He had no idea the mirror's fancy decorations hid one of the many Lambourian video camera around the Palace.

Minutes of waiting for someone to arrive dragged on, before Commander Liepmann arrived. Nothing either man said could be heard over the interference.

'The harmonics are wrong,' said Leo. 'I was a communications and radio officer for three years, I can fix that.' Leo minimized the window with the video and began running some software.

'It's a good job I could use my expertise to suppress your little chat over the radio on the night of the Black Masquerade. It's one of the reasons why I'm here.'

'I encrypted that to the twenty hells and back,' said Aneurin.

'Sorry Nye, you left too many breadcrumbs back to the source.'

There was a screech of complaint from the video and then full audio.

'So, Mr. Singleton, your employee will be able to perform the task for me?' the Commander asked.

'Oh, I wouldn't call him an employee, more like a free-lance associate who gets things done,' he said. 'We have an interesting business relationship.' This was true as it was actually one person. 'I will pass your fee to him, as it is best for both of you that you never meet.'

'OK, I understand. This task is important to my business, I need it done as quickly as possible.'

'Don't worry, Commander, once the fee is paid, it will be done within a limited period of time.'

'Thank you.'

The Commander had gone, leaving a big bag of untraceable money. Silvermann/Singleton returned to the highly decorative mirror on the wall.

'I might as well use this mirror,' he said before he pulled the implants for Charles Singleton out. For the first time ever, one of his transformations was recorded, as he became Reg Payntor.

'I assume the job the Commander wanted the associate to do was the murder of Baron Gilbert,' Leo said to Erik Franke, as the two men watched the recording again.

'You know, baby-sitting young Jadwiga, and her brother, was supposed to be a bit of a break for me. I can't do anything next door in Carlton until everything lines up over there. A few months away from the pressure of the Job,' said Erik Franke. 'Fat chance of that happening. I'll have to make a report to Commissioner Federn and Her Majesty.'

'Her Majesty?'

'Yes, Your Grace, she is very determined about winding down all the former Political Police's black-operations before they can mutate into Organised Crime gangs. She sees that as a clear and present danger to the security of the Kingdom.'

'Oh, I see,' said Leo. He didn't really care about that at the moment. All he cared about was Chantelle's safety. Where in the Hells was she?

'But proof that Stanley Silvermann is real, not just a Chessman myth is awesome. This will heat up so many cold cases.'

'Indeed. So tell me Chief Inspector, are we any closer to finding Lady Chantelle du Fauché?'

'Your Grace, I never lost her, that was a cover story for a cover story. I have friends in the Order of the Merciful Sisters, including Lady Chantelle's cousin, Cardinal Sister Vera. She arranged to smuggle her out of Fiandre. So I sent her off in a car full of Merciful Sisters going to the Mother House in Tintagel, dressed as a Novice of the Order. Thus rendering her invisible.'

'She's not decided to stay there and take the veil, has she?' Leo asked. Angels, please let that not be true, he thought.

'Of course not, that was only for part of the journey. To get her out of this Archduchy. Your grandfather's passing paralysed the courts here. Lady Chantelle's case was fast-tracked through a court in Carlton. That court decided in her favour yesterday.

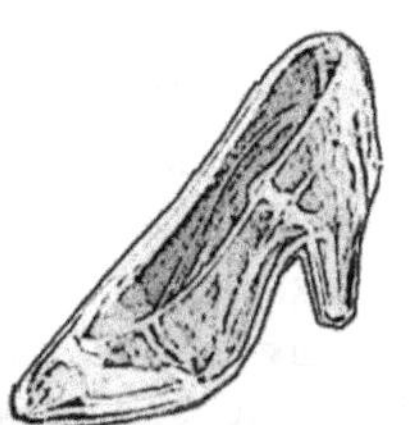 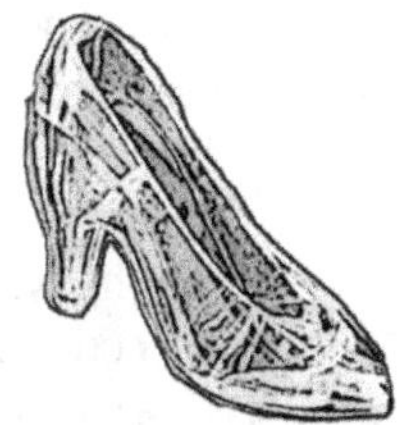

25

esterday, they had arrived at the town of Belmont, which was ten miles down the coast from Tintagel. Earl Leonard had flown them to Tintagel in his sub-orbital shuttle. They were then met by one of Archduke Gerald's luxury cars for the trip down the coast.

We can't feel comfortable without Chantelle, Aneurin thought. I suppose that means the journey is not really over until Mother and Mr. Franke have been to fetch Chantelle from Tintagel.

Friday, 11th September, 5885CGC. No, it could not really be that long. What had happened to the month of Augusta? Chantelle clearly remembered arriving at Tintagel at the end of the second week of Julia. She had stayed as a guest at the Mother-house for two weeks, until Mr. Franke's people came to collect her. Except it was not one of Mr. Franke's men. The last thing she remembered was being drugged.

She had woken up here at the Asylum that afternoon. She had been lucid enough to avoid swallowing any medication. After an incident with another patient, the nurse had forgotten her the dose of nightly sedative. Her basic Still Point Meditation trance looked like she was in a pharmalogically induced haze. Those ten lessons, twenty sureal hours, sitting cross legged in a leotard, wimple and veil with the novices had been eye openning. She now knew how Mrs. Glanville, still Sister Simone back then, had always been so calm in school. Surely Mrs. Glanville would help her study the art more thoroughly. She did not realise it had also blocking the brainwashing techniques being used on her.

The 11th September, She had not been here nearly six weeks, had she?

4am, everything was quiet. It was time to escape.

Each patient had a cubicle with a bed and a tiny cupboard for their meagre possessions. By the looks of things she was a good thirty years younger than any of the other patients, who were free to shuffle around the ward in a dazed stupor by day and kept sedated by night. None could leave the ward, which was locked with a key-code device Without the code, Chantelle wasn't going to get very far. She heard the footsteps, she was not going to be caught that easily, so she went into the room next to the exit, hoping the nurses would be too lazy to check. Her hope was not in vain.

She could hear voices behind her.

'Brozhnik! Ella's gone walkabout,' said one of the nurses.

'No need to worry, she won't get far,' said her male colleague 'She's drugged up to her eyeballs.'

She knew everyone called her Ella, they thought she was delusional claiming to be a Baron's daughter. Despite being true her protests only made her sound more delusional.

'That's true, then we get to punish her,' said the female nurse with far too much enthusiasm.

'They've changed the door code whilst I was on holiday, didn't bother to tell me,' said the woman. 'I'm desperate for a gasper.'

'It's five, two, nine, eight,' said her colleague. Its not very original

'The year the Boatbuilder was born, again. Twice in six months I think I can remember that.'

The door swung open. Chantelle heard two sets of footsteps walking away from the ward. Was this an elaborate trap. She would never know unless she tried to escape.

Her avatar and the charm bracelet had been taken when she had been admitted, but her psychic interface was unclouded by drugs. The charms were in range. She used them to set the security camera to duplicate a loop of an empty corridors from its memory card. After a few minutes she found the cupboard her avatar and the charms were stored, mistaken for cheap glass baubles.

Next she slipped into a store room for laundered nurses' uniforms Chantelle quickly changed out of her patient's nightdress and put on one of the bottle green kirtles with short white puffed sleaves. Sitting on other shelves were white aprons and green headscarves.

She spotted a small mirror on the back of the door, it showed in all its horrendous detail, the ruination of her hair, hacked into a patient's bob. Tying the headscarf hid the ruins and completed her disgiuse. A Dutiful Sister does not care about her hair, Chantelle thought. Then it's good job I'm not a Dutiful Sister, or ever likely to be. Where had that notion come from?

At 8am, the shift changed and most of the nurses headed to their accommodation. Chantelle blended in, however, she then kept on walking behind a group who continued out of the Sanatorium's grounds through suburbs. Eventually on she was heading deeper into the city of Tintagel, before the new shift realised she was not in the building.

Every time she heard a car she panicked slightly. What if it was from the Asylum, what if they caught her and took her back. Her disguise had been great in the Asylum, but was now a liability. Traditionally dressed in a city that was completely modern. When a car passed by, she let out her breath and just kept on walking. With the Ansersol rising to her right, she knew she was heading towards the heart of the city.

She was especially worried about walking past a police station. Surely the men inside would have been informed of her absence from the Asylum by the staff. Then she spotted the wanted poster. It had her face on it. She was wanted for absconding from her indenture. Just for once, the stupid woman had done something good for her. As soon as they checked her identity, the warrant for her arrest would outrank anything the Asylum said. So she walked through the heavy wooden doors, through thick stone walls into a thoroughly modern police station.

'Good morning, Sergeant,' she said cheerily, with a copy of the poster in hand. 'My name is Chantelle du Fauché, I believe you have been looking for me.'

'Indeed we are, Ella,' said desk sergeant. He had a familiar face and this was a familliar location. The sergeant was the man who had drugged her, after FPC Drake had delivered her here and gone off duty.

Chantelle turned to run, a buzzer sound and doors swung shut and clicked to locked before she had chance to escape.

'As I've told you,' said the man in a white coat sitting on the other side of the desk. 'There is no way that the woman you are looking for could possibly be in this establishment. We cater for geriatric patients exclusively.'

'And as I have told you, I don't believe you,' said Bronwen, who had taken as much flannel from Dr. Elliot Caithness, the director of the asylum, as she could stand. 'This is the nearest mental hospital to the Mother-house.'

'I've had enough of this, I am going to have to ask you to leave.' This finally pushed Dr. Caithness over the edge as well. 'If we listened to every moan from every lunatic, or their annoying relatives, we would get nothing done. You can go quietly, or I will call security.'

Erik Franke inwardly cringed, Bronwen was good, but still an amateur. The situation had become professional and he should have left Bronwen at the Mother-house. Not his first slip-up in this case. He had assumed that Lady Chantelle was safe with the Merciful Sisters without checking and had used this information to give false hope to his friend when she was ill.

'I wanted to do this quietly and politely, Dr. Silvermann,' said Erik Franke, 'I've always known who you really are. I was just going through the charade in the hope my team would not be necessary.' He took his warrant card and an impressive looking document from his briefcase, 'but I am the security. Royal Security and so by the powers vested in me by her most Anserian Majesty, Queen Johanna IV, I am ordering you to transfer to my colleagues all your admission registers, medical records, drug manifests, business accounts, personnel records and anything else they think might be relevant. This business is suspected of having connections to organised crime and is going to be thoroughly investigate.'

'Trying to frighten me into telling you where Ella is? It's not going to work,' said Doctor Caithness, unaware of his blunder.

'I never mentioned the name Ella. I simply know from your cousin Phyllis Silvermann, aka Reverend Mother Paula, that Ella had been delivered to Cousin Alfred.' He could see the man sag.

'I'll ask again. Where is Chantelle du Fauché?'

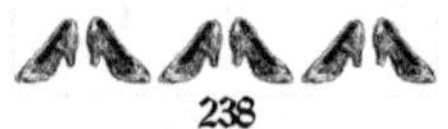

'So, if she has escaped from here, where is she?' Bronwen asked Erik as they left the asylum, heading towards Erik's car.

'She won't have got very far on foot,' replied Erik. 'This is worrisome, she was in no fit state to be wandering around in public.'

'You blame yourself?' asked Bronwen.

'Of course I do. I failed both of you with this.'

'So, this is no time for maudlin self-pity,' said Bronwen. 'You're not a superman, I wouldn't want you to be. Accept your mistake and try to correct it.'

'I've sent a group of my people to a local police station, to set it up as a base for our search, amongst other things. It's also the administrative headquarters of the Archduchy's Traffic Police.'

Erik fervently hoped Chantelle had not turned herself in at Penhill Station. He had done more than send men to set up a base. The Tintagel Traffic Police Department was the most corrupt branch of the Crown Police Service, anywhere in the Kingdom. This would be a full scale raid.

One of his plants within Penhill Station, FPC Drake had told him she had escorted Lady Chantelle from the Mother-house to a waiting unmarked vehicle, which had brought her here. Erik was confident his people were busy cleansing the rats from their nest. His phone rang.

'Hello, Dad,' said a female voice when he answered.

'Hello, Daughter. How's tricks?' he asked.

'Our parcel has just arrived, Dad,' she said. 'Turned up from nowhere. Drugged up to the eyeballs.'

'Well, you are about to be in the centre of a shit-storm. You have twenty minutes to get our parcel out of there. Failing that, keep the parcel safe.' Erik hung up. 'Ah Brozhnik!Brozhnik! Brozhnik! Brozhnik! Brozhnik!'

'Go on Erik, say what you really mean,' said Bronwen jokingly.

'Bronwen, this is no laughing matter. I've just been told Chantelle has walked into a known corrupt police station. Under the old regime, it had close ties to the Chessmen. One which is about to be raided by my men, in an operation it took months to arrange. I've been waiting for weeks for this and it can't be stopped now.'

'Who were yous a-talkin' to Drake?' asked Sergeant Bends. His origins made him stand out amongst the urban officers of the Crown Police Service in Tintagel.

'To my Dad, Sarge,' said FPC Drake. She knew even a dullard like Sergeant Bends would know that was a lie.

'Yous don't have no Dad. You be an orphan,' said the man, whose skin glowed scarlet when he was angry. It was reddening now.

'I was trying to be polite, it's none of your business,' said Holly-Lee Drake.

'You were a-makin' a private call while you were on duty. That make's it my business.'

'On my break, Sarge,' said Holly-Lee Drake. Tall and thin, she had been assigned to Penhill Station as her first assignment. Holly-Lee stood out from the lazy colleagues who shared the building with the corrupt Traffic Cops. She hated it and tried to be reassigned almost immediately. Sergeant Bends had also tried to get rid of her, both had failed. Then she met Constable Johnstone, who had introduced her to Chief Inspector Erik Franke, aka Dad, who had explained Johnstone was really Inspector Jarvice, who was working undercover at Penhill.

She was assigned a night shift patrolling the grounds around the Mother-house, which wasn't that unpleasant. She had spent the first twelve years of her life in the orphanage run by the Merciful Sisters in Ivybridge. She knew the way the nuns' minds worked and knew what she could or could not get away with, in any given circumstance.

After leaving the orphanage at thirteen she had got a job working for the Police Support Service, the organisation that supplied the cleaners and janitors for Crown Police stations. Her dream of joining the Force began. An impossible dream at a time when only men could join the Police. However, two years earlier, Queen Johanna had opened the service up to women. She was one of the first women to join and receive her Warrant Card.

'Evening Sarge,' said Johnstone, 'I understand we have a guest in Cell#3.'

'Johnstone, you're not supposed to know that.'

'Lots of things I'm not supposed to know. That's never stopped me in the past.'

'Well lad, you and Drake here can take our guest back to where she came from.'

'I'm right on it, Sarge. FPC Drake, go get our guest from Cell#3, I'll fire up the motor on the Squad car.'

Holly-Lee Drake tried to hide her surprise. Sometimes it was better to be born lucky than rich. No, she thought. It's not possible to be that lucky, or for the Sarge to be that stupid. The arrival of Inspector Washington, from Traffic, proved that she was neither lucky nor rich. The Inspector was the real brains in this operation.

'Not so fast,' Washington said. 'Johnstone, put that bitch in Cell#3 with the nutter.'

'Eh? What?' asked a bemused Sergeant Bends

'She's been working with Erik Franke and his crusade against corruption.' Inspector Washington said to Sergeants Bends, then sneered at Holly-Lee, his long and narrow scarred face looked demonic, 'did you think you could get away with betraying your colleagues?'

'Don't see any colleagues in this room, only a bunch of bent coppers,' replied Holly-Lee.

This earned her a viscous back-handed slap from Washington. 'Johnstone, get her out of my sight.'

Chantelle had been feeling sorry for herself. Her moods on a roller-coaster all day, as she went cold turkey from the drug that had kept her zombified in the Asylum. At the bottom of a deep pit of despair, she believed her luck had run out. Whatever these policemen were going to do with her, was not good. At best she would be taken back to the asylum. At worse they would hand her over to Silvermann and she would soon be re-united with her Father and meet her Mother. As she was rising out of the pit, she managed to put herself into a basic Still Point trance.

People were talking outside the cell door. Oh well, here goes, she thought. The door opened and a woman walked in.

'OK, we have a few minutes to get out of the building before the idiots realise things are going wrong,' said the female police officer who had taken her from the Mother-house. She was carrying a pair of hand-cuffs. 'Sorry about this.'

Chantelle didn't need to be told twice and left the cell. 'Only the Sarge and the Inspector know we're not supposed to be taking you anywhere. They're having a meeting in the Sarge's office and don't realise they're locked in and can't communicate with the rest of the station.'

Things were on the up. She followed the exit signs, with the woman, to the basement car park. One of the cars pulled out of its parking bay. An unknown policeman got out of his car and opened the back passenger door, and helped Chantelle into the car. As the car door slammed, the fire alarm began singing.

'Brozhnik, I thought we would be able to get out of the station! I'm Inspector Bill Jarvice, that is FPC Holly-Lee Drake. I take it you are Lady Chantelle, sorry Baroness Chantelle Angharad Cenerentola du Fauché.'

'Yes, that's right. I take it you are undercover from Mr. Franke's department?'

'The Chief Inspector sent him, I'm unfortunately permanently based in this rat's nest,' said Holly-Lee.

'OK folks, hold onto your breakfast,' said Jarvice, as the car shot forward. Chantelle could hear the engine's protest as it accelerated up the ramp. The reason was blindingly obvious, a heavy portcullis was slowly lowering at the exit. There was an unpleasant scraping noise as the portcullis took away the sirens and lights from the roof of the car. Another when the lid of the boot parted company with the vehicle. This was more than the vehicle could cope with, as this also wrecked its gas turbine engine.

'Charlie Sierra Whiskey 74 Indigo to Romeo Papa Alpha 1,' Bill Jarvice said in a calm tone. Too calm, Chantelle thought for a driver who had just lost half his car.

'Charlie Sierra Whiskey 74 Indigo, this is Romeo Papa Alpha One,' said Erik Franke over the radio, 'Report.'

'We have the Baroness,' he said.

That's all you have, Chantelle thought, Inspector Jarvice was a master of understatement.

'Excellent work Jarvice,' said Erik. 'What's your ETA?'

'Unknown, Sir. Our vehicle has been disabled.'

'Stay where you are, someone will come to collect you.'

'That might be a bit awkward, Sir.' Four of his former colleagues had surrounded what remained of the vehicle, pointing rifles at its three occupants. 'We have hostile company.'

'One day you are going to give me all the facts in one of your situation reports, and I won't believe it,' he said.

'I always give all the facts, Sir.'

'Yes, with a positive spin. That will get you killed one day.'

Chantelle could not help but notice the ironic sigh from Erik Franke. They had obviously worked together for a long time and learnt to cope with each other's difference in styles.

'Does your vehicle's armour still have its integrity?'

'Yes, Sir. I think they are pointing their weapons out of a false sense of bravado. They can't harm us.'

She had seen the officer fire his rifle and Chantelle ducked down into the well between the front and back seats. Holly-Lee Drake did the same. She heard the second shot. Sadly, Bill Jarvice, distracted by the radio did neither. The armour piercing bullet shattered the glass into a million pieces and was now lodged firmly in Jarvice's heart, stopping it forever.

There was noise then silence. Why had the corrupt policemen not driven home their advantage? Eventually, somebody opened the back door of the car. A man in uniform. Fear raced through Chantelle's mind.

'Don't worry, Baroness du Fauché, I'm with the Royal Protection Squad. I am here to rescue you,' said the man, which triggered her already unstable moods to swing from elation to depression and back up again, like a roller-coaster, several times. She felt the visibly shaking Holly-Lee put her arm around her and mumble something calming to her.

'We will have a doctor check you out, and take you back to the Mother-house, where your Aunt and the guv'nor are waiting for you.'

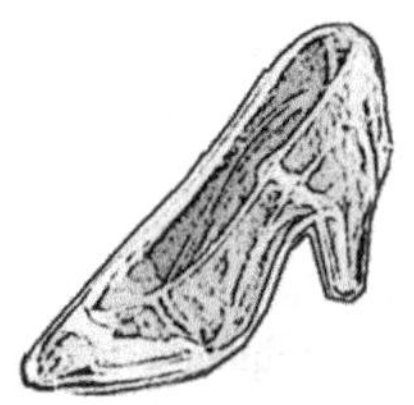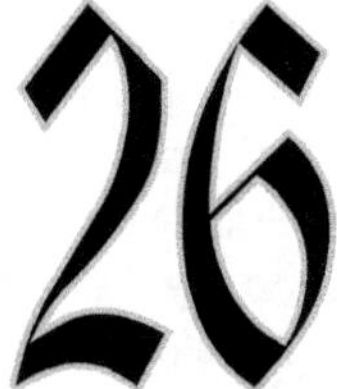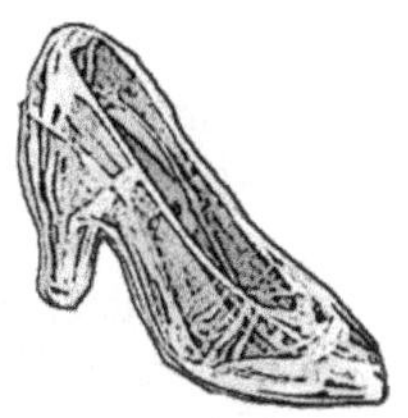

26

Chantelle had arrived at the safe-house four days ago wearing an old fashioned nurses uniform, splattered with blood. She had been very quiet, not herself at all. Today she was far more animated, back to her normal self. Aneurin decided to be discreet and not ask what had happened in the past few months.

He also chose to be discreet about how awful Chantelle looked in the City clothing everyone in Belmont wore. Chantelle had always been the poster girl for traditional dresses, effortlessly beautiful in a long skirt with a filmy veil on her head. What had happened to all her lovely hair, she looked like she had been attacked with a lawn-mower. Having grown up in a place where women wore their hair short, Aneurin had become fascinated with the longer Home-world styles. He was a little envious of a woman's ability to grow her hair all her life, and not go bald, as he eventually would.

'I would really like to visit the Jovian Baronies, and everywhere off the Home-world,' said Chantelle. 'The Silvermann Family was going to send me to one after Cousin Alfred finished with me.'

'There's not a lot of difference between here in Carlton and the Jovian Baronies,' he said. 'Pendragon, now that's a different story.'

'How could people live in space habitats?' asked Madeleine, 'with only metal walls between them and the void?'

'We managed it, I doubt you would have any problems,' said his Mother, recognisably back to her old self again, in modern city style clothes. So, let's go for lunch. I've booked a table in the Boar's Head Inn. A walk down to the beach and cable-car home.'

'No-one would disagree with that, Aunty Bron,' said Chantelle.

The post was waiting for them when they arrived home. Except, nobody was was supposed to know where they were. Yet there was an envelope, addressed to Madeleine. Chantelle recognised the handwriting.

'It's from Jadwiga. Mr. Franke must have left it here.'

'So what does she have to say?' asked Chantelle.

'Janek has had his service status changed from trainee to enlisted now, he has successfully been accepted into the Navy.'

'Something else I have missed whilst I was drugged to my eyeballs in Tintagel?'

'Of course, you didn't know. Sorry, Jadwiga says he's already specialised, training as a Navy Diver. He is also getting engaged to Eugenia du Pre at Jule, although they won't be getting married until they are both over twenty one. Look, here's a photo of them.' The picture showed Janek in a sailor's uniform, standing next to a pretty blond girl, in a traditional outfit that co-ordinated with Janek's uniform perfectly.

'She's only sixteen, that's a long engagement,' said Chantelle.

'It's one of the things about military life. They aren't keen on unofficial relationships, it has to be an official engagement or nothing.'

'Madeleine, I want you to sit down and tell me everything I've missed. Every piece of gossip, no matter how trivial for the past few months. Angel's I'm so out of the loop.'

'So let's start with the twins. Aunty Bron says Clementine is now Novice Emily of Secundo Quartam and Citronella is now Novice Alison of Quarta Quartam. I can understand why they can't both be Novice Livienne, so their using their grandmothers's names. I don't understand any of the rest. What does it mean?'

'I can answer that one. The Convent in Ponti is huge. So to make it easier, just like Tintagel it is split into four Quartam. The Twins have taken the entrance exam and done so well, they have avoided the Postulancy. I suspected they would. They have been put in different Quarta to finally seperate them. So enough of all that, on with the gossip.'

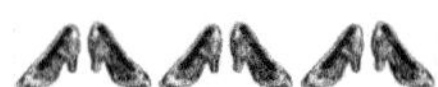

elmont looked so traditional. Whitewashed houses lining steep cobbled streets running down hill to the harbour below. Stanley Silvermann hated it, because beneath that traditional surface was a gleaming modernity that was against everything he believed in. The people wore horrible unisex clothing and had a horribly egalitarian attitude which seemed to be in a hurry to destroy traditional Anserian morality. Also, the traditional look had been permanently scarred by the cable cars that went up and down the wide main street of the town.

His own life was falling to pieces, and it was all down to those bitches. The police had somehow discovered so many of his secrets. The family crime empire he was building had been destroyed before it had chance to really establish itself. He still had enough resources to happily retire to a place the Law would never find him. This was his penultimate persona, the one with which he would kill the interfering women and boy, who had put an end to his lucrative career. They were currently too well protected by Erik Franke and his squad of Royal bodyguards. So he had killed that silly bitch Livienne du Fauché. He knew the family would abandon the safety of Belmont and return to Cenerentola House for the official mourning. They would be isolated and alone there on Silent Night, when the police, with all their surveillance equipment would be utterly useless, unable to protect them.

r. Franke and his colleagues at the Royal Protection Squad were monitoring everyone who came to the cottage, so Chantelle knew it was safe to answer the door. It was probably one of Mr. Franke's colleagues. Heavily vetted tradesmen delivered at the backdoor and they had not made any new friends on this visit to Belmont. The people were so friendly, but she and her family had to be so guarded in what they said and did, as well as being guarded by armed policemen. She would come here again, and she was determined to properly enjoy everything this town had to offer on her next visit.

To Chantelle's surprise, standing at the door was the Prime Viscount, no that was wrong, he was the Earl Leonard of Fiandre now. A million miles from childhood playmate Len. She had to be formal and curtseyed as etiquette demanded. 'Your Grace.'

'Oh please get up Ellabella,' the young man said. Nobody had called her that since their twelfth birthday. The first one he had missed, because he was at the Tintagel Naval Academy, and she sent to school in Ponte di Carla.

'I bet nobody calls you Len any more either?' she asked.

'No, it's usually Your Grace. Of course you can call me Len.'

'OK, Your Grace,' she formally replied, winked and continued 'how are you, Len? Is there anything I can do for you?'

'Become my wife. I didn't realise until I danced with you at the Black Masquerade, how much I loved you. That I have always loved you and wanted to share my life with you.'

'OK, I didn't see that coming. But you barely know me now. You are in love with an image in your head. I am Ella now, a lowly plebeian housemaid.'

'You know my Father married a plebeian housemaid when he was Viscount Edwin. He didn't care about rank, he loved my Mother for who she was, not what rank she was. If you really must be socially correct, you were born amongst the Gentry. Now your step-mother's heinous lies have been disproved, you are not a housemaid, you are a member of the Gentry again. By becoming my wife, you will enter the Aristocracy.'

'I should have told you everything at the Masquerade, but my pride got in the way. I wanted to prove my case myself. Gratitude for rescuing me is not enough to build a marriage on. Especially as I only had an image of you to work from. I will consent to being your friend and building a proper relationship first,' Chantelle told him.

'As always, you are right, Chantelle. We have so many years to catch up on.'

They were a millimetre away from kissing when the front door opened with a loud bang. Madeleine came bounding into the cottage with the Twins in tow.

'Madeleine, Clementine and Citronella, what's the panic. What's happened?' asked Chantelle. More importantly, what were the twins now dressed in their novice habits doing here. She knew that new Novices spent their first month almost constantly in church, praying and singing to Angels. They should be performing Prime now.

'It's our Mama,' said someone she thought was Clementine, but it could have been Citronella. In their robes they were now truly identical.

'She's been murdered,' said the other one.

'It's true. Her body was found in the Ellis River, ten miles from Elizaburg. Her throat...' Madeleine could not bring herself to say it, so changed the subject. 'They've sent the Twins home to bury and mourn our Mother,' said Madeleine. When she spotted the Earl. She curtseyed, 'Your Grace.'

The twins followed suit, and then began crying.

'Ladies,' said Leo diplomatically, 'I commiserate with you on your loss, and will leave you to your mourning.'

'I shall escort you to the door, Your Grace,' said Chantelle, who did not know what to make of the situation.

Leo seemed to remember something. From his jacket pocket he removed a black box, to large for a ring, so obviously a different piece of jewellery. 'I nearly forgot this. You left it at the Palace on the night of the Black Masquerade.'

'You mean the Lady Madeleine left it at the Palace,' said Chantelle who then laughed. 'No, the need for that pretence no longer exists. Thank you, Your Grace. This belonged to my Mother.' She looked at the charm, it appeared to be a glass shoe. 'I never knew what it really did. I suspect she didn't either. It was still the bad old days when any alien tech that survived the war was seen as witchcraft.'

'We know from the Queen that the Valentine Device mistook unwillingness to use the Psychic Interface as an inability to use it.' Leo could see that Chantelle was doing something to the charm. 'You are obviously more adept than I.'

'There you go. You keep this. I've got the other half of the pair. Primed to our emotions, I will know when you are thinking of me, and you will know when I am thinking of you.'

'Thank you, Baroness Chantelle.' They had just walked through the front door and out in the street, so they had to be far more formal than they wanted to be.'

'Your Grace?' Chantelle was shocked.

'Yes, Baroness Chantelle, you are now, and have been since your Father's death, the real Baroness du Fauché. The only person challenging that, despite all the facts is the recently departed Lady Livienne, who falsely claimed the title.'

This had not occurred to Chantelle. 'In which case, I have much to do,' she curtseyed. 'Your Grace will probably see me in a few days, at the Lady Livienne's funeral.'

'Until next time, Baroness,' Leo said, politely kissing her hand. It was like a bolt of electricity hitting her, but she knew she could not react. It would not be dignified.

'I have to say I am not happy about this, Bronny,' Erik Franke said to her. He was sitting in an office he had commandeered in Belmont's police station. He looked imperious behind the desk, now he was back in uniform. However he was regretting not taking the late Lady Livienne into protective custody. He had let his revulsion for the old witch over-ride his professionalism.

'Neither am I,' said Bronwen, who had been summoned here by the policeman, 'but I didn't like your jolly wheeze of us all going back home and pretending nothing had happened. Let Livienne lord it over Cenerentola House, as if sha had done nothing wrong, for as many weeks as it took to catch Silvermann.'

'In hindsight that was a bad idea also. However, it was the only operational plan we had,' said Erik Franke.

'Chantelle is insisting on it. She says despite everything her late Step-Mother did to her, she was a du Fauché and must be shown all the respect that that deserves.'

'That dreadful woman doesn't deserve a thing from Baroness Chantelle. But it shows the new Baroness is and always was the better person,' said Erik.

'I won't disagree with that. But isn't it obvious that Silvermann killed the Lady Livienne to force a return to Cenerentola.'

'Yes, Aunty Bron, Mr. Franke. As obvious as the plastic and carbon fibre nose on his artificially rebuilt face,' said Chantelle, who had walked into the room. 'The Sergeant let me in.' The Sergeant had obviously shown deference to the baronial chain Chantelle was wearing.

Bronwen could see Erik was not happy about Chantelle crossing the town without an escort. Especially as she knew the man who wanted to kill her was in town. However, he remained completely calm and polite.

'Yes, Baroness Chantelle,' said the policeman. 'Which is why you should remain here in Belmont, where it is safe.'

'I know he's already been to Belmont, and is long gone.' Chantelle pointed to one of the charms on her bracelet. 'I set this to go off whenever his DNA profile is less than a mile way.'

'A Lambourian Glass Slipper charm. Earl Leonard has a similar device. You left it in the Palace at Castello del Filippo when you were acquiring evidence in an undercover operation. So to speak.'

'I wish I had known all the features on these charms that night. It would have made things so much easier. You're trying to change the subject, aren't you Mr. Franke?' Chantelle asked the man. He said nothing in reply.

'At least delay the funeral for a week, dear,' Bronwen said to her niece. 'Until after Silent Night.'

'The Book of Care says that funerals must take place within two weeks of a person's death. These things have to be done properly.'

'Is that for her benefit or yours, Chantelle?' her Aunt asked.

'Definitely her. I won't be happy until the Biocrete has turned her body and the clothes she is burried to the same cold white stone her heart was made of.

'Isn't that a bit harsh and vengeful?' asked Erik Franke.

'I only objected to her resting next to my Mother and Father.' Madeleine and the twins want to watch as the newly formed solid stone statue is dropped into the deepest part of the Mare di Napoli.'

'So, off to Cenerentola we go then,' said Erik Franke.

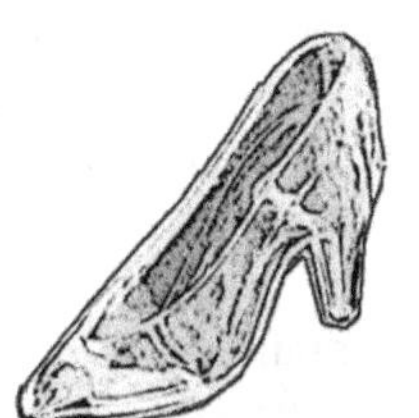 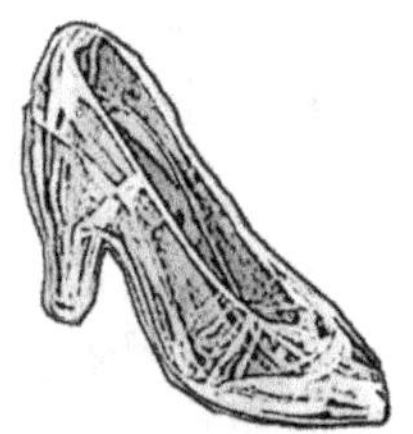

27

enerentola House sat on a tiny scrap of land in the middle of a small lake at the heart of the island. Very little other than conifers could grow on the Island, so the main source of income for the inhabitants was fishing in the calm, deep waters of Mare di Napoli. At the Island's highest point a stream of pure water rose and flowed down the light gradient to the east, where it entered the sea at Cenerentola village. The road to the village ran along this stream, crossing it twice at small stone bridges.

The Silent Night was reaching its peak. Despite it being 2am in the predawn morning, the sky was a bright as noon. The sky was, however, bright pink with yellow flashes. Each family member was taking turns as sentry. Chantelle had volunteered for this portion of the night, as her body clock was still skewed by the sedatives she had taken in the asylum. Chantelle stood looking at the first bridge, through an arrow slit in the top storey of the tower at Cenerentola House, safe in the knowledge nobody outside could see her. The bridge should have been crossed and recrossed by the policemen who had come to the Island when her family returned home. There had been no movement for the past ten minutes. This was deeply concerning, she should wake her family, so they could defend themselves as best they could, if Stanley Silvermann was going to pay them a visit.

First she woke Aunty Bronwen and Aneurin, who knew the Pendragon spacesuit sign language everyone who lived there learnt. With their gift for languages, Chantelle and Madeleine had quickly picked it up.

"What's happening?" signalled Aunty Bronwen.

"Something has happened to the police patroling the road," Chantelle replied with a flurry of hands and fingers.

"OK," signalled Aneurin. "Go and wake Madeleine. The Ugly Sisters are in the Chapel, praying."

"Don't call them that," gestured Chantelle.

"You've changed your tune," was Aneurin's digital reply.

"Stop wasting time," signalled Aunty Bron, with extra emphasis.

Chantelle woke Madeleine, who was sleeping in a chair.

'Haven't any of you thought about communicating through the psychic interface?' The sound of Madeleine's voice was almost deafening. 'It plugs straight into your brain, bypassing the ears.'

'That's impossible,' said Aneurin. 'None of the relays work.'

'None of the Anserian relays. Chantelle has a bracelet with ten of those fancy antique Lambourian relays.'

'Nine, I gave one to Leo,' said Chantelle.

'Does it matter. We have one big tactical advantage over Mr. Silvermann. An old dinosaur like that would never know how to use the Psychic Interface.'

'I'm afraid you are wrong there,' said a voice from the aether, 'I never regarded it as witchcraft. I hate it because it's not Ansarian, but that doesn't mean it doesn't have any uses.'

He stood there, gun in one hand, a bunch of handcuffs in the other. 'I've been here for hours, waiting for you all to be in the same room. Right, each of you take a pair of cuffs and put them on.' Then counting the people in the room asked, 'Where are the fat girls?'

'Behind you, stupid,' said Citronella as the sisters slammed into the man, pushing him of balance then into the pantry. They used the eerie silence to creep up behind Silvermann. They had studied Still Point meditation, which hid the mental chatter that might have given them away. He had dropped his gun, it went off silently. The bullet ricocheted around the room before embedding in the kitchen table. Clementine locked the pantry door.

'That's not going to hold him,' said Clementine. 'We have to get to the panic room in Papa's Solar. That is impregnable, we can sit in there until the police get here.' Then she screamed. Citronella was lying on the floor, bleeding profusely.

'It's OK Emily,' Citronella said. 'It's only a shallow wound, looks worse than it really is, but hurts like the hells.'

Every fortified manor house has a room or set of rooms called the Solar. Normally it was used by the lord of the manor as his private quarters, but if the manor ever came under attack, it would be the nerve centre of the defence and home for his Lordship's family.

'It doesn't matter if you lock yourself in there. I'm planning on blowing this place up. That Solar will go up with the rest of thi...' the disembodied voice of Silvermann was cut mid-sentence by the fall of a very modern looking security grill.

'We don't want to hear what he has to say, and we don't want him snooping on us,' said Clementine. 'The grill has Lunavapron varnish. He can't snoop on us. Unfortunately, we can't snoop on him either.'

Chantelle had never seen the Twins so connected with the real world. Was it the adrenalin rush or was it the absence of their dreadful mother. In the end they had rebelled against her as well. No wonder Lady Livienne had upped sticks back to Elizaburg.

'Good idea,' said Chantelle. 'It's 3am, we've hours until sunrise. Perhaps you can start singing Matins, to help pass the time.'

'Will you join with us, Myfanwy. We know you know the words now,' said Citronella, 'after your trip to Tintagel.'

'You should lead. Your time as a novice give you an older entry in the Nomina in Libro than us,' said Clementine.

'Do I, Emily?' asked Chantelle, that was all pretence.

'Yes, Sister Grace told us,' explaining the Twin's insistence on calling her Myfanwy.

'Then I would be honoured to,' said Chantelle and began singing in Latin.

Earl Leonard Edwin Griffin-Phillips hated Silent Night and its unnatural aura, even though he knew he had been conceived during a Silent Night twenty five years earlier. They continued marking major changes in his life, at eight his parents had been reunited, at sixteen he had become a Midshipman aboard FQV Ballytylor. This year he became the second most important person in the Archduchy.

He was having difficulty sleeping. The total absence of sound was unnerving him. The castle was quieter since his parents had moved to the grander Archduke's residence at Ponte di Carla. They had left him with a skeleton staff. Every member of this skeleton staff had gone out to enjoy the freak show. Leo could not understand why. What was the point of oohing and aahing at the light-show if no-one could hear you. Even without anyone else in the building, there should still be some noise at night. Unfathomable creaks and growns from the old place's structure, not this crazy audio vacuum.

Leo also had a headache, like something was drilling into his skull. He got out of bed. Thinking he could walk himself to sleep, he pulled on his dressing gown. He spotted the glass shoe on the dressing table. It was glowing, which meant that Chantelle was thinking about him. He picked it, the thing felt red hot, so dropped it back onto the table. In a flash he saw the scene inside Cenerentola House through Chantelle's eyes. The man Silvermann was standing in front of her and her family pointing a gun. He was unaware that the twins were creeping up behind him. He saw the two young women risk their lives and bundle Silvermann into the pantry, then he saw Chantelle and her family dash to the Solar and into the Baron's panic room. Amazingly, he heard Chantelle and the twins singing a prayer so beautifully, but through that he could feel her fear.

Ten minutes later Leo was sitting astride the fastest and most powerful motorcycle he owned. Normally he would not have used it at night, because it was also the noisiest vehicle he owned. Tonight, the roar of its gas turbine engine was hidden by the cosmic glitter.

Leo was armed to the teeth. Two pistols, four daggers and a sword. The streets of Castello del Filippo had been full of people gawking at the sky, unable to hear the horn blaring. However, once the crowd became aware of the bike's presence, passage for it. Soon Leo made his way onto a country road. The motorbike just eating up the miles between the city and Zucca. He would arrive at its port just as the first ferry of the day was about to depart.

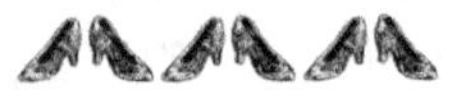

The ferryman had tried to stop him boarding. Holding up a sign saying that motor vehicles were prohibited on the island. Leo had lifted the visor on his helmet. One look at his face changed the ferryman's mind and he was signalled aboard.

The policeman was quite insistent. Leo would not be able to progress any further into Cenerentola Island. His use of naval diver's sign language marked him as a veteran of that service. Leo tried appealing as one ex-sailor to another. That didn't work. The ex-sailor said in signs that would only be used on a naval dive that was going horribly wrong that "His Grace, the Earl would have to wait until he spoke to the Chief Inspector before he could proceed."

So Leo followed the policeman into the bar of the Tavern, which Erik Franke was using as his headquarters.

'Good evening, Your Grace. To what do I owe this privilege.'

'You've got one of those experimental field dampeners, how in the twenty hells did you get that?'

A black box with flashing lights sat on the bar. Anserian scientists had been trying for decades to find a way to stop the auditory paralysis that accompanied the Silent Night.

'Her Majesty can be very persuasive, when she needs to be,' said the Policeman. 'She thinks this case takes priority over all else.'

Leo had met Queen Johanna once. A remarkable woman, who seemed to know precisely the right thing at the right time.

'Does Her Majesty want Silvermann taken alive?' Leo asked.

'Alive, by preference, but I told her that was unlikely to happen, given what we know of the man.'

'Well, he is currently at Cenerentola House, having been locked into a cupboard in the kitchen.'

'And exactly how do you know this?'

'This thing blasted an image of exactly what Chantelle was seeing straight into my brain.'

'Ah, Lambourian technology. If they could do that a century ago, the Angels only know what they are capable of now.' Erik touched the charm and saw two women kneeling in prayer. Then he heard a voice directly in his skull.

'Chief Inspector Franke, I see Leo has come to see you,' said Baroness Chantelle.'

'Yes,' he said.

'As you can see, we are in the Panic Room at Cenerentola House. Silvermann is not trying to gain entry, but he is on the premises. I think he is planting bombs. He mentioned blowing the place up. I think he is going to kill himself and everyone in the building.'

'Understood, Your Ladyship, I am about to mobilise a rescue for yourself, and your family.'

The link was cut. 'Well, did you hear that, Your Grace?'

'I heard it too, I think immediate action is required,' said Leo.

'It is suspected that Silvermann has two dozen Pilchard Mines in his possession.'

'Old and temperamental,' said Leo.

'Indeed, the Pilchards have to be wired in series, if one becomes disconnected, the whole chain fails. Although its more accurate to say cabled. The firing mechanism sends a pulse of light down fibre-optic cables connecting each bomb.'

'So they aren't affected by the Silent Night,' said Leo. 'I have to get there as quickly as possible.'

'Your Grace, as a member of the Royal Protection Squad, I am also charged with stopping Aristocrats putting themselves in harms way. I cannot allow you to go on such a dangerous mission.'

'And how do you plan on stopping me?'

'I...' everything went silent as Erik was speaking. He turned to the bar, the machine sitting on it was running through a diagnostic routine before rebooting. He looked out the pub door, to see a powerful motorcycle silently travelling up the narrow road to Cenerentola House.'

'...dozy brozhnik young Ristoze idiot,' Erik said as the machine finished re-booting.

'Chief Inspector, Sir, that Navy diver has arrived, do you want to add him to the briefing?' asked Erik's underling.

'Yes, Wilson, that's what he's here for.'

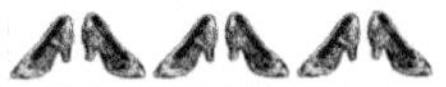

He had dumped the bike at the lower bridge, by the bodies of three policemen. Using the bridge as cover, he got out a pair of binoculars and studied the building. He saw a man planting explosives at selected places around the building. The man obviously had a little knowledge of demolition theory, but not much.

Leo stealthily approached the bridge to Cenerentola House. He knew the man was at the other side of the structure, as he disarmed the explosive devices in front of him, breaking their circuit. When the man tried to detonate them, the entire enterprise would fail. Leo hid himself in the undergrowth and waited for the man to press the shutter release button. Leo could hear a stream of expletives. Of course, the man had some sort of alien tech with him that over rode the effect of the Silent Night.

'I would advise you, Sir, to drop what you are doing, and put your hands up,' said Leo, the sound of his voice was good.

'You know, I should have expected you, you little bastard. Earl Leonard indeed! Your tart of a mother did well for herself.'

'If you're thinking you're going to make me angry and do something stupid, think again, you pile of brozhnik,' said Leo.

'Once a pleb, always a pleb. No true Ristoze would ever use that word.'

'You've obviously never been aboard a naval vessel in a storm then. Old Otto tried to kill the founder of the Anserian navy. There's a reason Archduke Andrew Rushton-Browne is known as the Boatbuilder.'

'Otto Brozhnik was loyal to his Queen and almost sabotaged his rich friend's revolution. I am so much better than old Otto. I not only succeeded in killing my rich friend's wife, I'm about to kill his daughter.'

'What? You're ignoring killing your rich friend?'

'I did not kill Gilbert. Unless you count supplying his killer with the untraceable poison and a means to block any investigation into the murder. Anyway, must dash. Things to do.'

'How? You're not going anywhere,' said Leo.

'I beg to differ,' said the man as he dived into the lake to avoid capture. Leo watched as someone swam to one of the buttresses and climbed out of the water. Leo took aim and fired his pistol. The bullet passed a few inches from the man's ear.

'You have gained no advantage, in fact you have taken several steps backwards,' said Leo.

'You are so smug, aren't you. What a shame you are pinning down a policeman.'

Leo looked at his victim, who was wearing a wetsuit and could not possibly be the assassin. He saw something moving to his left and felt the rush of air as a bullet whizzed soundlessly a few inches from his heart. Leo took cover.

His opponent must be feeling the effects of his dive. It might be as bright as a Summer day, but it was still an October night with cold winds blowing from the sea. He must have been shivering so badly his aim was out. Leo spotted a line of wet footprints heading towards the main doorway and spotted the assassin's profile in a window. He fired. Damn, another miss. He quickly glanced behind him, seeing the police frogman take position.

There are voids within the nebula, when part of the surface of the planet passed through one of these voids even at its height, the Silent Night could become very noisy.

'I'm Earl Leonard Edwin Griffin-Phillips,' he shouted. 'The target has entered the building.'

'I hear you, Your Grace,' replied the policeman.

'Sorry about earlier,' said Leo sheepishly.

'Not to worry. These things happen,' said the policeman. 'Do you know where Baroness Chantelle and here family are located?'

'I believe they locked themselves into the panic room in the manor house's solar.'

'Cover me, Your Grace, I'm coming to your position.'

Leo could see that the assassin had made his way to the first floor and was crouching beneath a window looking out onto the garden. As the assassin raised his head to take a shot at the moving policeman Leo took a shot with his pistol. It hit the assassin in the shoulder and he saw the man fall to the floor, which must now be covered with the glass from the window.

'Target is down, repeat target is down. Approach Cenerentola

House but proceed with extreme caution.' The man had reached Leo's position. He was not a policeman, that was a navy wetsuit. 'Good shooting, Your Grace.'

'Janek,' said Leo, who had recognised the man's face, 'what are you doing here?'

'Luckily, my ship is currently moored at Castello del Filippo, one of our regular ports of call. Uncle Erik requested I be here using up a favour with the Captain. I'm supposed to be a friendly face for the women when we spring them.'

'Ah, I see,' said Leo, satisfied with the answer.

'Your Grace,' said a voice over the radio, 'this is Inspector Havers. The astronomers say this is a major void, the aural interference will be absent for the next twenty minutes.'

'Inspector, I have to warn you, he tried to blow up the building. He might have set up booby traps in case that option failed.'

'A bomb disposal unit is on its way, Your Grace, to make the building safe. We have orders to try and bring Silvermann in alive. We realise how dangerous he is and we were expecting more of a fight. We will proceed with caution.'

'Very good. Carry on, Inspector.'

Chantelle, I can hear you,' Madeleine said to her sister as she finished the last verse of the hymn.

'Of course you can, said Citronella, 'that sicky in your face thingy is doing something to your head.'

'No, Citronella, I can really hear what Chantelle was singing. And everything else. It sounds like a herd of elephants has invaded the house.'

'Baroness Chantelle, this is Janek Smitz. The police have taken control of the building and apprehended Stanley Silvermann. It is safe for you to leave the panic room.'

'How can we trust you? You might be Silvermann impersonating Janek's voices badly? It's too deep.'

'Tell Lady Madeleine her pearl came from the second oyster.'

There was no movement at the door.

'He is who he says he is Ellabella, dear.'

'Len, is that you?' Chantelle asked.

'Yes, hurry up, the silence will be returning soon,' said Leo.

'Where's Brilly Bobbery?'

'In the boat house. It's the statue of an angel with a fishing rod. Ellabella'

Chantelle threw the door open, flung her arms around Leo, and kissed him.

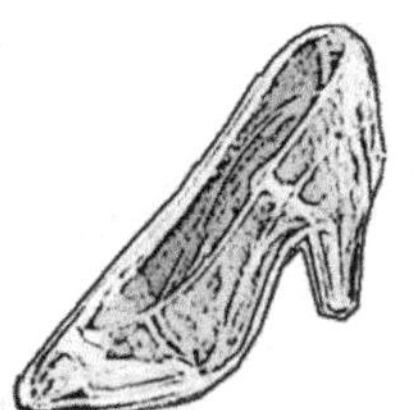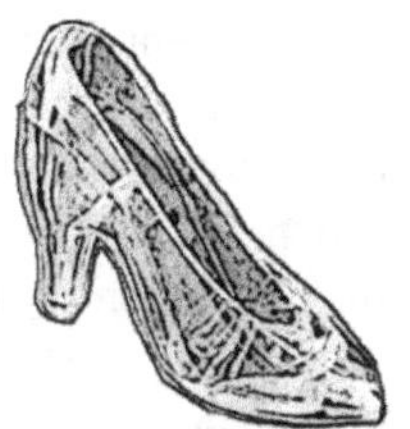

28

'If Silvermann didn't kill Gilbert, who did?' Bronwen asked, 'who exactly did?'

'It wasn't my Mother, Angels give her rest,' said Madeleine. Everyone in the room turned and stared at her. 'Well, even after all the horrible things she did, she didn't deserve to be murdered by a man like Silverman.' Tears were now rolling down Madeleine's face, 'and despite it all, she was my Mother.'

Chantelle put her arm around the sobbing girl.

'Well, Silvermann will hang for that, and all his other crimes,' said Erik Franke.

'There only remains one suspect,' said Aneurin, 'Commander Hans Liepmann.'

'And all we have on him is the word of Stanley Silverman,' said Erik, 'which is too weak a case to take to Court.'

'We know he bought the poison he used from Silverman,' said Madeleine. 'We have the video recording of the meeting, between the Commander and two of Silverman's alternate personalities.'

'Which shows Silvermann agreeing to sell things to the Commander, it doesn't say what or why. We have to prove it was the sale of the poison.'

'I'm afraid we all have a funeral to attend,' said Bronwen. 'Followed by seven days of mourning for Livienne du Fauché may the Angels give the foolish woman rest.'

Her daughters had agreed that the original plan of dropping their biocrete encased body into the Mother's depths of the Mare di Napoli was excessive. She would instead be interred at the Cemetery in the village, and not at the du Fauchés' family vault close to Cenerentola House. Unlike her late Husband's funeral, only the immediate family were present. The late Lady Livienne du Fauché had no friends at all. She had a magnificent talent for alienating people. There was no lawyer to read the Will, as André Nouveauté had been arrested and the office raided by a very well informed police squad, following the instructions of Jadwiga Smitz.

The seven days of mourning had passed. The twins were leaving to start their new life. This time in Tingagel wearing novice habits and using their new names, after passing the Order's entrance examination. Chantelle had come to the Priory to see them off.

'So, no mistaking which one of us is which now,' said Clementine. 'Novice Alison has a three inch scar on her left cheek, I do not.'

'In a few weeks it will be barely noticeable, Novice Emily,' said Citronella.

'While it lasts, it will help us develop the inner uniqueness we currently lack.' said Clementine.

There was no squabbling, no angry name calling. The Twins were being calm and grownup.

'Being separated has done us the world of good. Hasn't it Novice Emily?'

'Indeed it has,' said a voice from the car similar to the car she had travelled in earlier that year, it was brown and had the same shabby functionality. This car was larger as it had to accommodate more passengers and had solar panels on the roof to augment its gas turbine.

'Sister Maud, how nice to see you again.' Chantelle said as she fought the urge to raise her hand for permission to speak. This time she was not a passenger, pretending to be Novice Myfanwy.

That, however, had not stop Sister Anne. 'You are wearing a white veil and wimple. I have said we need women like you. We have time for you to change into a brown tunic and come with us as a novice.'

'Oh put a sock in it Sister. She is also wearing a Baronial Chain. She has a different vocation.' said Sister Maud, then turning to Chantelle, 'It is good to see you too, Baroness.'

'How was the Northern Continent?' Chantelle asked her cousin who had attended Lady Livienne's funeral.

'Too hot and humid, I was so glad to come home to Zucca, even if it was for tragic reasons. Cardinal Sister Anne must be off her head, going there to replace me.'

'It is the will of the Angels,' said Sister Anne.

Chantelle realised what was different about the driver. She now wore a black veil, a sign she had filled the vacant place in the Council of Cardinal Sisters created by the death of Cardinal Sister Amanda.

'May I ask, why you are travelling to Tintagel, Sister Grace.'

'Reverend Mother Paula has resigned. She jumped before she was pushed. Your cousin and I had arranged for you to be safely transferred to the protection of Mr. Franke, and not bundled away to a private asylum,' said Sister Grace. 'Former Reverend Mother Paula confessed to plotting with her cousin.'

'What the former Reverend Mother Paula did was monstrous, she deserves to forfeit her position of authority,' said 'Sister Maude. Sister Grace will receive her black veil.'

'And now the Cardinal Sisters are going to Tintagel. There we will appoint Acting Mother Frances as Reverend Mother of the Order of the Merciful Sisters of the Charity of the Angels to all Children,' said Sister Anne, now with the steel of authority in her voice.

'And I shall return to Seconda Quartam, Angels be praised,' said Sister Vera, 'I was only sent to the North because the former Reverend Mother saw me as a threat.'

'What happen to Reverend Mother Paula?' Chantelle asked.

'She is starting to live the life she tried to banish you to. She will spend the rest of her days as Sister Patrick of the Order of the Dutiful Sisters of Perpetual Poverty, in their most northerly convent, on the Lonely Islands. Like all their other establishments it is properly austere. She will never return to us. We have found all the money she stole. If she left religious life now she would be a pauper, living in true poverty.'

Chantelle considered this punishment. She made no comment, even now, the workings of the monastic mindset was a mystery to her.

'Goodbye, my dear half-sisters,' Chantelle said to the Twins, who had climbed into the third row of seats at the back of the big brown car and were both sitting patiently. Clemintine would become Novice Emily in Ponti de Carlo, Citronella was heading north, with the older nuns, on the transcontinental glider service, to become Novice Alison in Tintagel. 'You already know about living a destructive life with your Mother. I hope you achieve your aim of living a constructive Indentical Life within the Order, unique on the inside but perfectly identical on the outside.' This was another aspect of Anserian Monasticism she would never understand.

'We are all on a journey, only the Angels know our destinations,' they said in unison, as the door slid shut.

Sister Anne, once more silent in the driver's seat, cranked the vehicle's gas turbine. The big brown car pulled away from the curb silently. Chantelle stayed to watch the car disappeared from sight, so very glad she was not a passenger this time.

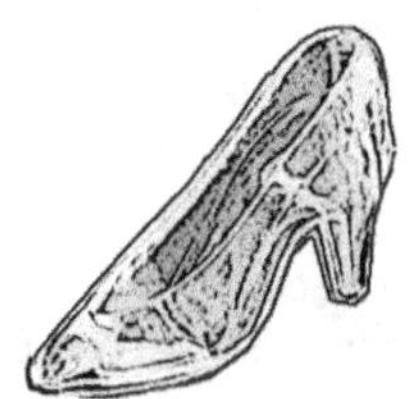 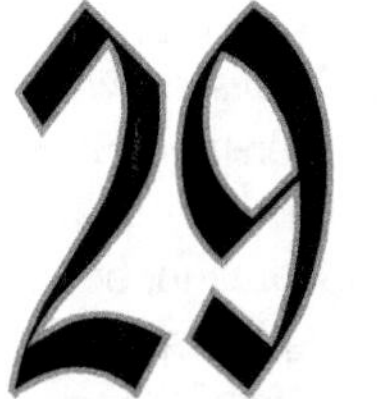 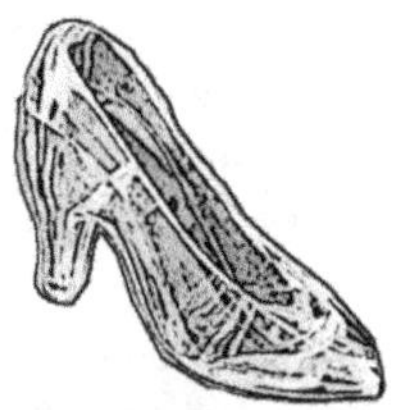

29

ans Liepmann was not a happy man. Murder is rarely good practice in business. What had he been thinking. Stanley Silvermann was supposed to be the best fixer in the Kingdom. Silvermann would not do the deed himself, but he would supply you with the tools that made the crime look like death from natural causes and then set up measures to prevent an overly suspicious Police enquiry into the killing. And with the odious Lady Livienne dead, in whose tedious company he had wasted too many hours enduring, it had all been a waste of time and money. Chantelle had become Baroness, and would not sell her shares in the fishing commune to him. Lady Madeleine had fallen out with her Mother and would vote with her half-sister, and the Twins, who inherited their Mother's shares, had become Ugly Sisters, so their Order now controlled those votes. It had appointed Baroness Chantelle as its voting proxy.

The Royal Council, the newly elected government of the Kingdom, wanted the combines to loosen their monopolies on fishing areas they controlled. They could either do this voluntarily, or have it forced on them by a new law passed in the Legislative Congress. What was worse, Lady Madeleine had inherited the shares in the Combine he had sold to her mother. This would cause problems.

Also Silvermann had gone and got himself arrested for a string of crimes. Tripped up by his irrational hatred of Fenzrians, focussed on Gilbert's first wife and her daughter. Fortunately the Crown Police were convinced Silvermann had killed Gilbert.

The official mourning for Lady Livienne was over, Liepmann found himself on the Island, going to see the du Fauché Girls.

'You've got a cheek, showing your face around here,' said Archduchess Jacqueline as Mr. Bottles showed Commander Liepmann into the sitting room at Cenerentola House. 'You're unpleasant business practices are not welcome here or anywhere else in Fiandre.'

'Your Grace,' said Liepmann, bowing the most correct full bow protocol demanded. He also spotted the Archduchess's sister, Dr. Avril Hartford-Smyth, wife of the research chemist Lord Denis.

'Excuse my Aunt's bluntness,' said a young woman who had just walked into the room. She had remove a wimple to reveal exceptionally short hair, and was unpinning the heavy formal baronial chain, 'but exactly what are you doing here?'

'I was a friend of your late Father and Step-mother for many years, Your Ladyship.' Liepmann recognised her as the new Baroness du Fauché. Of course, Baroness Chantelle claimed kinship with these appalling gold-diggers, where none existed.

Also the rumours about Chantelle shaving her head and hiding in a nunnery were true. 'I was unable to attend her funeral, so I have come to pay my respects at the first available time.'

'You know she was killed by the same assassin who killed my Father,' said Chantelle.

'You think I had something to do with your Father's death, because we had a business disagreement?' Liepmann asked, trying to gage if these women were on to him.

'You once told me there was no friendship in business.'

'There's more to life than Business, Your Ladyship,' he said. 'Outside of the disagreement over fishing rights in the Mare di Napoli, we were great friends, and had been since we served as Royal Pages together.'

Commander Liepmann was now certain that Baroness Chantelle and her family had no idea he was behind the death of Baron Gilbert du Fauché.

'If you'll excuse me, I must change out of these robes.'

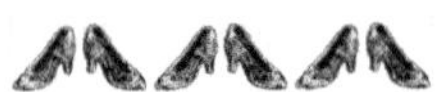

'So, Commander, would you like a cup of tea?' asked Chantelle. She had returned to the room, in a modern lilac dress. Chantelle could hardly bring herself to be civil to this loathsome man, but had to find out if the Commander knew they suspected him, without tipping him off that they did.

'I understand your Maletbon tree is in competition again this year?' Aunty Avril asked, making polite conversation.

'Yes, up for a prize in the "Best Kept Tree" category and the "Best Fruit" category at the Archduke's Agricultural Show. The judges for Best Kept Tree are visiting my estate this afternoon. Obviously it can't be taken to the show ground for judging. They visit three times a year to see the tree in various stages in its cycle.'

'I have a bonsai Maletbon tree in my office back in Elizaburg,' said Aunty Avril, 'my husband is trying to extract and artificially duplicate the fruit's remarkable properties.'

'There is more to the Maletbon fruit than just its chemistry, Your Ladyship. The magic is infused in the actual fresh fruit. You'll never catch that in a bottle.'

'Oh!' said Chantelle. She had just remembered that it was the Commander who had given her Father the poisoned fruit on that fateful day. 'If you will excuse me for a few minutes.'

From the way he was talking about that blessed plant, it was obvious Commander Liepmann had no idea she knew how he had killed her Father.

Previously, Chantelle had never seen the point of the secure phone line in her Father's office. Now she was firmly of the opinion that just because you are not paranoid, does not mean somebody is not out to get you.

'Yes, Aunty Bron,' Chantelle said to her Aunt, who was in her house in Zucca. 'It was definitely Commander Liepmann who gave my Father the poisoned Maletbon fruit. It came from his own tree.'

'You have no way of proving that.' said Mr. Franke, recently appointed as Estate Manager at Cenerentola. 'A good brief will draw doubt onto the validity of your memory.'

'Well, I've just received the advanced toxicology report on the recycling bin. It confirms massive levels of Palpadino, but the worms were killed by the presence of Maletbon fruit in the bin.'

'And there is no way of proving that it came from a fruit picked from the Commander's tree,' Erik added gloomily. 'The fruit had deteriorated too far for a genetic profile.'

'However, a friend at the Royal in Elizaburg tells me that Silvermann was treated as a teenager for a violent reaction to Maletbon fruit,' said Erik. 'He can't even touch them without developing a body encompassing rash.'

'Congratulations, we've just done the job of Silverman's defence team and got him off one count of Murder.'

'My late Step-mother detested drunkenness and anything that encouraged it. She would not have given my Father the fruit, so that just leaves Hans Liepmann.'

'Have you ever considered a career in the Police, Your Ladyship?'

'Oh brozhnik, I had better go back to the sitting room. My Aunts are there, they are here to talk about my plans. Marrying Leon and teacher training.'

'So you're still going ahead with that?' asked Bronwen. 'I thought that was an idea implanted at that that asylum.'

'They were trying to brainwash me, but not about that. I'd already told my Sister Monique about my descision at the Mother-house.'

'Are you sure?' ask asked Erik.

'Yes, three years to get a History Degree, then a year studying teaching theory in college, followed by a year studying teaching in practice.'

'That checks out,' said her Aunt. 'Sorry dear, we have to be careful.'

'I still can't believe I'm an atheist. I go to church every Sunday.' Chantelle could see Erik struggling to keep a straight face. She could imagine her Aunt in a similar situation. 'Oh brozhnik.'

'You would not have made a good Dutiful Sister, with language like that,' said her Aunt.

'You've lost me,' said Erik.

'The nightmares she has had recently about myself, Aneurin and

Madeleine dying in a plane crash, are part of another fake memory implanted in your head by Silverman's cousins, at his private asylum. Now you know its a lie, it will fade away. However, if you had not escaped it would have become her true memory. She would have been delivered to the Central Convent of the Order of the Dutiful Sisters of Poverty by another of Silverman's cousins, Reverend Mother Paula. The Dutiful Sisters would believe you were a devout young lady, all alone in the world. Where else would you turn. Once in that place, our Fenzrian ancestry's genetic predisposition to anonymous mind-think would have seen you become a novice nun for real. Untraceable, as you would have a new random male name, chosen for you by the Order.'

'Who, Reverend Mother Paula is Silverman's cousin?' asked Chantelle.

'Yes, original name Felicia Paula Tintagel Silvermann,' said Erik as Mr. Bottle ushered two plain clothed policemen into the office. 'And it looks as if the Queen has sent more people to try to make me reconsider my change in career,'

Of course, Chantelle knew Erik had not really changed his career. Running the du Fauché Estate was the latest cover for his real job. These policemen were carrying a quiet different message from the Queen. Chantelle was more than willing to let him moonlight here while his real job took him to Fiandre and its neighbouring archduchies on the Eastern Continent.

There was the sound of arguing coming from the sitting room, followed by Commander Liepmann storming into the hallway.

'I'm not staying here to be insulted,' said the Commander. 'That woman called me a murderer because I said I gave Gilbert a Maletbon fruit from my tree, the day he fell ill. I'm not staying here to be insulted.'

'No, sunshine,' said Erik, 'but you will be staying here to be arrested. Sasha, you know the score.'

'Eh! What? How? Why?' said the Commander in rapid succession. Then he realised what he had just said, and who he had just said it to.

'Commander Hans Howard Sorrento Liepmann, I am arresting you for the Crime of Murder, the most heinous Breach of the Queen's

Peace, of Gilbert François Cenerentola du Fauché, the forty second Baron of Cenerentola, on Wednesday, 9th April, 5885CGC. You do not have to say anything, but anything you do say during questioning, upto...' said Inspector Alexandr Bakharinov, quickly remembering torture had been banned recently, before continuing. 'Er, will be recorded and may be used in Court against you. You are entitled to contact a lawyer. If you cannot afford one, a public defender will be appointed for you.'

'You do realise I am the richest man in the Archduchy, do you think I need a public defender?' Some of the Commander's usual bluff and bluster had returned.

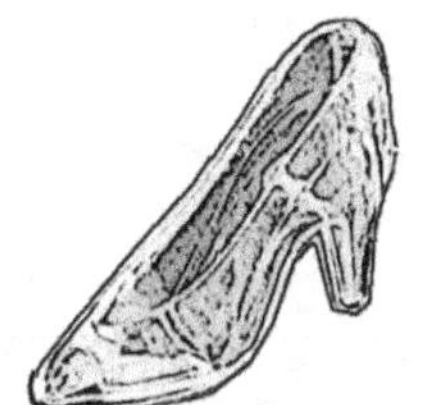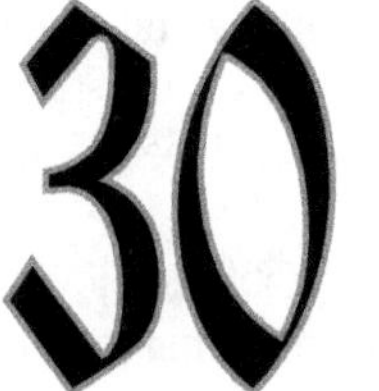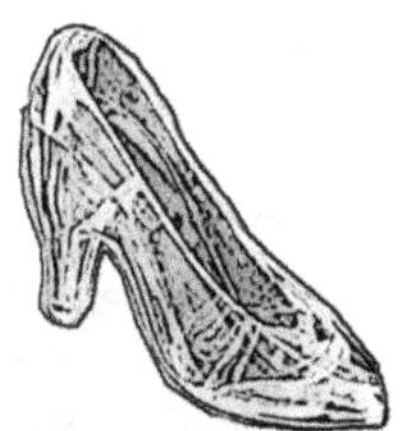

J adwiga looked at the young family, sitting at a kitchen table. Father keeping the baby in the high chair entertained while the mother tried to feed the baby pureed gloop. It looked so normal, so average. They could be her family, if she were six inches taller and several dress sizes smaller and had eight pints of blue blood, because it was not as it seemed. Despite the modernity of the kitchen, the parents were wearing traditional medieval dress and both had crowns on. They were not her family, even though she felt closer to them than her own.

'You look rested, dear, I wish I felt the same. Madame here woke at 3.30am, and unusually would not go back to sleep,' said the Mother.

'Yes, Your Majesty, I heard her.'

It's funny, Jadwiga thought, any other time in this kitchen, she would not be curtseying and calling her friend "Your Majesty", but Imogen was still wearing her crown and using her posh voice, so she was still playing the role of Queen Johanna IV.

Pretend I bain't got no bling on, gotta make an official decision when finished here be I,' said Imogen. 'So, what d'yer reckon about them du Fauchés? I heard there was a bit of fiddle faddle happenin, m'dear.'

'That my dear, is putting it mildly,' said the father.

'I have to agree with you, Carlo.' She should have bowed to Prince Regent Carlo, addressing him as "Your Royal Highness", but her Queen had just removed the need for formality. 'Baroness Chantelle was almost duped out of her inheritance by her wicked step-mother, who paid the ultimate price for her evil plan.'

'It all worked out in the end, I be glad to say. Though, I'll miss Gilbert du Fauché, he always had his finger on the pulse.'

'Not as much as Chantelle and Madeleine are missing him,' said Jadwiga.

'That be true. However, I be askin' you 'bout 'em as a fam'ly, ain't I?'

'Now they are a very stable and lovin' one, wivout de du Carrefour element,' said Jadwiga, reverting to her old Elizaburg Scouse accent. 'No, maybe dat is a little harsh on them Twins' but do they still count, as they left that family by becomin' Novice Merciful Sisters and were never the problem their mother was?'

'The late Baron Gilbert turned his family fortunes around, do yous reckon the current generation will keep up the proper job of a-managin' their estate?'

'How should I know Imogen, I'm not an economist,' said Jadwiga.

'I reckon, little sister, have a good think and take a wise stab at it, given all what 'yous've seen.'

'Excellent, I would say. I read the history, it was only the one profligate generation, over two centuries ago. I think the current generation will handle the income from the pearls better than the earlier one did with the emeralds,' said Jadwiga.

'Imogen is not inquiring about history and the past, she is interested in learning about the future, aren't you, dearest?'

'Yes, Carlo. So Jadwiga?' ask Imogen, back in Queen mode.

'Well, Ma'am,' Jadwiga replied formally. 'Lady Madeleine was delighted when Baroness Chantelle announced she was going to become a teacher. Maddy has always been planning on studying Law and Economics at University, now she says she wants to do an MBA after her degree, and take over running the estate. Chantelle says when she eventually marries Leo, she will hand the title of Baroness over to Madeleine. She doesn't have to.'

'So when I restore the du Fauché family to the Aristocracy as Minor House Griffin-Charles, they will be happy?'

'Ma'am, Why bother, the Aristocracy has lost all its power?'

'No, Jadwiga, it has lost direct access to the apparatus of government,' said the Queen. 'However, they are all still wealthy and have a great deal of indirect access through the Aristocratic Council. I am one of the most progressive individuals in the Kingdom, and as the leader of that deeply conservative organization, I want to ensure that at least some of its members are progressives and my supporters.'

'In which case, I suggest you include Bronwen and Aneurin, making it House Phillips-Tudor.'

'Ah, the indefatigable Aunt, I can't wait to meet her,' said Imogen.

'As yourself or in an official capacity?' asked Carlo.

'Both,' said Imogen, 'and raising them to the Aristocracy would show that there really is no differences between people of Terran and Fenzrian origins any more.'

'Long overdue,' said Jadwiga, 'because we all originated on Earth anyway.'

'But Jadzie dear, you appear to have left something behind.'

'I have?' asked a bemused Jadwiga.

'Yes little sister, my Head Bodyguard,' said the Queen.

'Imogen, Uncle Erik is still in constant touch with you. And it is better that he is based in the East while ridding it of corrupt policemen.'

'Did you have to let facts spoil a good sulk, Jadzie?'

'You were the one who suggested he go with me. But I suppose you never expected Uncle Erik to meet Aunt Bronwen.'

'I didn't think he had a romantic bone in his body,' said Prince Carlo.

'Neither did he. Of course they are still telling each other they are just good friends.'

'Naturally, Little Sister.'

I wish she would stop calling me that, Jadwiga thought. Yes she has been like a big sister to me for the past three years, taking me in when my Mother refused to take me back. Helped me with my homework and gave me more encouragement than my parents ever did. But I am not, nor never can be her little sister in reality.

'You had another bust-up with your Mother?' asked Imogen.

'Yes, she blames me for what Janek did. Says I filled his head with radical ideas. She wasn't the problem. Dad sided with mother this time. He said I had made Janek disobey family tradition, that he never really wanted to join-up until I encouraged him. So I told him that if he had ever, paid attention to what his son really wanted, he would know that was a lie.'

'Your father didn't take that well?' asked Imogen, who could see Jadwiga was close to tears. 'I'm sorry dear, sorry for upsetting you.'

'It's all right, Imogen, you would have found out any way,' said Jadwiga, 'I've never seen my father so angry. He was so angry with both of us. We have both been disowned. A full legal repudiation, he got Uncle Barney to expell us from the clan.

'I still have Janek. He told our father to go to the twentieth hell. Janek says he will never return to Elizaburg. That he will change his name to du Pré when he marries Eugenia. He says old man du Pré is more than happy for me to join his clan. As my mother has disowned me, so I was going to rename myself Jadwiga Adelina Orlov du Pré.'

'I already know all this. I have spoken to Janek, and your parents. Janek was perfectly reasonable, your father was as pigheaded as your mother.'

'They're not my mother and father any more.'

'You have us, darling, so will no longer be a private joke,' said Imogen, 'I love you like a sister, and as she grows, Princess Marion will love you as her radical Aunt, Princess Jadwiga. Just as I loved my radical Aunt, Princess Marie-Anne'

'But how? I accept that I stopped being an ordinary girl from Elizaburg years ago, but I am still not royalty, you have to be born into that.'

'Don't worry about the how and the when. Your clan has repudiated you, and your mother and father cursed you,' said Carlo. 'It was quite a spat, so Imogen said, with full royal splendour, "If you don't want her in your family, then she will become part of mine." which silenced both your parents, for a minute, and then your father said, "fair enough, she's been yours since the day you met." and signed a Deed of Transfer.'

'A Deed of Transfer, they haven't been used since the colonial days. I didn't know they were still legal,' Jadwiga said. 'That is why I need to go to law school, there are still aspects of Anserian Law I have only a glancing knowledge of.'

'Don't change the subject. I have accepted the Deed, which bring you into the Great House of Ellisford-Castle and the Royal Family.

You will legally become my sister, Her Royal Highness, the Princess Jadwiga Gertrude Eirwen Orlov Ellisford-Castle of Anseris, or Princess Jadwiga. I know my mother would be proud to have you as a daughter.'

'This will change so many things,' said Jadwiga, considering her new name. Had Imogen thought is up on the spur of the moment.

'I have so much to ask, like when does this all happen.'

'Tomorrow morning,' said Carlo. 'When the Royal Decree is issued. Although in a few months there will be a big initiation ceremony. Then we party.'

'What about my studies?'

'Well, Elizaburg University has always been academically rigorous. Its the quality of your work, not the rank of your family that matters. So there should be no problem,' said Imogen.

'And me being a Princess will have an effect on Janek and the Navy?'

'No, Jadzie, nothing changes for him. And even if it did, there is a long history of aristocrats and gentry who couldn't get into officer training who enlisted and spent their careers as ordinary seamen,' said Carlo. It always has been the most egalitarian service.'

'Then it's a good thing I've never been a republican,' said Jadwiga.

'Yes, Princess Jadwiga, it is,' said the Queen.

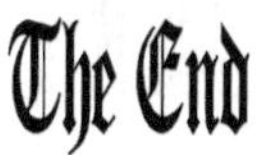

The End

5885 CGC

Jenavieve

S	M	T	W	T	F	S
				1	2	3
4	5	6	7	8	9	10
11	12	13	14	15	16	17
18	19	20	21	22	23	24
25	26	27	28	29	30	31

Fevriona

S	M	T	W	T	F	S
1	2	3	4	5	6	7
8	9	10	11	12	13	14
15	16	17	18	19	20	21
22	23	24	25	26	27	28

Marcia

S	M	T	W	T	F	S
1	2	3	4	5	6	7
8	9	10	11	12	13	14
15	16	17	18	19	20	21
22	23	24	25	26	27	28
29	30	31				

Avril

S	M	T	W	T	F	S
			1	2	3	4
5	6	7	8	9	10	11
12	13	14	15	16	17	18
19	20	21	22	23	24	25
26	27	28	29	30		

Maia

S	M	T	W	T	F	S
31					1	2
3	4	5	6	7	8	9
10	11	12	13	14	15	16
17	18	19	20	21	22	23
24	25	26	27	28	29	30

Junia

S	M	T	W	T	F	S
		1	2	3	4	5	6
7	8	9	10	11	12	13
14	15	16	17	18	19	20
21	22	23	24	25	26	27
28	29	30	31			

Luglia

S	M	T	W	T	F	S
			1	2	3	4
5	6	7	8	9	10	11
12	13	14	15	16	17	18
19	20	21	22	23	24	25
26	27	28	29	30	31	

Augusta

S	M	T	W	T	F	S
30	31					1
2	3	4	5	6	7	8
9	10	11	12	13	14	15
16	17	18	19	20	21	22
23	24	25	26	27	28	29

September

S	M	T	W	T	F	S
		1	2	3	4	5
6	7	8	9	10	11	12
13	14	15	16	17	18	19
20	21	22	23	24	25	26
27	28	29	30			

Ochember

S	M	T	W	T	F	S
				1	2	3
4	5	6	7	8	9	10
11	12	13	14	15	16	17
18	19	20	21	22	23	24
25	26	27	28	29	30	31

November

S	M	T	W	T	F	S
1	2	3	4	5	6	7
8	9	10	11	12	13	14
15	16	17	18	19	20	21
22	23	24	25	26	27	28
29	30					

December

S	M	T	W	T	F	S
		1	2	3	4	5
6	7	8	9	10	11	12
13	14	15	16	17	18	19
20	21	22	23	24	25	26
27	28	29	30	31		

Anseris uses the Common Galactic Calendar, which is four days ahead of the Gregorian Calendar. The seasons are Winter, which starts on 1st Jenavieve; Spring begins on 1st Avril. Summer starts on 1st Julia and ends on 31st Augusta, making it two months-long; The Embers, which opens on 1st September. October was changed to October, to match the other months in the season.

The first eight months of the year have all been changed to female names. Traditionally girls born on the first day of one of these months are named after them.

Two Astronomical holidays Black Masquerade and White Jule occur on the Solstices The Anserian equivalent of the Christmas Holiday is Jule, which begins on the Sunday before the Solstice and ends at Midnight on 31st December.

All of Augusta is a school holiday. This dates back to when children were expected to work with their families bringing in the harvest.

Veterans Day is the 1st Julia. In the days of conscription, it was the day young men called up began their military service.

Glossary

This novel is set on a world based on a psychopathic nut-job's vision of the European Middle Ages. To help paint a picture, the text has been peppered with words from that era. Their definitions can be found below.

Also included is a translation and pronunciation guide for the Welsh words used in this novel.

Articles of clothing worn by a single gender is marked (F) or (M), otherwise marked (C). Welsh words are marked (W).

Bandeau (F)	A strip of cloth wound around the torso to support the breasts.
Barbette (F)	Narrow strip of cloth worn vertically around the face for attaching veils.
Beth sy'n bod? (W)	What's the matter? (Bayth seen bawd)
Braies (M)	Baggy knee-length underpants to which hose were attached.
Bycocket (C)	Robin Hood's hat pointed at each end with a feather. Worn by men and women.
Cape (C)Caul (F)	An outdoor garment fastened by a pin or broach at the shoulders. Sometimes with a hood.
Cariad (W)	Dearest, darling, loved one. (Carryad) Leggings attached to Braies with a garter at

CHAUSE (M) — the knee to stop the garment sagging.

CHEMISE (F) — Full-length undergarment.

CLOAK — An overcoat, with or without hood.

CODPIECE (M) — A pouch to which Hose were attached at the crotch to accommodate male anatomy.

COIF (C) — Close-fitting, semi-circular hat.

COTEHARDIE (C) — A short tunic.

DRIST IAWN (W) — Very sad. *(Drist Yee-ow-en)*

ERS (W) — Since.

FILLET (F) — Narrow strip of cloth worn horizontally around the forehead for attaching veils.

FURLONG — An unit of distance equalling one-eighth of a mile. Literally a furrow long, as it was the length of the strips of land used in English agriculture in the Middle Ages.

FY NHAD — My Father *(Vur nhard)*

GAMBESON (M) — Quilted jacket worn as armour by archers.

GORGETTE (F) — Similar to a Wimple but looser and made of more lavish material.

HOOD (C) — Large collar and hood.

HOSE (C) — Thick woollen tights similar to leggings.

JETTYING (A) — Constructing each story of a building to overhang the one below.

KIRTLE (F) — Basic dress with detachable sleeves. Worn over Chemise and Bandeau but under Surcote. The long draped peak of a hood.

LIRIPIPE (C)

SCAPULAR — A loose apron like vestment, part of the habit of nuns and monks as a demonstration of faith.

SHILLER (J) — The apparent luminescence of a gem caused by the refraction of light within it.

STEEPLE HENNIN (F) — Clichéd woman's pointy medieval hat with veil.

SURCOTE (C) — Topmost indoor garment.

TEMPLAR (F) — A pair of tubular latticed baskets for dressing hair. Attached to either a crown or fillet, on either side of the face.

TAD CU (W) — Grandfather (*Tard key*)

TOCQUE (F) — Circular hat with inwardly sloping sides.

WIMPLE (F) — Oblong cloth covering the neck, chin and ears, leaving only the face visible.

Acknowlegements

The influence of my late Father, Alderman Gwynfryn Rees, cannot be measured. He is here, in things major and minor. I would not have been to a fraction of the place I have visited, nor seen anything like the amazing things I have seen, had it not been for him. A case in point is the Black Sea coast of Bulgaria, on which the coast of the Mare di Napoli is based. Back in 1986, in the dying days of Communism, Bulgaria was first opening up to the West. Little was known about it in the UK. Without him the would be no Brozhnik. When we arrived, we could taste the paranoia in the empty shops and restaurants desperate to hide their lack of stock or ingredients. My father still managed to find humour in the situation. Somewhere along the line, he heard the word "brozhnik" which I am told means "brew". He decided it would be a great joke to tell his work colleagues when he returned home that "brozhnik" was a popular greeting in Bulgaria. This strange word stuck in my mind, and I started using it the way my charcacters do in the novel.

Of course, I also have to say a big thank you to my Mother, Patricia. Starting a book is a solitary effort, but finishing it is a collaborative effort. She is first person to read the manuscript after it has left the creative stage and entered the polishing stage of the writing process. Without her assistance, proof reading and making suggestions for changes to the text to improve the flow and make the story more readable, my novels would be half the works they are today. Also my sisters Janet Guy and Carolyn Davies for their continued support, encouragement and suggestions.

Once again I would like to thank Lynda Carter, the first person outside my family to proof read my manuscripts. Her fresh perspective is always extremely useful.

Also I have to thank Timothy Farr, for his help, encouragement and yet another perspective during the proof reading stage of all my novels. Another person I would like to thank is my friend Ian Meredith, a Linguist. He made sure the French and Welsh used in the dialogue was a present and correct.

I have, in relied on the Mr. Dialect web site [https://mr-dialect.com/en-gb/translator/] to give the accents a make-over.

In my research into things Medieval, I discovered a fascinating YouTube video [http://www.youtube.com/watch?v=ulcLSntbEF0] created by historical costumer Morgan Donner, who was recreating the outfit of a late Regency portrait. The subject lady, Fräulein Christina Antonietta Cornelia Vetterlein bore a striking resemblance Ms. Donner. In the portrait Fräulein Vetterlein is wearing a Renaissance dress with a hairstyle from the Fourteenth Century. I have to thank Ms. Donner for drawing my attention to this perfectly Anserian mish-mash. Of course I had to find way to incorporate the picture into this book. Especially as the subjects full name sounds so Anserian.

Finally, a big thank you to the Committee, Guests and Attendees at the annual ArmadaCon Science Fiction Convention in Plymouth. Without their friendship over the past three decades, I would never have started writing science fiction.

John Campbell Rees,
31st October, 2019